INDIAN CUISINE
Diabetes Cookbook

Savory Spices and Bold Flavors from South Asia

MAY ABRAHAM FRIDEL

American Diabetes Association®

Director, Book Publishing, Abe Ogden; *Managing Editor,* Rebekah Renshaw; *Acquisitions Editor,* Victor Van Beuren; *Editor,* Lauren Wilson; *Production Manager,* Melissa Sprott; *Composition and Cover Design,* pixiedesign llc; *Photographer,* Renee Comet Photography; *Printer,* Versa Press.

Printed in the United States of America
1 3 5 7 9 10 8 6 4 2

The suggestions and information contained in this publication are generally consistent with the *Standards of Medical Care in Diabetes* and other policies of the American Diabetes Association, but they do not represent the policy or position of the Association or any of its boards or committees. Reasonable steps have been taken to ensure the accuracy of the information presented. However, the American Diabetes Association cannot ensure the safety or efficacy of any product or service described in this publication. Individuals are advised to consult a physician or other appropriate health care professional before undertaking any diet or exercise program or taking any medication referred to in this publication. Professionals must use and apply their own professional judgment, experience, and training and should not rely solely on the information contained in this publication before prescribing any diet, exercise, or medication. The American Diabetes Association—its officers, directors, employees, volunteers, and members—assumes no responsibility or liability for personal or other injury, loss, or damage that may result from the suggestions or information in this publication.

Madelyn Wheeler conducted the internal review of this book to ensure that it meets American Diabetes Association guidelines.

♾ The paper in this publication meets the requirements of the ANSI Standard Z39.48-1992 (permanence of paper).

ADA titles may be purchased for business or promotional use or for special sales. To purchase more than 50 copies of this book at a discount, or for custom editions of this book with your logo, contact the American Diabetes Association at the address below, at booksales@diabetes.org, or by calling 703-299-2046.

American Diabetes Association
2451 Crystal Drive, Suite 900
Arlington, VA 22202

DOI: 10.2337/9781580405997

Library of Congress Cataloging-in-Publication Data

Names: Fridel, May Abraham, author.
Title: Indian cuisine diabetes cookbook : savory spices and bold flavors from
   South Asia / May Abraham Fridel.
Description: Alexandria : American Diabetes Association, [2017] | Includes
   index.
Identifiers: LCCN 2016033227 | ISBN 9781580405997
Subjects: LCSH: Diabetes--Diet therapy--Recipes. | Cooking, Indian. | LCGFT:
   Cookbooks.
Classification: LCC RC662 .F54 2017 | DDC 641.5/6314--dc23
LC record available at https://lccn.loc.gov/2016033227

Contents

Acknowledgments

I want to express my love and deepest gratitude for everyone who has supported, inspired, and guided me on this incredible journey. You have made the experience of writing my first book one I'll never forget.

I want to dedicate this book to my late father, Abraham Mathew, who made sure that every meal in our household was given the attention and care it deserved, and my mom, Sara Abraham, who is an amazing cook and has been a wonderful resource for me in writing this book. My father was especially particular about the way meals were prepared and always encouraged us to eat healthy. I grew up in a "foodie" family, and I am so grateful for all of the culinary knowledge and inspiration I gained during my childhood. Special thanks also to my husband, Frank Fridel, and son, Matthew, for their endless support and love during this process. Thank you to my sisters, Annu and Susan, for constantly sharing tips, recipe

ideas, and childhood memories with me. This book wouldn't have been possible without them.

I'd like to acknowledge my maternal and paternal grandmothers, who were both fantastic cooks. Thank you to my great aunt, a well-known culinary expert in Kerala, the late Mrs. K.M. Mathew. She always inspired us with her cookbook collection and culinary aspirations.

My sincerest thanks to my friends Christina Amundson, who was instrumental to the development of this book and guided me through the process, and Susan Grates, who spent her time helping me through many stages of editing. Thanks to Passion for Spice, the Sustainable Test Kitchen team, chef Robert Vanderbeek—who helped me during the recipe-testing process—and culinary interns Carlos Cabral and Amanda Lamperti. Thank you to the chef who gave me more insight into authentic Keralan cuisine, chef Jose Varkey. Special thanks to Executive Chef

Ashish Bhasin of The Oberoi Rajvilas in Jaipur, India and The Oberoi Group.

To Abe Ogden: thank you for believing in me and inviting me to share my passion for cooking and spices. It has been a pleasure to write this book for the American Diabetes Association. Thank you to Victor Van Beuren, who was my guide through the development and book production process; whenever I felt lost, his wisdom and advice got me back on track. Thank you to my editor Lauren Wilson, who labored over this book with care and enthusiasm, attention to detail, and organizing skills. I am so impressed with the entire team at the American Diabetes Association, as well as photographer Renee Comet, food stylist Lisa Cherkasky, and prop stylist Audrey Kenney. I hope to work with the Association again in the future and I offer my continued support to the Association's mission.

I hope this book will inspire many all over the globe and help them to lead a healthy and happy life.

Thank you to food author and historian Colleen Sen, renowned cookbook author James Peterson, and Dr. Jothydev Kesavadev for taking the time to review this book. I appreciate their expertise and feedback.

Thank you to everyone I've had the opportunity to meet throughout this process and the countless friends and family members who have offered their support. All of you have my gratitude and affection forever. You've made my dream of being an author come true, and you've encouraged me to write more books! Lastly, thank you to my readers for taking an interest in a healthy lifestyle and Indian cuisine.

I'm also grateful for my childhood experiences with food—growing up around incredible cooks, who taught me to enjoy cooking and value India's wealth of ingredients and spices. I want to share those positive experiences through this book. I've always thought that cooking is an expression of love, a way of connecting with friends and family, and I wrote this book to inspire everyone to cook and live with passion and continue the tradition of family and amazing food!

May Fridel

Introduction

There is a beautiful ancient Sanskrit expression—"Atithi devo bhava"—that essentially means that your guest (*atithi*) is your God (*devo*), and God will treat you as you treat your guests. This is the guiding principle of Indian philosophy and hospitality—from the way we receive guests and entertain them to the way we feed them.

Indian Culinary Philosophy

In Indian society, food plays a primary role in connecting people with each other. Family members cook meals in a collaborative manner and eat food together. Welcoming and sharing a meal with others is paramount to Indian culture, and we believe that eating together helps develop and strengthen bonds. In India, food is an essential part of all occasions in the human life cycle (birth, marriage, pregnancy, etc.). An individual's relationship with food begins at birth with the ritual of putting a drop of honey on the tongue of the newborn baby prior to his or her first feeding. Indian ceremonies and customs showcase the special lifelong connection that human beings have with food.

In India, families used to shop together and take pride in selecting the freshest local and seasonal ingredients. Food is considered sacred in India and is treated with reverence because it nourishes the body and the soul. Indian cuisine was designed to honor the soil, the sea, the farmers, and the fishermen. Indian cooking customs have been passed down through generations, and each family has its own unique cooking styles. This created a rich legacy of culinary knowledge. Unfortunately, things are changing in India; buying fresh ingredients and cooking at home is becoming less and less common. My hope is that this book will keep that legacy alive and inspire people to get back in the kitchen.

I grew up in South India and moved to the United States as an adult when I was hired as a knowledge engineer. With my high-powered corporate job, my lifestyle changed dramatically. Because of my hectic work schedule, I began to take advantage of the convenience foods that are readily available in the U.S. today. Eventually, I realized that highly processed foods, however convenient, were having a negative effect on my health and on my young child's immune system.

I decided to take a break from my career and began to focus on tapping back into my culinary roots and philosophy, and reestablish my native food culture in my home. How did I make this happen while living in the U.S.? I replaced processed foods with fresh, organic foods (whenever possible) and started cooking everything from scratch. I began to utilize my culinary knowledge, passed down through my family, gleaned from the nutritional resources available in the U.S., and learned through lessons with various culinary experts. I combined this knowledge with the gadgets and conveniences of the modern Western kitchen to create easy, well-balanced, flavorful meals with delicious Indian spices. (In addition to enhancing flavor, spices also have nutritional benefits and antioxidant and anti-inflammatory properties.) In other words, I adapted my traditional family recipes to my modern life.

I am so fortunate to have had the experience of preparing and relishing wholesome food with my family in India, following the guiding principles of Ayurveda—including the nutritional aspects of this practice. Ayurveda is a collection of lifestyle practices developed during the Vedic period in India. It is considered in India to be an art of appropriate living—a way of balancing the body and mind to optimize one's life. In terms of nutrition, Ayurvedic principles are common-sense practices that can help guide an individual's diet, taking into account the different stages of life, seasonal changes in foods, and how different ingredients interact with the body. One simple example of how this works: Ayurvedic principles teach that people should not consume yogurt at night because it is thought to lead to the production of excess phlegm in the body. Today, I practice Ayurveda with my American family. My experience with and knowledge of these practices, and of the cooking traditions passed down by my family, have been instrumental in writing this book.

All of my family members—especially my mother and grandparents—were excellent cooks, and I am very fortunate to have learned from their expertise.

Ayurveda: an Ancient Lifestyle Practice

Ayurveda is an ancient school of thought about nutrition and wellness. Ayurvedic practices teach you to pay attention to your body, and integrate good nutrition into everyday life.

Growing up in Kerala in South India, my family practiced the Ayurvedic way of life, and I have wonderful memories of my parents and grandparents sharing words of wisdom about how vital food is to a person's well-being. They explained the "dos" and "don'ts" of selecting ingredients based on the guiding principles of Ayurveda. My maternal grandfather was especially into the Ayurvedic lifestyle. He enjoyed a long, healthy life and managed to avoid chronic diseases. He lived to be a centenarian. His lifestyle practices served as valuable lesson for the rest of the family.

Indian philosophy recognizes three *gunas* (or qualities) that are often applied to nutrition and eating principles. The three gunas are *sattvic*, *rajasic*, and *tamasic*, and each guna is associated with certain foods that are thought to bring about the quality of that guna in the person who eats them. The sattvic guna, for example, is associated with purity, and sattvic foods include fresh produce, some whole grains (rice, barley, wheat), some nuts and seeds, milk, fresh yogurt, and ghee. The rajasic guna is one of passion and sensuality. Some rajasic foods include fish, eggs, fermented foods, white sugar, spices, and salty, sour, and/or spicy foods. Tamasic foods include leftover, preserved, or fried foods, fast food, meat, and intoxicants such as alcohol. This is the guna associated with lethargy.

While the three gunas do not actually come from the Ayurvedic tradition, people who practice Ayurvedic principles should be familiar with the concept of the gunas and the foods associated with them.

Ayurveda also encourages the use of seasonal ingredients. Our bodies benefit from different nutrients and ingredients at different times of year. Eating seasonal foods and using cooking techniques that take advantage of seasonal ingredients allows the body to adjust to changes in the outside environment. Ingredients taste better and are more nutritious when eaten in season.

In terms of nutrition, Ayurveda encourages people to eat fresh, seasonal, unprocessed foods as often as possible. This simple healthy eating principle makes very good sense when you think about it. It's something that I practice in my kitchen.

My family introduced my sisters and me to a lot of exotic, rare ingredients that enhanced our palates and repertoire of foods. My dad was a big "foodie" who always emphasized the importance of healthy eating and had us try many traditional recipes. He was particular about the quality of his food and had a very discerning palate. I used to go with him to the farmers' market, fishmonger, and butcher where he would introduce us to new ingredients and teach me how to select best fresh-caught seafood and cuts of meat. Those lessons formed the foundation of my passion for cooking and my culinary philosophy.

The kitchen in my house growing up was a beautiful space with a wood-burning stove that was always full of people working on the next meal. I remember the sounds and smells of people grinding grains, preparing spices, making batters, and pickling and preserving different foods. We had our own cows, so we always had fresh milk and butter was churned each day. Our water was drawn from a large well and was left in earthenware pots in our kitchen to cool; even the well water tasted incredibly pure and sweet. On holidays, the kitchen was full of sweets—such as rich English fruitcakes with fruit soaked in brandy and the scent of fragrant spices—that were made to be exchanged with friends and neighbors. I hope the recipes in this book can bring that same warm atmosphere to your kitchen.

Food played such an important role in my early life and I have beautiful memories of sharing meals—which were made from scratch with great care for both special occasions and everyday meals—with my family growing up. In fact, my mother would prepare fresh meals, including snacks, for me every day when I was young. We ate such nutrient-rich foods, that none of us had to take vitamins or other dietary supplements. I also remember my parents hosting beautiful parties with an elaborate spread of traditional dishes including cocktails and desserts. These experiences inspired my love of cooking. I am thrilled to share my recipes and cooking traditions with you.

How to Use This Book

The *Indian Cuisine Diabetes Cookbook* is meant to serve as a guide to eating well for people whose lives have been affected by diabetes (or other chronic or lifestyle diseases) and for anyone who is trying to embrace a healthy lifestyle and be proactive about preventing illness. The recipes in this book combine healthy ingredients with traditional Indian flavors, regional cooking techniques, and modern conveniences of the Western kitchen.

I am excited to work with the American Diabetes Association to bring you this book. The Association is a nonprofit organization with the mission to fight diabetes and improve the lives of all people affected by this disease. The Association takes a wonderful approach to diabetes nutrition—focusing on healthy, nutrient-dense foods eaten in moderation—that correlates well with the traditional way of cooking and eating in India. If a person with diabetes wants to cook a meal in India, they have a lot of traditional recipes at their disposal, but they may not know how to eat to best manage their diabetes. The marriage of the Association's nutrition guidelines with India's culinary philosophy, which emphasizes the use of spices, is what makes this book an invaluable resource for every diabetes-friendly kitchen worldwide.

If you are trying to add some choice and variety to your meals, this cookbook is for you! My recipe collection includes something to please every palate. Children, families, young professionals, novice cooks, and even experienced chefs can all enjoy the flavors and techniques used in this book. Whether you are looking for a breakfast dish, a one-pot meal, an elegant entrée, or an exotic seafood recipe, this book has

a dish for you. In the following pages, you'll find classic regional Indian recipes, many of which have been adapted to make them healthier and easier to prepare. This collection is a good sample of the diversity of Indian cuisine, with dishes for special occasions and busy weeknight meals alike. There are also several options for vegetarians and vegans. If you want to master the art of Indian roti-making, we have recipes for that as well! I have taken classic Indian flatbread recipes and made them easier to prepare and incorporated more whole grains (see the Indian Flatbreads chapter on p. 157). Roti-making is a fun activity for the whole family!

This book has several features to make your introduction to healthy Indian cooking as straightforward as possible. The Spice Guide (p. 16) and Pantry List (p. 22) will help you ensure that you have everything you need to get started. The How-To Recipes (p. 28) will teach you to prepare some of the staple elements of Indian cuisine. For your convenience, I have also marked recipes that are gluten-free and/or vegan. All of these features have been added to help people get excited about cooking. You will be surprised how easy it is to prepare the recipes in this book. Start with some simple, crowd-pleasing recipes, such as the Spiced Turkey Meatballs on p. 148, for example. You will love the bright exotic flavors of my recipes and the joyful feeling of preparing and serving a delicious, healthy homemade dish!

This book is also my opportunity to preserve my culinary heritage and Indian cooking traditions by passing them along to you. I hope to inspire every reader of this book to practice the Indian art of home cooking, and to share tips that make healthy eating easy and fun.

Diabetes: A Global Issue

The Centers for Disease Control and Prevention estimates that over 29 million people are suffering from diabetes (diagnosed and undiagnosed) in the U.S. today. According to International Diabetes Federation estimates, Europe is home to over 59 million people with diabetes, and India has the second-largest number of adults living with diabetes worldwide, and these numbers are only growing. Prediabetes and Diabetes have reached epidemic proportions worldwide. (For more information on diabetes statistics, visit http://www.idf.org/about-diabetes/facts-figures.)

These alarming statistics demonstrate the need for a return to healthy eating practices worldwide. Health organizations like the American Diabetes Association are creating programs and initiatives to try to stop this epidemic, and have resources available to help people prevent and manage diabetes.

The good news is that type 2 diabetes can be prevented and managed with a healthy diet and lifestyle changes. People with prediabetes have the opportunity to improve their health before they progress to diabetes. My hope is that the cooking principles and diabetes-friendly recipes in this book will motivate people everywhere to make healthier eating choices and teach them how to live well with this disease. I believe the traditional Indian cooking philosophy laid out in this book, centered around the proper use of nutritious ingredients and spices, may help reduce the prevalence rates of diabetes (and other chronic/lifestyle diseases) for future generations.

The Importance of Nutrition in Indian Cuisine

Many people are overwhelmed by the idea of healthy eating, especially people with diabetes or prediabetes. Today we are experiencing information overload when it comes to the topic of eating and living well. We are constantly confronted with news stories and online articles about the latest food and diet trends and exercise fads. But eating a healthy, balanced diet does not need to be complicated. When I was growing up in India, people were not easily caught up in diet trends and fads; they were more concerned with eating fresh nourishing meals. I prefer the simple principle of combining wholesome, natural foods with spices and exciting flavors. If you make every effort to minimize processed foods in your diet and choose quality ingredients, then you will not have to spend a lot of time agonizing over food labels at the store.

The recipes in this book have been carefully selected and adapted to be healthy, easy, and flavorful options for everyone, especially those with diabetes. The healthy eating guidelines and strategies implemented in this book have been designed to maintain (and hopefully improve) the health of the entire family. Traditional Indian cuisine focuses on fresh, nutrient-dense ingredients and well-balanced meals—all of which may help you maintain good health and reduce the risk of chronic diseases. Another key to eating well is to be conscious of portion size. You can eat a variety of foods, but you always need to enjoy these foods in moderation.

The guiding principles I followed while writing this book come from my Indian heritage, family knowledge, and the nutrition guidelines of the American Diabetes Association. They are simple, easy-to-follow, versatile practices that are appropriate for anyone who is trying to embrace healthy eating.

Some of these guiding principles include:
- Incorporating a wide variety of vegetables, including tubers and legumes, and trying to choose options with a lot of fiber
- Choosing seasonal, locally grown vegetables
- Making an effort to grow your own vegetables and herbs
- Keeping added sugar to a minimum and using ingredients like maple syrup and local honey instead (though people with diabetes should note that these ingredients still contain sugar and carbohydrate)
- Creating balanced plates with healthy proteins like fish, lean meat, or vegetarian proteins
- Choosing wild-caught, sustainably grown seafood
- Choosing grass-fed, local, and organic meats, if possible (or at least choosing options raised without antibiotics)
- Including colors and vibrancy in meals by adding colorful fruits, vegetables, and herbs
- Choosing quality spices and herbs, preferably organic
- Using healthy cooking techniques, such as roasting, grilling, steaming, and marinating (which add flavor without a lot of added fat and salt) and using the right vessels/tools for each cooking method

CREATING A HEALTHY INDIAN PLATE

The traditional Indian meal offers a variety of dishes—incorporating multiple vegetarian dishes, a nonvegetarian option, yogurt, a high-fiber carbohydrate such as brown rice or whole-grain bread, and condiments such as raita or chutney—but the meals are nutritionally balanced, and the portions are relatively small. The Indian plate is rich in fiber and other important nutrients. The spices, ingredients, and cooking methods used in Indian cuisine create layers of complex flavors to satisfy the palate so there is no need for large portion sizes. Portion control is essential for healthy eating. Here are some tips to help you control portions and maximize the flavor of your meals:

- *Select quality ingredients:* Whether you're shopping for fruits and vegetables, proteins, or staple ingredients such as spices, herbs, and oils, high-quality ingredients provide great flavor in small quantities
- *Use nice cuts of meat whenever possible, preferably from a local butcher:* They taste so incredible that you'll be satisfied with smaller portions
- *Eat with your eyes:* Creating a beautiful, colorful plate that you can enjoy visually will enhance your eating experience regardless of portion size

PRESERVING THE INDIAN COOKING TRADITION

The modern diet, in both India and Western cultures, has been trending toward the consumption of processed, convenience foods and restaurant eating. The high-stress, fast-paced lifestyle of today seems to leave little room for nutritious, home-cooked meals; many people think that they do not have time to cook. But home cooking is a vital part of both the Indian culinary philosophy and a healthy lifestyle in general. For the sake of our health and well-being, we all need to make an effort to cook at home. But modern Indian families and those who emigrated to Western countries have started moving away from this tradition in favor of convenient foods, larger portions, and less balanced meals. It is so easy to get pulled into the modern way of eating, but it comes at a price. Diabetes prevalence rates have been on the rise in both India and Western countries for many years now.

Processed foods and many restaurant meals are often loaded with artificial ingredients, sodium, fat, and sugar. Even some store-bought spices can be loaded with these things. Just because a food label claims that a product is "healthy," "whole-grain," or "low-fat," doesn't mean this is a quality product or that it's good for your health. Eating a diet that relies heavily on processed foods can hinder your health and well-being. So cooking from scratch using fresh, whole ingredients is a great alternative. Despite what people think, it does not have to be an inconvenience! This book was designed to showcase strategies and techniques to make home cooking easy and enjoyable for you.

Many of the recipes in this book are easy to prepare and fast enough to make even on busy weeknights. I try to take advantage of the many kitchen tools and gadgets available on the market today to make the preparation and cooking of my recipes as simple as possible. Using a food processor, grater, chopper, or spice grinder to prepare ingredients is a great time-saver! And many of the recipes in this book have steps (such as marinating, or letting dough rest) that can be started ahead of time to cut down the time spent in the kitchen on a busy night.

Part of my focus in writing this book is to make it possible for individuals and families to get back in the kitchen. Traditionally, Indian meals were prepared by and for the family; shopping and cooking were an essential part of Indian life. Sadly, many people in India today, especially younger people, have stopped cooking. We need to preserve the Indian tradition of home cooking. In addition to the health benefits of cooking healthy meals over eating processed foods, cooking together gives families and friends the opportunity to interact and connect. Learning to cook is especially fun and beneficial for children. It is a good opportunity for parents to educate them about basic nutrition and it helps them to expand their palates and take on an active role in their own health. (This is very valuable for children with diabetes for whom practicing a healthy lifestyle at a young age is particularly important.) It also gives them a skill set that will continue to benefit them throughout their lives.

The Indian cooking tradition promotes a healthy lifestyle and fosters a strong sense of wellness for the family and community. Whether you're cooking Indian dishes or your favorite healthy family recipes, it is time for all of us to start cooking from scratch and stop sacrificing our health for convenience!

A SUSTAINABLE LIFESTYLE
Growing up in India, I was fortunate enough to live in a sustainable environment. My family grew a lot of our own produce and bought local ingredients and fresh seafood. So for me, a sustainable lifestyle is not new. My family and the generations before us lived this way. I have memories of the incredible taste of the fresh foods we ate. I remember that even families

with very modest incomes had access to cheap, fresh, and extremely nutritious ingredients such as jackfruit, yucca, and sardines; you did not have to have a lot of money to enjoy fresh, healthy ingredients. I want to help bring those same experiences into modern life.

Buying local, sustainable ingredients is a great first step toward living a healthy lifestyle. It allows you to support local farmers, enjoy fresh, delicious, seasonal foods, and may even reduce your carbon footprint. I try to buy local produce and fresh, sustainably raised meat, poultry, and seafood whenever possible. I recommend buying organic produce, eggs, and dairy products that are sourced locally when you can. Organic products can be a little more expensive, so if you can't afford to buy everything organic, that's ok. Buying organic foods is a good thing to work toward, but the most important thing is to buy fresh, nutritious ingredients— preferably local—and then get into the kitchen and cook with them!

If you enjoy gardening, try growing your own herbs and produce at home. Growing your own food guarantees that you have access to the very freshest ingredients. Because you control the growing process, you know exactly what is going into the food you're eating. I find gardening to be very therapeutic.

There's nothing like the feeling of preparing a meal using ingredients you grew yourself.

Personally, I have noticed a shift away from local, sustainable eating in modern India. People in India, especially young people, are relying on restaurant meals and processed convenience foods more and more these days. I believe that this shift away from a sustainable lifestyle has coincided with a large increase in chronic diseases in India. On the other hand, there seems to be a growing awareness in the U.S. about the benefits of fresh, local eating. It is part of my mission to help spread awareness worldwide about sustainable eating and share my positive experiences with that lifestyle.

Tips and Strategies for Healthy Eating

Eating healthy isn't just about choosing quality ingredients and recipes that work with your meal plan, it is a *lifestyle*. Here you will find a few techniques that I've implemented in my own life to help you make healthy eating a joyful experience.

PLAN AHEAD
Take a few minutes at the beginning of the week to plan your meals and see what can be prepared early. Taking the time to find healthy recipes, prepare a shopping list, and maybe start preparing

elements of your dishes ahead of time can save you time in the kitchen and money at the grocery store. If you have some free time on the weekends, you can cook a few meals and keep them in the refrigerator until you're ready to eat them during the week; then all you'll need to do is reheat for a delicious, healthy meal.

A well-stocked pantry of staple ingredients (oils, spices, herbs, legumes, and grains) and produce (such as carrots, onions, garlic, and ginger) will allow you to pull together a quick meal even on a night when you don't have anything prepared. (For more information on how to stock your pantry, see The Indian Pantry on p. 22.)

SHOP SMART

Think about the layout of your favorite grocery store. Where are the fresh and frozen whole ingredients located? Usually the healthiest and most essential ingredients, such as fresh produce, dairy, eggs, meat and seafood, can be found around the perimeter of the store. The aisles in the center of the store contain a lot packaged, processed foods. With the exception of a few foods, spices, and products, you can find most of the ingredients you need to create healthy satisfying meals without venturing into the center of the store.

Don't be fooled by sale prices. When you buy things on sale, make sure you're still buying good-quality ingredients. Don't sacrifice quality just to cut costs. It's always better to avoid low-quality, mass-produced ingredients.

When you're shopping, don't be afraid to ask questions like where the food is coming from or what is in season. You can even ask your butcher or the person working the seafood counter to help you get the exact cuts of meat or fish you want.

DON'T BE AFRAID TO EXPERIMENT

Tired of eating the same meat and potatoes meals for dinner every night? Change up your routine once in a while by trying new, unusual ingredients and finding healthy recipes, like the ones in this book, that feature those ingredients. Experiment with new textures and flavors and let yourself get excited about healthy eating. If grocery shopping feels like a chore, try planning an outing to a local farmers' market. Bring friends or family and have fun browsing, sampling, and chatting with local vendors. It's a great opportunity to learn more about food and select truly fresh, nutritious ingredients. Food shopping can be fun!

THE ART OF COOKING

Food literacy—the knowledge of food and the art of cooking—is essential for everyone. Cooking is an important life skill that should be taught from a young age. I have been teaching food literacy programs for children and organizations for years, and have noticed big changes in the children who participate in these programs: they begin to eat a wider variety of foods and they start cooking at home. It's important to teach children how to be "conscious cooks"; they should be aware of what is going into their food, and understand basic cooking techniques. If you have children, spend time with them in the kitchen and give them the opportunity to learn about different ingredients and where they come from.

Adults also benefit from a culinary education and the concept of conscious cooking. I recommend that adults who don't know how to cook sign up for a cooking class. Any opportunity you have to enhance your knowledge of food, and learn basic cooking techniques will help make your time in the kitchen more enjoyable. If you have the opportunity to travel and experience different cultures, it's a great idea to take the time to learn about the cuisine and local ingredients and cooking styles. This is a great way to expand your culinary knowledge.

As with any skill, practice makes perfect. The more time you spend practicing cooking techniques, the better you'll become and the more you'll enjoy the process. A culinary education, at any age, will encourage you to be more engaged in the kitchen and aware of what you're eating. Try signing up for cooking classes alone or as a family, or find cookbooks that will teach you essential cooking techniques. It will go a long way toward making you feel comfortable and relaxed in the kitchen.

Indian cuisine can be healthy, fun, and light and is not as complicated to prepare as it looks. Let the information and recipes in this book guide you on your path toward a healthy lifestyle. I have a deep love of learning about different foods and cultures, especially Indian culture. Sharing my knowledge with my friends and family and putting it into practice in my Western kitchen has made my life happier and healthier. It brings me joy every day! I hope that my passion for food, and for life, will inspire you to start cooking and make healthy, flavorful food a priority.

Spices: An Indian Culinary Heritage

In terms of world culinary history, India is noted for spices and the spice trade, and it is recognized as one of the first international cuisines of the world. India is incredibly diverse in both geography and climate. It is home to many different landscapes that have produced a wide variety of spices and ingredients. For centuries India has been a site of cultural and culinary exchange. The spice trade in India was an essential part of the development and evolution of Indian cuisine. Spice trade routes fostered the spread of Indian ingredients across the globe, and the multitudes of spice traders and colonists who came to India over the course of the country's history shaped Indian cuisine. Ingredients, flavor profiles, and cooking styles vary greatly among regions in India, but Indian cuisine is united by the use of spices to create complex flavors.

Evidence shows that from the time of the Indus valley civilization, the Indian subcontinent was one of the world's first global economies. It has a vast network of land and sea routes and a wealth of natural resources that attracted many foreign travelers and traders. Indian cuisine has been influenced by the cultures of Afghanistan, Persia, Central Asia, the Middle East, Africa, China, Indonesia, and more.

One of the driving forces behind the spice trade in India was black pepper. Peppercorns and a flowering plant called long pepper, which produces a spice similar to black pepper, are native to the Malabar Coast on the southern part of India's west coast. Long pepper has a pungent, earthy taste. It used to be the most popular form of pepper but today it has been replaced by black pepper and various chilies. In ancient times, the ports along this coast traded black pepper, long pepper, and other Asian spices with empires such as Egypt, Babylon, Greece, and Rome.

Several key ingredients to Indian cuisine were introduced to India through the spice trade. For example, black pepper was exchanged for cloves, nutmeg, and mace, which grew only in Malacca, Malaysia. In addition to pepper, India merchants traded ingredients such as turmeric, tamarind, garlic, ginger, cardamom, and curry leaves to other parts of Southeast Asia in exchange for herbs and spices like lemongrass and galangal. Later, European colonists introduced ingredients from the western hemisphere to the subcontinent, including tomatoes, pineapple, cashews, and chilies.

Today, India exports around 60 varieties of spices to 150 countries. India is the largest exporter of turmeric in the world. Thanks in large part to the spice trade, Indian cuisine has influenced many civilizations of the world such as the Greeks and the Romans. Indian cooking is a mainstay in modern-day Britain and has become popular in many other Western cultures as well.

Spices are the heart and soul of Indian cuisine. Simple ingredients come alive when spices and herbs are used correctly in a dish. This book will introduce you to Indian spices and serve as a practical guide on how to integrate these spices into your everyday meals. My philosophy when cooking is to use less fat and salt and instead create layers of flavor using spices. The recipes in this book have been selected to showcase authentic Indian spices and while keeping the dishes as healthy and easy to prepare as possible.

As a culinary educator, I teach food literacy courses all over the country that focus on how and when to use spices. I illustrate techniques for incorporating spices into your everyday cooking. I have tried to share that same knowledge with you through the recipes and information in this book. My goal is to introduce Indian spices to a Western audience and promote healthy and flavorful cooking that is good for both the body and soul.

My ancestors were part of the spice trade in India, so I have a long family history with spices. Growing up, I had the opportunity to see the entire process of preparing spice, from harvesting to the final product. The spices my family used were incredibly pure and flavorful. When I moved to the U.S., I was not able to find spices of the same quality that I was used to back in India. This inspired me to launch my own line of organic, kosher spices through my company Passion for Spices (www.passionforspices.com). I wanted to share my knowledge about spices with the community, and use this line as a platform to discuss the importance of healthy eating and flavorful cuisine.

Many people in Western cultures

have misconceptions about how spices are used in Indian cuisine. When they think of Indian food, they think of strong flavors and *spicy* foods. Indian cuisine isn't necessarily spicy. The heat in some of the spicier Indian dishes comes from different varieties of chilies (which can be omitted if you don't like spicy foods). But there are many dishes that have a zesty, earthy, or smoky flavor rather than a lot of heat. The use of spices in traditional Indian cooking can actually be quite subtle. The trick is to use herbs and spices in the right amounts and the right combinations to create exciting, balanced flavors without overwhelming the palate. Here are a few rules of thumb that guide the use of herbs, spices, and other flavoring ingredients in Indian cooking:

- Light, simple spices are used in many Indian vegetable and meat dishes. Spices with delicate flavors—such as fennel, cumin, mustard seeds, coriander, and turmeric—enhance the natural flavors of the main ingredients without overpowering them.

- Stronger, more pungent, warm spices such as cardamom, cinnamon, cloves, nutmeg, and black pepper are generally used whole or ground and some combination of these spices is mixed into an Indian spice blend called garam masala. (The ingredients in garam masala vary from region to region in India.) Using these spices whole while cooking and then removing them from the dish before serving is the more subtle way to incorporate them into a dish; this method allows the spices to create depth of flavor without becoming too strong. The ground versions of these spices have a more intense flavor.

- Fresh, aromatic herbs such as curry leaves, cilantro, bay leaves, and mint are often combined with spices and ingredients like coconut or fresh green chilies to give dishes another layer of bright, herbaceous flavor. These herbs are often used to create a green masala base for dishes. It's easy to overlook the importance of fresh herbs in Indian cooking, but they are essential.

- Ginger paste and/or garlic paste are used as a base for *many* Indian dishes. Souring agents such as lemon juice, lime juice, tamarind paste, and yogurt are frequently used in marinades in Indian cuisine.

- It's important to always taste your food before serving to make sure that the herbs, spices, and flavors are balanced correctly!

Using spices correctly is a great skill to practice in any kitchen, regardless of the type of food you're preparing. For more information on specific spices, please see the Spice Guide on p. 16.

Spice Guide

In Indian cuisine, a masala (or spice blend) is a balanced combination of herbs and spices used to enhance the flavor and aroma of dishes. Indian cooks often come up with their own spice blends as expressions of their personal taste. The term masala in Indian cuisine simply means to rub between two surfaces; it refers to the process of grinding spices and herbs into powder form (dry masala) or paste form (wet masala). For those who don't have a lot of experience using spices or creating masalas, I've included some information on a few of the most common spices in Indian cuisine. You'll also find tips and techniques for creating masalas and using certain spices in Cooking Techniques on p. 25.

TURMERIC (*Curcuma Longa*)

Turmeric, often referred to as the spice of life in India, is a member of the ginger family, and comes from the underground rhizomes of the turmeric plant. Turmeric is native to the Indian subcontinent. Turmeric is the ingredient that gives many Indian dishes their bright yellow color. Even today, India is the largest producer and exporter of turmeric in the world.

There are two types of turmeric on the market, Madras and Alleppey turmeric. Madras turmeric is grown in the southern state of Tamil Nadu, and Alleppey turmeric is grown in the Alleppey district in the state of Kerala. Madras turmeric has a bright yellowish-orange color and a warm, bitter taste. Alleppey turmeric has darker tone of yellow, is more aromatic and earthy, and also has a bitter taste.

The most common way of using turmeric is in powder form. Ground turmeric can be found in both Indian and regular supermarkets. The raw and dried turmeric roots can be found in Indian markets.

A major component of turmeric is curcumin, which is the source of turmeric's brilliant color. In Ayurveda, curcumin is believed to have both anti-inflammatory and antioxidant properties. Antioxidants have been found to reduce, potentially even prevent, some of the damage to the body's cells caused by free radicals. Some research suggests that other components of turmeric may also be beneficial. There are turmeric supplements on the market today that are becoming popular, but these supplements may not contain all of the components of regular turmeric. Rather than using these supplements, it's important to ingest fresh or powdered turmeric.

BLACK PEPPER (*Piper Nigrum*)

Black pepper, often referred to as the king of spices or black gold in India, dominated the spice trade for centuries. It is one of the most widely used spices in the world.

There are several different varieties of pepper. Black, green, white, and pink peppercorns are all fruits of a climbing vine native to the southern Indian state of Kerala. Green pepper berries are picked, treated, and dried in the sun to produce the black peppercorns that we're all familiar with. White peppercorns come from berries that are picked when they're slightly riper than the ones used to produce black pepper. The outer husk of the berries is removed before drying the pepper, which gives this variety of pepper its white color and a milder flavor.

Pink peppercorns come from berries that are allowed to ripen fully on the vine before they are preserved. But true pink peppercorns are not commonly available in stores. The "pink peppercorns" available in supermarkets are actually not peppercorns; they come from a plant that is not related to *piper nigrum*. These berries are harvested from pepper trees native to South America. They are preserved in brine then freeze-dried and marketed as pink peppercorns.

The flavor of each of these types of pepper varies. Black pepper has a warm, pungent aroma and a bit of heat; the white pepper tastes hotter and sharper than black pepper. Unpreserved green pepper berries have a mild and fresh taste and are often put in a brine and pickled in India. The best varieties of black pepper available in western markets—including Malabar and Tellicherry pepper—come from India.

CORIANDER (*Coriandrum Sativum*)

Coriander is the seed of the herbaceous cilantro plant, a member of the carrot family. Many people think of this spice in connection with Asian and Mexican cuisine, but this spice originated in the Mediterranean region. Coriander's history dates back thousands of years (it was even mentioned in the bible and ancient Sanskrit texts). It was cultivated for both medicinal and culinary uses. The ancient Greeks and Romans brought coriander to Europe and Arab traders transported this spice to India, China, and other Asian countries.

Coriander seeds have a different aroma and taste from fresh cilantro leaves. The seeds have an earthy and citrusy flavor. The seeds are harvested when they are mature and then dried and processed. They are often toasted and powdered when used in Indian cuisine. Common varieties of coriander seeds on the market today are Moroccan (*kazbarah*) coriander and Indian (*dhania*) coriander.

This spice is the base of many India masalas and spice blends from other countries and cultures—like the North African blend called ras el hanout, for example. In Ayurveda, coriander is thought to be a very valuable ingredient that may help with digestion.

CINNAMON (*Cinnamomum Verum*)

The use of cinnamon can be traced back to ancient Egypt, Greece, and Rome. Cinnamon comes from the bark of an evergreen tree, a member of the laurel family, native to Sri Lanka. Sri Lankan cinnamon, also known as Ceylon cinnamon, is considered to be the best in quality. The aroma of cinnamon bark is sweet and warm, and the spice is delicate enough to be used in desserts. It has a savory yet bittersweet flavor.

Cinnamon is used in many spice blends around the world such as Chinese five-spice, the Middle Eastern seven spice blend called baharat, and the Indian spice blend garam masala. In India, this spice can be used either ground or whole.

Cassia, a similar spice often confused with cinnamon, also comes from the bark of an evergreen tree. Cassia is cultivated in India, and China. The dried cassia bark is thicker and darker than Sri Lankan cinnamon bark. The taste is similar, but cassia is less aromatic than cinnamon. In Western supermarkets the spice sold as "cinnamon" is often actually cassia, which is usually imported from Indonesia or China. Saigon cinnamon, from Vietnam, is a medium-quality cinnamon that is also on the market today. Most of the cinnamon you'll find in stores is either cassia or Saigon cinnamon. Ceylon or Sri Lankan cinnamon is rare to see in stores because it's expensive, but I recommend buying Ceylon cinnamon when you can.

NUTMEG AND MACE (*Myristica Fragrans*)

Nutmeg and mace are two distinct spices that come from the same fruit of a tall tropical evergreen tree native to the Maluku Islands, also known as the spice islands, in Indonesia. The largest producers of nutmeg and mace today include the Indian state of Kerala, the West Indies, Sri Lanka, and Malaysia.

Nutmeg is a wrinkled brown nut that can be found inside the outer shell of a nutmeg seed. The outer shell must be removed to harvest the nutmeg. Mace is the red web-like covering wrapped around the outside of the nutmeg shell. Mace is harvested, dried, and sold whole or ground.

Both nutmeg and mace can be used in sweet and savory dishes. Nutmeg has a warm, bittersweet flavor and a citrusy aroma. The flavor profile of mace is similar, but it's slightly sweeter and a bit more subtle. These spices are often used to flavor stocks and season meats, and they work well in dairy-based dishes and sauces.

OTHER SPICES

Ajwain Seeds

Ajwain or Ajowan seeds are small aromatic seeds from an umbelliferous plant native to India. When crushed they release a strong scent similar to that of thyme, and when eaten raw they have a very distinctive flavor, like anise with a hint of spiciness. Ajwain seeds are thought to help relieve gas pain, and they are often chewed raw in India to cleanse the palate.

Amchoor (Mango) Powder

Amchoor is a finely ground powder made from sun-dried tart green mangoes. As they dry in the sun, the mangoes turn light brown, giving the powder its color. Amchoor powder is available in Indian markets and is used as a souring agent in many Indian vegetarian dishes.

Asafoetida Powder

Asafoetida (also called *hing*) is not a spice, but it is used in dishes just like spices; it's usually cooked in oil and then incorporated into dishes. It is an aromatic resinous gum from the root-stalk of a giant fennel-like perennial herb. It has a bitter taste and a very pungent, slightly sulfurous smell. But when cooked, it has a pleasant garlic-like flavor. Asafoetida powder can be found in block or powder form in the Indian markets.

Black Salt (*Kaala Namak*)

Black salt is a rock salt that comes in irregular dark gray or pink pieces. It has an unpleasant, sulfurous odor due to the mineral compounds in the salt. However, when it is added to food, it dramatically enhances their flavors. It is often used as a finishing salt. You'll see it on a lot of street food in India and in chaat masala. Black salt can be purchased in Indian markets.

Cardamom Pods

Cardamom pods, often called the queen of spices in India, are considered a staple of Indian cuisine. Cardamom is available in many grocery stores, but in Indian markets you may see two distinct types of cardamom pods: small green pods and large black pods. Green cardamom pods are small ovals, each with three segments containing 18–20 seeds. Green pods are highly aromatic when crushed. Black cardamom pods are six to eight times larger and are milder in flavor than the green variety. Each black pod contains three segments, with 30–40 seeds.

Cloves

Cloves have a strong, pungent smell and a bittersweet flavor. They are dried, black, unopened flower buds from a tropical variety of evergreen tree. Cloves are available in both Indian markets and regular grocery stores and are usually sold whole and ground. Cloves can burn easily, so they are generally added to recipes after other whole spices, such as cinnamon.

Cumin
Cumin seeds are brown, ridged, elongated seeds that come from an herb related to parsley. They have a spicy aroma and a bitter taste. In the Indian markets you will often see two types of cumin seeds: the brown seeds and the black variety. Black cumin seeds are a rare variety of cumin with thinner, darker seeds that grows in India, Pakistan, and Iran. The black seeds have a sweet aroma.

Curry Leaves
Curry leaves come from the curry leaf tree, which is native to southern India and Sri Lanka. These leaves have a warm, citrus aroma when crushed or chopped. You'll find that many recipes in this book call for curry leaves. It's a wonderful ingredient. Curry leaves, with their slightly bitter flavor, are often used to season various Indian dishes (usually South Indian dishes), but they are not an ingredient in curry powders. They are generally removed from a dish before serving.

Fennel Seeds
Fennel seeds come from the same family as anise, dill, cumin, and caraway. These light greenish seeds look similar to cumin seeds. Fennel seeds have a licorice-like flavor and aroma. They are often eaten raw, dry-roasted, or sugar-coated in India, where they are thought to help with digestion and gas.

Fenugreek
In Indian cooking you will see three forms of fenugreek used: the seeds, the greens (or *hari methi*), and the leaves (called *kasoori methi*). Fenugreek seeds are very bitter when eaten raw, but their flavor changes when they are cooked. Fenugreek greens are very aromatic and bitter in flavor. When used in leaf form, Indian cooks crush dried fenugreek leaves between their hands to release the aroma of the ingredient before adding it to a dish. Fenugreek seeds can be found in many high-end supermarkets, but you will have to go to an Indian market to find fenugreek greens and leaves.

Jaggery
Jaggery is the unrefined brown sugar produced from the sap of sugarcane. It is available in large blocks in Indian markets. If you can't find jaggery, it can be replaced with regular or dark brown sugar in recipes.

Kokum

Kokum is the sun-dried rind of the fruit of a plant in the mangosteen family. Pieces of kokum are used as a souring agent in Indian cuisine. Kokum is mainly used in sauces for fish and seafood dishes. If you don't have kokum, you can substitute tamarind.

Tamarind

Tamarind is the fruit contained inside the pods of the tamarind tree. This ingredient can be found in the Indian and Asian markets in several forms: blocks, tamarind paste, or tamarind pulp.

The Indian Pantry

One of the first steps to creating a well-stocked pantry is to check your inventory. Go through all the ingredients you already have. How old are your spices? They lose potency over time. Do you have everything you need on hand? Springtime is a great time to clean out your pantry, discard stale or old products, and restock. Let this list guide you as you're building your Indian pantry.

WHOLE SPICES:

Black pepper
Cinnamon sticks
Green cardamom pods
Saffron
Star anise
Whole cloves

WHOLE SEEDS:

Ajwain seeds
Black mustard seeds
Brown mustard seeds
Coriander seeds
Cumin seeds
Fennel seeds

Fenugreek seeds
Nigella seeds

GROUND SPICES:

Amchoor (mango) powder
Asafoetida powder
Cayenne pepper
Chat masala
Curry powder (mild)
Garam masala
Ground black pepper
Ground cardamom
Ground cloves
Ground turmeric
Smoked paprika

CHILIES:

Dried red chilies
Guajillo or Kashmiri chilies
Red chili flakes

FRESH STAPLES:

Green chilies

AROMATICS, SOURING AGENTS, AND HERBS:

Apple cider vinegar

Bay leaves
Cilantro leaves
Curry leaves
Fresh garlic
Fresh ginger
Jaggery
Kokum
Lemons
Limes
Methi (dried fenugreek leaves)
Mint leaves
Red onions
Shallots
Tamarind paste
White vinegar

OILS:
Cold-pressed extra-virgin olive oil
Cold-pressed sunflower oil
Ghee (clarified butter)

IN THE REFRIGERATOR:
Butter
Light coconut milk
Low-fat buttermilk
Low-fat milk
Low-fat yogurt
Paneer
Reduced-fat sour cream

HOME-MADE INGREDIENTS:
Ghee (see p. 30)
Ginger-garlic paste (see p. 34)
Paneer (see p. 32)

RICE, PULSES, AND GRAINS:
Black (forbidden) rice

Brown basmati rice
Chana dal (split chickpeas/split Bengal gram)
Chickpeas
Farro
Freekeh
Masoor dal (red/pink lentils)
Mung dal (green gram dal/mung beans)
Quinoa
Toor/tuvar/arhar dal (split pigeon peas)
Urad dal (black gram/black lentils)

SALTS:
Black salt (kala namak)
Himalayan pink salt
Sea salt

SWEETENERS:
Honey
Maple syrup
Stevia bakeable blend (Pyure)
Stevia sugar blend
Superfine raw stevia blend
Truvia brown sugar blend

KITCHEN TOOLS:
Cast iron griddle
Chopper
Food processor
Grater
Heavy-bottomed pots and pans (preferably cast iron)
Idli stacker/cooker (or poacher)
Mortar and pestle
Pressure cooker
Spice/coffee grinder
Steamer

Dal Varieties

Dal, a Hindi word that means raw and prepared lentils, is a staple of Indian cuisine and is eaten throughout the country. India is the largest producer of pulses (beans, peas, lentils) today, and it is believed that some forms of dal have been consumed in India since ancient times. Some of the recipes in this book call for several different types of dal. Here is a guide to the different varieties:

Mung Dal (Mung Beans or Green Gram)

Mung dal is a small, kidney-shaped legume with green skin. In the Indian markets you'll often see three forms of this ingredient: whole green mung beans with skin on (green mung dal), split green mung beans with skin on, and skinned and split mung beans (yellow mung dal).

Masoor Dal

This type of dal is available in Indian markets as either whole green-brown lentils with the skin on (*sabut masoor*), whole red lentils without the skin, or red skinned and split lentils (*dhuli masoor* or *red masoor dal*)

Toor Dal (Tuvar/Arhar Dal, Pigeon Peas, or Yellow Split Peas)

These pale green pigeon peas are most commonly available in stores as skinned and split yellow-gold beans.

Chana (Chickpeas, Garbanzo Beans, Bengal Gram, or Chole)

Chana is the Indian term for chickpeas. There are two varieties available in the Indian market: *kala chana* and *kabuli chana*. Kala chana, or black chickpeas, are a smaller, darker variety and kabuli chana are larger, paler, and look like the chickpeas most people are familiar with.

Chana Dal (Split Chickpeas or Split Bengal Gram)

This variety of dal is very similar in appearance to yellow split peas, but is actually made from black chickpeas (*kala chana* or Bengal gram). Some recipes in this book call for roasted chana dal. You can usually find this already roasted in grocery stores. But if you can't find the roasted variety, you can buy plain chana dal and roast it yourself in a heavy-bottomed pan over medium heat for 2–3 minutes. Chana dal flour is a flour made from the skinned and split black chickpeas.

Urad Dal (Black Gram)

These small black beans resemble green mung dal in appearance when whole. They are available in Indian markets either as whole black urad beans (*sabut urad* or black urad dal), as split black urad beans with skin on (*chilkewali urad dal* or split black urad dal), or as white, skinned and split urad beans (*dhuli urad* or white urad dal).

Rajma (Red Kidney Beans)

These are available everywhere in supermarkets and Indian markets.

Indian Cooking Techniques

Cooking with Your Senses

Indian cooks rely heavily on their sense of sight and smell while cooking. An experienced Indian cook gets a feel for the doneness of the food from visual cues and aromas. This is something that takes time and practice to master, but once you get used to the techniques of Indian cooking, it becomes second nature.

Toasting and Grinding Spices

This is an important Indian cooking technique to learn, because many of the spices used in Indian cuisine should be toasted and ground before they are added to a dish. Whenever the recipes in this book call for spices or seeds to be toasted and crushed or ground, this is the procedure you should follow.

TO TOAST SPICES: Take a dry heavy-bottomed, preferably cast iron pan, and add the spices. Toast the spices over medium heat, stirring and shaking the pan constantly, to get an even toast of spices and prevent burning. During the first 2 minutes or so you won't notice a visual change in the spices, but as the moisture in the spices dries up, they will release their aroma and start to brown. Watch the spices carefully and remove them from the heat before they burn. (Please note that cumin seeds might take less time to roast than other seeds, such as coriander seeds.)

TO GRIND SPICES: It's best to grind small quantities of spices using a mortar and pestle. But it you have a large amount of spice to crush, you can use a spice grinder or coffee grinder to powder them. You can also put the spices in between two pieces of wax paper or onto a clean cutting board and crush using a mallet, rolling pin, or the bottom of a clean heavy pan.

Making Bhuna or Indian Sauce/ Curry Bases

Curry (the sauce, not the spice) is a gravy base used to cook various ingredients such as seafood, meats, and vegetables. Curries have distinct flavors and aromas based on the various regions of India in which they are prepared. The word curry comes from the Tamil word *kari*, meaning blends of spices cooked with vegetables. The British created the variation of the dish with various spices and added meat that is popular today, and hence curry came into the culinary world.

The traditional way to make curry sauces is to first heat oil in a wok or pan, then chopped onion, cumin, and other flavors such as ginger and/or garlic and add them to the pan. Once the onions are browned, any desired herbs and spices, and even tomatoes, can be added. Finally, small quantities of water, yogurt, coconut milk, or stock are introduced to the pan if/when the ingredients start to stick. After the oil separates from the rest of the mixture, the main ingredient (meat or vegetable) is added to the sauce and cooked.

Tadka (Tempering Spices)

This is an age-old technique in Indian cooking used for seasoning dal, vegetarian dishes, and some meat preparations.

Tadka, or tempering, is achieved by heating oil or ghee over medium-high heat then adding aromatic seasonings like cumin seeds, asafoetida (a powdered gum resin with an onion/garlic flavor), garlic, onions, mustard seeds, curry leaves, etc. The oil or ghee extracts the essence of the other ingredients during tempering. The seasoned oil is then added to dishes, usually towards the end of the cooking process to give the best aroma and flavor.

Dum (Steaming) Method

This cooking process showcases the ingenuity of the Indian chefs; it is the Indian traditional method of pot roasting. The process starts with adding spices to a heavy-bottom pan and building the flavor base. Then the other ingredients are added, making sure there is enough liquid in the pan to steam the ingredients, and the heat is increased to high. Then a dough is used to cover and seal the pan, essentially creating an oven, and a tight lid is placed over the dough to prevent the escape of any steam.

Tandoori-Style Cooking

Tandoori-style cooking has a long history; it originated in ancient India and is one of the mainstays of Indian cuisine.

A tandoor is a dome-shaped oven that imparts a unique taste and flavor to foods. The Indian tandoor is usually made of clay and can reach temperatures as high as 550°F / 288°C. It looks like a rounded beehive. Tandoori is a hotter and faster form of cooking than the western barbecue. Tandoors are used to make naan breads, kebabs, and tandoori meats and seafood. Today there are two types of tandoors available in the Indian markets: home-style tandoors and commercial tandoors for restaurants.

Tandoori cooking requires a tenderization process and a good flavorful marinade, which are the keys to enhancing the flavor and texture of the primary ingredient. If you don't have a tandoor, a similar effect can be achieved by heating your oven or grill to a high temperature (400°F / 205°C or higher for an oven).

Korma (Braising)

This cooking technique is similar to the western method of braising. This technique was influenced by the Mughlai style of cooking during the Mughal Empire. The main ingredient in a korma dish is often seared, then it is cooked in a small amount of a liquid base in a covered container. The base for Indian korma is usually made with yogurt, spices, and/or nuts.

LEARNING THE BASICS
How-To Recipes

How to make
Mung Dal Sprouts Ⓥ ⓰

Mung dal sprouts (or sprouted mung beans) have a long culinary history in Indian and Asian cuisine due to their nutritional properties. Today, sprouts continue to be a staple in the diets of Americans of Asian descent. Although accounts of eating sprouts appear early in human history, it took centuries for the Western world to fully realize their culinary merits. Sprouts are a source of vitamin C, and it is said that sailors in the 18th century would eat bean sprouts, along with lemons and limes, to ward off scurvy.

SERVES: 6 • SERVING SIZE: ⅓ CUP / 50 G • PREP TIME: AT LEAST 72 HOURS • COOKING TIME: NONE

1 cup / 120 g **dried mung beans**
1½ cups / 350 mL **cold water**

COOK'S NOTES
You can spray or sprinkle the cloth with water to keep it moist while the beans are sprouting. You can use this same method with other dried beans like chickpeas. Make sure the beans (or seeds) you select for sprouting are free of fungicides or pesticides. I use organic varieties to be on the safe side. Make sure to refrigerate the mung dal after it sprouts to avoid bacteria.

CHOICES/EXCHANGES
Free Food

Calories	10
Calories from Fat	0
Total Fat	0.0 g
Saturated Fat	0.0 g
Trans Fat	0.0 g
Cholesterol	0 mg
Sodium	0 mg
Potassium	50 mg
Total Carbohydrate	2 g
Dietary Fiber	1 g
Sugars	1 g
Protein	1 g
Phosphorus	20 mg

1 Take the whole mung beans and spread on a plate. Pick and clean the mung beans. Wash the beans in water 3–4 times, until water runs clear.

2 In a large bowl, add mung beans and enough water to cover and reach 1 inch / 2½ cm above the mung beans. Cover and let rest overnight at room temperature.

3 The next day, drain water from the soaked mung beans. Rinse beans thoroughly with cold water.

4 Wet a clean cloth or kitchen napkin with water and squeeze the excess water from it. Take this damp cloth and add the soaked mung beans to the damp cloth. Tightly wrap the cloth around the mung beans and put it into a covered container for 2 days.

5 After one day, you will begin to see small sprouts. They will have grown longer after 2 days. For even longer sprouts, you can keep the beans in the container for an additional day.

6 Sprouted beans will stay fresh in the refrigerator for 1–2 days. Keep them in the refrigerator after they have sprouted if you don't intend to use them the same day.

How to make

Homemade Ghee (Indian Clarified Butter)

Ghee is a form of clarified butter that originated in ancient India and is commonly used in South Asian cuisines and religious rituals. Ghee is used in many parts of India, in both sweet and savory dishes. Several communities outside the Indian subcontinent make ghee. For example, Egyptians make a similar product called samna baladi.

SERVES: 72 • SERVING SIZE: 1 TSP / 5 G • PREP TIME: NONE • COOKING TIME: ABOUT 10 MINUTES

1 lb / 450 g **unsalted butter**

1 Place butter in a medium saucepan over medium-high heat.

2 After approximately 2–3 minutes, butter will come to a boil.

3 Once boiling, reduce heat to medium. Butter will form a foam, which will disappear, and milk solids will separate.

4 Ghee is done when butter forms a second foam and milk solids turn golden. At approximately 7–8 minutes, brown milk solids will settle in the bottom of pan.

5 Gently pour ghee into a heatproof container through a fine mesh strainer or cheesecloth.

6 Store in an airtight container and keep free from moisture.

CHOICES/EXCHANGES
1 Fat

Calories	35
Calories from Fat	35
Total Fat	4.0 g
Saturated Fat	2.6 g
Trans Fat	0.0 g
Cholesterol	10 mg
Sodium	0 mg
Potassium	0 mg
Total Carbohydrate	0 g
Dietary Fiber	0 g
Sugars	0 g
Protein	0 g
Phosphorus	0 mg

COOK'S NOTES

Ghee does not need refrigeration and will keep in an airtight container at room temperature for up to 1–2 months. I prefer to use organic (and local, when possible) butter and milk products in my kitchen. They taste wonderful!

How to make

Dahi (Indian Plain Yogurt) GF

Dahi, Indian yogurt, originated in India and was later introduced to the West. Yogurt is used extensively in everyday Indian meals, often as a meat tenderizer or souring agent.

SERVES: 8 • SERVING SIZE: ½ CUP / 122.5 G • PREP TIME: ABOUT 12 HOURS • COOKING TIME: ABOUT 5 MINUTES

4 cups / 950 mL **organic 2% milk**
2 Tbsp / 30.6 g **yogurt with live cultures**

1 Add milk to a large saucepan, bring just to a boil, then set aside to cool.

2 Cool just enough so that the liquid is just over lukewarm (about 120°F / 49°C).

3 Pour warm milk in a glass or pyrex bowl and add the plain yogurt with live culture. Mix well and cover the bowl completely—top and bottom—with clean dish towels to maintain an even temperature.

4 Keep covered at room temperature until mixture has set, about 4 hours.

5 Once it is set, transfer the yogurt to the refrigerator. Refrigerate for 8 hours before serving.

6 Store finished dahi in an airtight container in the refrigerator for up to 4 days.

CHOICES/EXCHANGES
½ Reduced-Fat Milk

Calories	60
Calories from Fat	20
Total Fat	2.5 g
Saturated Fat	1.6 g
Trans Fat	0.1 g
Cholesterol	10 mg
Sodium	60 mg
Potassium	180 mg
Total Carbohydrate	6 g
Dietary Fiber	0 g
Sugars	6 g
Protein	4 g
Phosphorus	120 mg

COOK'S NOTES

You can use yogurt starter in this recipe instead of yogurt with live culture. Add fruits or other flavorings to this recipe (incorporate them just before allowing the yogurt to set) and enjoy dahi as a dessert. Indian hung curd can be made by taking dahi, placing it in sieve, and leaving it in the refrigerator overnight to drain the excess liquid.

You can use any leftover dahi from your first batch of this recipe as the live culture for the next batch; no need to buy more yogurt.

How to make

Paneer (Indian Cottage Cheese)

A staple in Indian cuisine, paneer is a fresh cottage cheese usually made from cow or buffalo milk. The word *paneer* is of Persian origin, and the ingredient is also known by the name *chenna* in many parts of India. Unlike many other cheeses, paneer does not use rennet—a complex of enzymes produced in the stomachs of unweaned calves, lambs, or goats—for coagulation. Paneer is made by heating milk and adding a souring agent like lemon juice or vinegar, causing the milk to curdle and the whey to separate from the curds. This makes it a suitable protein source for lacto-vegetarians, the primary type of vegetarians in India.

SERVES: 8 • SERVING SIZE: 2 TBSP / 15.3 G • PREP TIME: ABOUT 2 HOURS • COOKING TIME: ABOUT 5 MINUTES

½ cup / 120 mL **water**

½ gallon / 1.9 L **organic fat-free milk**

½ cup / 120 mL **lemon juice** (juice of 3 lemons)

KITCHEN TOOLS
Cheesecloth

CHOICES/EXCHANGES
1 Lean Protein

Calories	30
Calories from Fat	0
Total Fat	**0.0 g**
Saturated Fat	0.0 g
Trans Fat	0.0 g
Cholesterol	5 mg
Sodium	0 mg
Potassium	75 mg
Total Carbohydrate	1 g
Dietary Fiber	0 g
Sugars	1 g
Protein	7 g
Phosphorus	80 mg

1 Preheat a heavy-bottomed 5-quart pan over medium-high heat and add water, then milk to the pan. Let the mixture cook.

2 Meanwhile, juice lemons. Strain to remove pulp and seeds, and set juice aside.

3 Moisten a large piece of cheesecloth and set over a mesh strainer. Set the strainer over a large container to contain the whey.

4 When the milk just starts to boil, remove from heat and immediately add the lemon juice. Stir milk mixture to ensure that the acid is well mixed. You should see the milk curdle almost instantly.

5 Allow mixture to cool for about 5 minutes. Pour curdled mix into the cheesecloth-covered strainer. Gather the corners of the cloth to make a round bundle and squeeze out as much whey as you can.

6   Once most of the whey has been squeezed out and the cheese is cool enough to handle with your bare hands, gently squeeze cheesecloth again and completely cover the round block of cheese with it. Place a very heavy pot/pan over the cheese until it cools completely. This helps to press the liquid out and solidify the cheese. (Add heavy cans to the pot/pan to increase the weight if possible.)

7   Paneer will be formed, set, and ready for use after 2 hours. The texture will be firm, but yielding. This is great if you're looking to use a crumbled form of paneer for your recipe.

8   To get a firm consistency for cutting into cubes, wrap the round block of paneer with some sturdy kitchen paper towel (to wick away any stray moisture) then wrap tightly in plastic wrap and refrigerate overnight.

COOK'S NOTES

Adding milk directly to the pan and heating it tends to scorch the bottom, resulting in brown bits of caramelized milk solids. I add the milk to water in this recipe in order to minimize that problem. If the milk does not curdle immediately, add more lemon juice. You should see the whey separating; and it will be a light green color.

How to make

Ginger-Garlic Paste Ⓥ ⒼⒻ

Ginger garlic paste is a key ingredient in many Indian dishes; it's used for marinating seafood and meats and sautéing vegetables, among other things. This paste is often sautéed in oil to form the base of many curries and stews. It adds layers of flavor to many dishes. If you're not a fan of the ginger-garlic combination, you can use a ginger paste *or* garlic paste for the same purposes (see below).

SERVES: 16 • SERVING SIZE: 1 TBSP / 15 G • PREP TIME: ABOUT 5 MINUTES • COOKING TIME: NONE

1 cup / 150 g **peeled, chopped garlic**
1 cup / 150 g **peeled, chopped fresh ginger**
1 Tbsp / 15 mL **sunflower oil**
1 Tbsp / 15 mL **lemon juice**

1 Process all ingredients in a food processor until paste reaches a smooth consistency.

2 Store in the refrigerator for up to 1 week.

COOK'S NOTES

You can add up to 1 Tbsp / 15 mL water if needed for a smoother texture. If you freeze the paste, it will keep for months.

CHOICES/EXCHANGES
1 Nonstarchy Vegetable

Calories	30
Calories from Fat	10
Total Fat	**1.0 g**
Saturated Fat	0.1 g
Trans Fat	0.0 g
Cholesterol	**0 mg**
Sodium	**0 mg**
Potassium	**75 mg**
Total Carbohydrate	**5 g**
Dietary Fiber	0 g
Sugars	0 g
Protein	**1 g**
Phosphorus	**15 mg**

For Ginger Paste
SERVES: 8 • SERVING SIZE: 1 TBSP / 15 G

1 cup / 150 g **peeled, chopped fresh ginger**
½ Tbsp / 7.5 mL **sunflower oil**
½ Tbsp / 7.5 mL **lemon juice**

For Garlic Paste
SERVES: 8 • SERVING SIZE: 1 TBSP / 15 G

1 cup / 150 g **peeled, chopped fresh garlic**
½ Tbsp / 7.5 mL **sunflower oil**
½ Tbsp / 7.5 mL **lemon juice**

GINGER PASTE CHOICES/EXCHANGES 1 Nonstarchy Vegetable		GARLIC PASTE CHOICES/EXCHANGES 1 Nonstarchy Vegetable	
Calories	25	Calories	35
Calories from Fat	10	Calories from Fat	10
Total Fat	**1.0 g**	**Total Fat**	**1.0 g**
Saturated Fat	0.1 g	Saturated Fat	0.1 g
Trans Fat	0.0 g	Trans Fat	0.0 g
Cholesterol	**0 mg**	**Cholesterol**	**0 mg**
Sodium	**0 mg**	**Sodium**	**0 mg**
Potassium	**80 mg**	**Potassium**	**75 mg**
Total Carbohydrate	**3 g**	**Total Carbohydrate**	**6 g**
Dietary Fiber	0 g	Dietary Fiber	0 g
Sugars	0 g	Sugars	0 g
Protein	**0 g**	**Protein**	**1 g**
Phosphorus	**5 mg**	**Phosphorus**	**30 mg**

How to make

Brown Basmati Rice Ⓥ 🅖🅕

The word *basmati* comes from a Sanskrit word meaning "fragrant." Basmati rice is an aromatic variety of rice with long, thin grains. It is a staple in Indian cuisine.

SERVES: 21 • SERVING SIZE: ⅓ CUP / 68.3 G • PREP TIME: 20 MINUTES • COOKING TIME: ABOUT 55 MINUTES

2 cups / 380 g **brown basmati rice**
4 cups / 950 mL **water**

1 Add rice to a container and add enough cold water to cover the rice. Soak rice for at least 15 minutes.

2 After soaking, gently rinse the rice until water runs clear. Drain rice and set aside.

3 In a Dutch oven with a tight-fitting lid, combine drained rice and 4 cups / 950 mL water, and bring to a boil.

4 Once rice is boiling, stir once, cover, and reduce heat to low. Simmer for 40 minutes (do not lift the lid).

5 Remove from heat and let stand, covered, for 10 minutes. Fluff rice with a fork and serve.

CHOICES/EXCHANGES
1 Starch

Calories	60
Calories from Fat	5
Total Fat	0.5 g
Saturated Fat	0.1 g
Trans Fat	0.0 g
Cholesterol	0 mg
Sodium	0 mg
Potassium	40 mg
Total Carbohydrate	13 g
Dietary Fiber	1 g
Sugars	0 g
Protein	2 g
Phosphorus	60 mg

COOK'S NOTES

Try carefully covering the Dutch oven lid with a towel while the rice is resting for 10 minutes. This method, called dum cooking, helps the rice cook more evenly.

CHAPTER 1
Healthy Breakfasts

Spiced Apple Pancakes

SERVES: 4 • SERVING SIZE: 1 PANCAKE • PREP TIME: 5 MINUTES • COOKING TIME: 5 MINUTES PER PANCAKE

½ cup / 60 g **whole-wheat flour**

½ cup / 52 g **oat flour**

½ tsp / 2.3 g **baking powder**

½ tsp / 2.5 g **baking soda**

1½ Tbsp / 31.1 g **maple syrup**

1 cup / 240 mL **low-fat (1%) buttermilk**

2 Tbsp / 30 mL **low-fat (1%) milk**

1 **egg**

1 cup / 150 g **grated Granny Smith apple**

½ tsp / 2.5 g **ground cinnamon**

¼ tsp / 1.3 g **ground cardamom**

1 Tbsp / 15 mL **sunflower oil**

1. In a large bowl, sift together both flours, baking powder, and baking soda, and incorporate well. Set aside.

2. In a medium bowl, mix maple syrup, buttermilk, milk, and egg together. Whisk to incorporate well.

3. Add wet ingredients to dry ingredients and fold gently to form a smooth batter with no lumps. Add the apple and spices to the batter and mix well.

5. Heat a skillet over medium-high heat. Carefully grease skillet with the sunflower oil using a paper towel. Pour ¼ cup / 60 mL batter into skillet, cover with a lid, and reduce heat to medium for 3 minutes.

6. Once bubbles form on surface of pancake, flip and cook for an additional 2 minutes on medium heat. Serve hot.

CHOICES/EXCHANGES
1 Starch
1 Carbohydrate
1 Fat

Calories	200
Calories from Fat	50
Total Fat	6.0 g
Saturated Fat	1.3 g
Trans Fat	0.0 g
Cholesterol	50 mg
Sodium	290 mg
Potassium	270 mg
Total Carbohydrate	30 g
Dietary Fiber	4 g
Sugars	11 g
Protein	8 g
Phosphorus	250 mg

COOK'S NOTES

You can make these pancakes ahead of time! To reheat, preheat oven to 200°F / 94°C and layer the pancakes. Then top the stack with a wet paper towel and seal with heavy-duty aluminum foil. Heat in the oven for 10 minutes. These taste great topped with powdered sugar and grated apple.

Bulgur Wheat Upma Ⓥ

This savory breakfast grain dish is called *upma* in North India and *uppumavu* or *uppittu* in South India. In many Dravidian languages (the language in South India and parts of eastern and central India), the word "uppu" means salt and the words "mavu" or "hittu" mean flour. Upma is usually made with semolina or rava (cream of wheat), but I use hearty bulgur wheat in this version of the recipe.

SERVES: 9 • SERVING SIZE: ⅓ CUP / 60.6 G • PREP TIME: NONE • COOKING TIME: 50 MINUTES

4 cups / 950 mL **water**
2 cups /280 g **medium-grain bulgur wheat**
¼ tsp / 1.7 g **sea salt**

TADKA

1 Tbsp / 15 mL **sunflower oil**
1 tsp / 3.5 g **mustard seeds**
1 **sprig curry leaves**

MASALA

1 **medium onion, finely chopped**
1 **green chili, chopped, seeds removed**
1 (½-inch / 13-mm) **piece ginger, peeled and grated or finely chopped**
7 **unsalted cashews, finely chopped**
1 **sprig curry leaves**
¼ tsp /1.7 g **salt**

COOK'S NOTES

You can add about 1 Tbsp / 1 g chopped cilantro leaves instead of the curry leaves.

CHOICES/EXCHANGES

2 Starch

Calories	150
Calories from Fat	20
Total Fat	2.5 g
Saturated Fat	0.4 g
Trans Fat	0.0 g
Cholesterol	0 mg
Sodium	135 mg
Potassium	200 mg
Total Carbohydrate	30 g
Dietary Fiber	7 g
Sugars	1 g
Protein	5 g
Phosphorus	125 mg

1   Add water, bulgur wheat, and salt to a heavy-bottomed saucepan and bring to a boil. Once the water boils, reduce to simmer and cook for 15 minutes.

2   Turn off the heat, cover with a lid, and allow mixture to steam for about 30 minutes, until all the water is absorbed. Fluff the bulgur wheat and set aside.

3   To make the tadka, heat a heavy-bottomed wide pan over medium-high heat and add sunflower oil. Add the remaining tadka ingredients. When the mustard seeds begin to splutter, add all the masala ingredients and sauté well for about 3 minutes. Remove curry leaf sprigs.

4   Add the cooked bulgur wheat to the pan and stir well to combine. Serve.

Gujarati Khaman Dhokla (Steamed Chickpea Cake) (GF)

SERVES: 10 • SERVING SIZE: 1 PIECE • PREP TIME: 4 HOURS • COOKING TIME: 15 MINUTES

2 cups /240 g **chickpea flour or garbanzo flour**
1 tsp / 4.2 g **sugar**
1 cup / 245 g **plain low-fat yogurt**
1 cup / 240 mL **warm water**
¼ tsp / 1.7 g **salt**
½ tsp / 2.5 g **turmeric**
1 tsp / 5 g **green chili paste**
1tsp / 5 g **ginger paste (p. 34)**
1 Tbsp / 15 mL **lemon juice**
1 tsp / 5 g **baking soda**
1 tsp plus ⅛ tsp / 5.6 mL **sunflower oil**

GARNISH
1 Tbsp / 1 g **finely chopped cilantro leaves**

KITCHEN TOOLS
Steamer, Thali (or shallow baking pan)

CHOICES/EXCHANGES
1 Carbohydrate
½ Fat

Calories	90
Calories from Fat	20
Total Fat	2.0 g
Saturated Fat	0.4 g
Trans Fat	0.0 g
Cholesterol	0 mg
Sodium	230 mg
Potassium	220 mg
Total Carbohydrate	13 g
Dietary Fiber	2 g
Sugars	4 g
Protein	5 g
Phosphorus	95 mg

1 Add chickpea flour and sugar to a medium bowl then add yogurt and warm water. Mix well, making sure not to leave any lumps. Add salt and mix again. Set batter aside for 4 hours at room temperature to ferment.

2 Once batter is fermented, add turmeric, green chili paste, and ginger paste and mix well.

3 Heat a large steamer over medium heat.

4 In a small bowl, mix together lemon juice, baking soda, and 1 tsp / 5 mL sunflower oil. Add the lemon juice mixture to the batter and mix well.

5 Grease a thali (a traditional steel plate or a plate with edges) or a shallow baking pan with remaining ⅛ tsp / 0.6 mL oil.

6 Pour the batter into the prepared pan and place it in the steamer. Cover and steam for about 15 minutes, or until a toothpick inserted into the cake comes out clean.

7 Let cake cool and then cut into 10 square pieces. Garnish with cilantro.

COOK'S NOTES

Do not save any unused batter once the lemon juice/baking soda mixture has been added.

Traditional Idli
(Steamed Urad Dal Dumplings) Ⓥ ⒼⒻ

Idli is a steamed lentil and rice dumpling that is famous in southern India. Idli is mentioned in several ancient Indian works, though not in the modern form we see today. Ancient texts and authors describe idli as being prepared by soaking urad dal (black gram/black lentils) in buttermilk, grinding it to a fine paste, and mixing it with the clear water of curd and spices. Food historian K.T. Achaya speculates that modern idli recipes might have originated in the area that is present-day Indonesia. This is a breakfast/snack staple in many southern Indian homes even today. Idli is very light and can generally even be eaten by people with poor digestion.

SERVES: 10 • SERVING SIZE: 3 IDLIS • PREP TIME: 7 HOURS + OVERNIGHT • COOKING TIME: 15 MINUTES

2 cups / 380 g **long-grain rice**

1 Tbsp / 11 g **fenugreek seeds**

1 cup / 190 g **skinned and split urad dal (black lentils)**

½ cup / 102.5 g **cooked brown rice**

1 tsp / 6.7 g **sea salt**

KITCHEN TOOLS
Food processor, Idli cooker/steamer, Idli stacker

CHOICES/EXCHANGES
3 Starch

Calories	220
Calories from Fat	5
Total Fat	0.5 g
Saturated Fat	0.1 g
Trans Fat	0.0 g
Cholesterol	0 mg
Sodium	230 mg
Potassium	190 mg
Total Carbohydrate	44 g
Dietary Fiber	1 g
Sugars	0 g
Protein	8 g
Phosphorus	110 mg

1 Add long-grain rice and fenugreek seeds to a large bowl, cover with water, and soak for a minimum of 5 hours. Soak urad dal in a separate bowl also for a minimum of 5 hours.

2 After soaking, rinse both the soaked rice and dal and wash until water runs clear.

3 Using a food processor, grind the urad dal, adding small amounts of water, as needed, to get the consistency of a smooth paste. Set aside.

4 Clean the food processor and use it to grind the long-grain rice, fenugreek seeds, and cooked brown rice, adding small amounts of water, as needed, to get the consistency of a smooth paste.

5 In a baking pan or oven-safe vessel with well-fitting lid, combine the urad dal paste and rice paste and fold gently.

Fold in the salt. The batter will have a thick consistency.

6   To ferment the batter, preheat oven to 200°F / 93°C. Once it is preheated, turn oven off and place batter in the oven, covered, for about 2 hours.

7   Remove batter from oven, mix well, and let rest in the refrigerator, covered, overnight. Remove from the refrigerator 1 hour before cooking the idlis to allow batter to reach room temperature.

8   Fill the bottom of a traditional idli cooker or steamer with just enough water to reach just below the idli stacker or poacher. Oil the idli stacker and pour the batter to the brim. Place the filled stackers into the idli cooker or steamer and steam for about 15 minutes, until idlis are cooked through. (If you don't have an idli stacker or poacher, you can use a cake pan instead. See Cook's Notes.)

9   Allow idlis to cool for a few minutes then carefully remove the idlis from the stacker using a knife. Serve hot.

COOK'S NOTES

You can use a 9-inch cake pan instead of a stacker to cook the idli, but the batter will take more time to steam (about 20 minutes). Pour the batter into the pan and place the pan inside the steamer. Once the batter is done steaming, allow to cool and cut into 30 equal pieces (3 per serving).

Idli rice, available in Indian markets, can be used instead of long-grain rice in this recipe.

Rava Idli
(Steamed Semolina Dumplings)

This is a quick version of the traditional Indian dish Idli. It is very commonly eaten for breakfast in the southern region of India.

SERVES: 8 • SERVING SIZE: 2 IDLIS • PREP TIME: ABOUT 5 MINUTES • COOKING TIME: 30 MINUTES

2 cups / 334 g **rava (coarse white semolina)**

1 Tbsp plus 1 tsp / 20 mL **sunflower oil, divided**

2 Tbsp / 20 g **chopped raw cashews**

1 (½-inch / 13-mm) **piece ginger, peeled, finely minced**

1 **Thai green chili, seeds removed and finely minced**

½ cup / 72 g **frozen peas**

½ tsp / 3.3 g **salt, divided**

4 cups / 980 g **low-fat plain yogurt**

1 tsp / 5 g **baking soda**

Juice of ½ **lemon**

1 Tbsp / 1 g **finely minced cilantro leaves**

KITCHEN TOOLS

Idli cooker/steamer, Idli stacker

CHOICES/EXCHANGES
2 Starch
1 Fat-Free Milk
½ Fat

Calories	270
Calories from Fat	50
Total Fat	6.0 g
Saturated Fat	1.7 g
Trans Fat	0.0 g
Cholesterol	5 mg
Sodium	390 mg
Potassium	390 mg
Total Carbohydrate	41 g
Dietary Fiber	2 g
Sugars	9 g
Protein	12 g
Phosphorus	255 mg

1. Preheat a heavy-bottomed pan over medium heat and toast the rava (semolina) for about 10 minutes, stirring constantly to make sure it does not burn. Remove from heat and set aside.

2. To a small pan over medium-low heat add 1 Tbsp / 15 mL sunflower oil, cashews, ginger, minced chili, and peas and sauté well until the mixture is a light brown color. Add ¼ tsp / 1.7 g salt, mix well, and set aside.

3. In a large bowl, combine 1 tsp / 5 mL sunflower oil, yogurt, baking soda, lemon juice, and remaining salt. Add the toasted rava and mix well.

4. Fill the bottom of a traditional idli cooker or steamer with just enough water to reach just below the idli stacker or poacher. Oil the idli stacker and pour the batter to the brim. Add the cashew mixture on top of the batter before you steam. Place the filled stackers into idli cooker or steamer and steam for about 15 minutes, until idlis are cooked through. (If you don't have an idli stacker or poacher, you can use a cake pan instead. See Cook's Notes.)

5. Allow idlis to cool for a few minutes then carefully remove the idlis from the stacker using a knife. Serve hot.

COOK'S NOTES

You can use a 9-inch cake pan instead of a stacker to cook the idli, but the batter will take more time to steam (about 20 minutes). Pour the batter into the pan and place the pan inside the steamer. Once the batter is done steaming, allow to cool and cut into 8 pieces.

You can toast a large amount of rava ahead of time and keep it in an airtight container for later use.

Roasted Plantain

Plantains are native to the Malayo-Polynesian islands and were introduced to India via the Indian Ocean. Plantains are a staple in the southern part of India where they are eaten raw as well as ripe and cooked, as they're prepared in this recipe.

SERVES: 6 • SERVING SIZE: ⅓ PLANTAIN • PREP TIME: ABOUT 5 MINUTES • COOKING TIME: 30–35 MINUTES

2 ripe medium (about 13-oz / 368-g) **plantains**
¼ cup / 20.8 g **freshly grated coconut**
1 tsp / 4.2 g **granulated sugar**
¼ tsp / 1.3 g **ground cardamom**

1 Preheat oven to 400°F / 200°C.

2 Place whole plantains (skin on) on a baking sheet. Roast whole plantain for about 30–35 minutes, or until the inside of the plantains are caramelized.

3 Meanwhile, mix the garnish ingredients together in a small bowl and set aside.

4 Remove plantains from oven. Serve by cutting the skin open and sprinkling the garnish on top.

CHOICES/EXCHANGES
2 Starch

Calories	110
Calories from Fat	15
Total Fat	1.5 g
Saturated Fat	1.0 g
Trans Fat	0.0 g
Cholesterol	0 mg
Sodium	0 mg
Potassium	380 mg
Total Carbohydrate	26 g
Dietary Fiber	2 g
Sugars	12 g
Protein	1 g
Phosphorus	25 mg

COOK'S NOTES

Freshly grated coconut can be found in the frozen section of many grocery stores and in Indian markets.

Masala Sweet Potatoes (V) (GF)

SERVES: 12 • SERVING SIZE: ¼ CUP / 63.8 G • PREP TIME: NONE • COOKING TIME: ABOUT 20 MINUTES

1½ lb / 680 g **sweet potato**
1 cup / 240 mL **water**
½ tsp / 3.3 g **salt**
1 tsp /5 g **ground turmeric**

TADKA

1 Tbsp / 15 mL **grapeseed oil**
1 tsp / 3.5 g **black mustard seeds**
1 **dried red chili**
1 **green chili, finely chopped**
2 medium **onions, peeled, ½-inch / 13-mm dice**
1 tsp / 1.7 g **grated ginger**
6 **curry leaves**

GARNISH

½ cup / 8 g **roughly chopped cilantro leaves**
Juice of ½ **lemon**

1. Add sweet potato cubes, water, salt, and turmeric to a heavy-bottomed pot over medium-high heat and cook until fork tender, about 10–15 minutes. Most of the water should have evaporated by that point. Set aside.

2. To make the tadka, heat oil in a heavy-bottomed skillet and add the mustard seeds. Once the mustard seeds start spluttering, add the red chili. Stir in the green chili, onions, ginger, and curry leaves. Fry until onions are golden brown. Remove red chili.

3. Pour contents from skillet into the cooked sweet potato and stir well.

4. Garnish with cilantro leaves and lemon juice. Serve.

CHOICES/EXCHANGES
½ Starch
1 Nonstarchy Vegetable

Calories	60
Calories from Fat	15
Total Fat	1.5 g
Saturated Fat	0.1 g
Trans Fat	0.0 g
Cholesterol	0 mg
Sodium	115 mg
Potassium	190 mg
Total Carbohydrate	12 g
Dietary Fiber	2 g
Sugars	4 g
Protein	1 g
Phosphorus	30 mg

COOK'S NOTES

This may be served with any Indian flatbread (see recipes in chapter 9). White mustard seeds can be used instead of black mustard seeds. Any heart-healthy oil will work in this recipe.

Spiced Muesli with Fresh Fruit ⓖⒻ

This classic cold grain dish is said to have been invented by Swiss physician and nutritionist Maximilian Bircher-Benner for his patients in the late 19th century. I first experienced this delicious dish at a resort in India, and the chef was kind enough to share the recipe!

SERVES: 4 • SERVING SIZE: ½ CUP / 140 G • PREP TIME: 10 MINUTES • COOKING TIME: NONE

MUESLI

1½ cups / 135 g **old-fashioned rolled oats**

½ cup / 120 mL **cold low-fat milk (or soy or rice milk)**

¼ cup / 60 mL **apple juice**

¼ cup / 61.3 g **plain fat-free Greek yogurt**

1 large **Granny Smith apple, cored and roughly grated**

1 Tbsp / 21.2 g **honey**

3 **dried apricots, finely chopped**

½ tsp / 2.5 mL **vanilla extract**

1 tsp / 5 g **ground cinnamon**

Juice of 1 **lime**

GARNISH

2 Tbsp / 20 g **roughly chopped walnuts, lightly toasted**

3 **dried apricots, finely chopped**

1 In a large mixing bowl, combine oats, milk, and apple juice. Stir and set aside at room temperature for 10 minutes to soften. (Or you can let oats soak overnight in the refrigerator to get a softer texture.)

2 When ready to serve, add the yogurt, grated apple, honey, apricots, vanilla, cinnamon, and lime juice and mix well.

3 Stir and transfer to serving bowls. Garnish muesli with walnuts and apricots.

COOK'S NOTES

You can replace honey in this recipe with agave nectar, if desired. Instead of the apple, use any fresh fruit of your choice.

CHOICES/EXCHANGES

1½ Starch
1 Fruit
½ Carbohydrate
1 Lean Protein

Calories	250
Calories from Fat	45
Total Fat	5.0 g
Saturated Fat	0.8 g
Trans Fat	0.0 g
Cholesterol	0 mg
Sodium	25 mg
Potassium	410 mg
Total Carbohydrate	45 g
Dietary Fiber	6 g
Sugars	20 g
Protein	8 g
Phosphorus	200 mg

Masala Omelette with Mixed Veggies 🅖🅕

SERVES: 2 • SERVING SIZE: ½ OMELETTE • PREP TIME: NONE • COOKING TIME: ABOUT 10 MINUTES

2 tsp / 10 mL **sunflower oil**

1 medium **red onion, finely minced**

1 **fresh green chili, finely minced**

1 **clove garlic, finely chopped**

¼ tsp / 1.3 g **ground turmeric**

1 tsp / 5 g **ground cumin**

1 small **ripe tomato, finely minced**

2 large **eggs, beaten**

¼ tsp / 1.7 g **salt**

1 Tbsp / 1 g **freshly chopped cilantro**

1. Heat oil in a cast iron frying pan over medium-high heat. Add red onion, chili, garlic, and turmeric and sauté until soft.

2. Reduce heat to medium and add cumin and tomato. Sauté for 2 minutes, stirring occasionally.

3. Add the beaten eggs, swirling the pan to help the eggs set on the bottom. Cook for about 2–3 minutes.

4. When eggs are cooked through, fold the omelet and sprinkle with salt and fresh cilantro. Serve hot.

CHOICES/EXCHANGES
2 Nonstarchy Vegetable
1 Medium-Fat Protein
1 Fat

Calories	170
Calories from Fat	90
Total Fat	10.0 g
Saturated Fat	2.1 g
Trans Fat	0.0 g
Cholesterol	185 mg
Sodium	370 mg
Potassium	390 mg
Total Carbohydrate	13 g
Dietary Fiber	2 g
Sugars	6 g
Protein	8 g
Phosphorus	145 mg

COOK'S NOTES

You can serve this with any Indian bread. You can use curry leaves instead of cilantro leaves to garnish the omelet, if desired.

Parsi Scrambled Eggs (GF)

This dish is a popular breakfast item among the Parsi community in the western part of India. It is usually served with toast or with homemade parthas (see recipes in chapter 9).

SERVES: 8 • SERVING SIZE: 2 OZ / 56 G • PREP TIME: NONE • COOKING TIME: 25 MINUTES

1 Tbsp / 15 mL **sunflower oil**

1 small **white onion, finely chopped**

1 **serrano chili, stemmed, seeded, and finely chopped**

2 **cloves garlic, finely chopped**

2 **plum tomatoes, cored and chopped**

8 **eggs, beaten**

¼ cup plus 1 Tbsp / 5 g **chopped cilantro, divided**

1 Tbsp / 15 mL **whole milk**

¼ tsp / 1.7 g **salt**

1 Heat oil in a heavy-bottomed skillet over medium-high heat.

2 Add onion and cook, stirring occasionally, until soft, about 10 minutes.

3 Add chilies and garlic and cook, stirring frequently, until they begin to soften and brown lightly, about 3 minutes.

4 Add the tomatoes and cook, stirring occasionally, until tomatoes release their juices, about 6 minutes.

5 Add eggs, ¼ cup / 4 g cilantro, milk, and the salt. Reduce heat to medium and slowly cook the eggs, stirring frequently with a wooden spoon, until soft curds form and the eggs are just set, about 6 minutes.

6 Transfer eggs to a platter. Sprinkle remaining 1 Tbsp / 1 g cilantro over eggs and serve hot.

COOK'S NOTES

You can replace whole eggs with the equivalent amount of egg whites.

CHOICES/EXCHANGES
1 Medium-Fat Protein
½ Fat

Calories	100
Calories from Fat	60
Total Fat	7.0 g
Saturated Fat	1.8 g
Trans Fat	0.0 g
Cholesterol	185 mg
Sodium	150 mg
Potassium	135 mg
Total Carbohydrate	3 g
Dietary Fiber	0 g
Sugars	1 g
Protein	7 g
Phosphorus	110 mg

Tofu Bhurj (Scrambled Tofu) Ⓥ

In the traditional Bhurj recipe, paneer or cottage cheese is used instead of tofu. This is a healthier alternative to the traditional dish, but it doesn't sacrifice protein or flavor!

SERVES: 2 • SERVING SIZE: ABOUT 1 CUP / 200 G • PREP TIME: NONE • COOKING TIME: ABOUT 10 MINUTES

2 tsp / 10 mL **sunflower oil**

1 tsp / 2 g **cumin seeds**

1 medium **red onion, finely minced**

1 tsp / 5 g **ginger-garlic paste (p. 34)**

2 small **ripe tomatoes, finely minced**

½ tsp / 2.5 g **ground turmeric**

1 tsp / 5 g **ground coriander**

1 tsp / 5 g **smoked paprika**

1 (16.4-oz / 464-g) block **soft organic tofu, crumbled into small pieces**

½ tsp / 2.5 g **garam masala**

¼ tsp / 1.7 g **salt**

1 Tbsp / 1 g **freshly chopped cilantro**

1 Heat oil in a heavy-bottomed pan over medium-high heat.

2 Add cumin seeds and cook until they start to release their aroma. Then add onion and stir well.

3 Reduce heat to medium and add ginger-garlic paste and tomato and fry for 2 minutes, stirring occasionally.

4 Add turmeric, coriander, and paprika and sauté well for 1 minute.

5 Add crumbled tofu and mix well. Sauté for another 2 minutes.

6 Add garam masala stir quickly. Top with salt and cilantro, remove from heat, and serve.

CHOICES/EXCHANGES
3 Nonstarchy Vegetable
2 Medium-Fat Protein
½ Fat

Calories	250
Calories from Fat	130
Total Fat	14.0 g
Saturated Fat	1.8 g
Trans Fat	0.0 g
Cholesterol	0 mg
Sodium	320 mg
Potassium	700 mg
Total Carbohydrate	17 g
Dietary Fiber	4 g
Sugars	7 g
Protein	19 g
Phosphorus	275 mg

COOK'S NOTES

This dish can be served with any Indian bread.

Eggs in Tomato-Based Sauce GF

SERVES: 7 • SERVING SIZE: 1 EGG + ABOUT 1 TBSP / 15.6 G SAUCE • PREP TIME: 5 MINUTES • COOKING TIME: 10 MINUTES

7 **eggs, boiled medium hard**

1 Tbsp / 15 mL **grapeseed oil**

2 medium **onions, thinly sliced**

2 **green chilies, slit open**

1 tsp / 6.7 g **salt**

1 **sprig curry leaves**

3 **cloves garlic, thinly sliced**

1 (1-inch / 2.5-cm) **piece fresh ginger, thinly sliced**

2 **ripe tomatoes, finely chopped**

1 tsp / 5 g **ground turmeric**

1 tsp / 5 g **cayenne pepper**

1 tsp / 5 g **ground coriander**

1 tsp / 5 g **smoked paprika**

1 tsp / 5 g **ground black pepper**

⅓ cup / 80 mL **light coconut milk**

1. Peel the cooked eggs and set aside.

2. Add grapeseed oil to heavy-bottomed pan over medium-high heat. Sauté the onions, green chilies, salt, and the curry leaves until onions are translucent. Then add the garlic and the ginger, stir, and cook for about 2 minutes.

3. In a small bowl, combine the turmeric, cayenne pepper, coriander, paprika, and black pepper. Mix well.

4. Add tomatoes and spice mixture to the pan and sauté for about 3 minutes, stirring frequently. (If tomatoes begin to stick to the pan, add a few drops of water.)

5. Add coconut milk, reduce heat to medium-low, and stir. Remove curry leaves and green chilies.

6. Take the boiled eggs and score them. Add them gently to the tomato mixture and simmer until eggs are coated and sauce starts to thicken, about 2 minutes.

COOK'S NOTES

To reduce the heat level of this recipe, reduce the amount of cayenne pepper, or leave it out completely. Also, the seeds of the chilies can be removed, but keep the chili skins to retain the flavor.

This dish can be served with regular bread, parathas, or any flatbread. The light coconut milk can be replaced by low-fat evaporated milk.

CHOICES/EXCHANGES
2 Nonstarchy Vegetable
1 Medium-Fat Protein
½ Fat

Calories	130
Calories from Fat	70
Total Fat	8.0 g
Saturated Fat	2.4 g
Trans Fat	0.0 g
Cholesterol	185 mg
Sodium	410 mg
Potassium	340 mg
Total Carbohydrate	9 g
Dietary Fiber	2 g
Sugars	4 g
Protein	8 g
Phosphorus	145 mg

Fresh Papaya with Lime and Mint (V) (GF)

SERVES: 4 • SERVING SIZE: ¼ PAPAYA • PREP TIME: ABOUT 2 HOURS • COOKING TIME: NONE

1 medium (1-lb / 450-g) **ripe papaya**

½ tsp / 2.5 g **chaat masala**

1 **lime, cut into 4 wedges**

1 **bunch mint, stems removed, leaves cut into a chiffonade**

1   Cut the papaya in half lengthwise and remove the seeds and white pith with a spoon. Then cut into 4 wedges.

2   Chill papaya in the refrigerator for 1–2 hours and take out a few minutes before serving.

3   Sprinkle wedges with chaat masala. Serve with lime wedges and garnish with mint leaves.

CHOICES/EXCHANGES

½ Fruit

Calories	35
Calories from Fat	5
Total Fat	0.5 g
Saturated Fat	0.1 g
Trans Fat	0.0 g
Cholesterol	0 mg
Sodium	80 mg
Potassium	160 mg
Total Carbohydrate	9 g
Dietary Fiber	2 g
Sugars	6 g
Protein	1 g
Phosphorus	10 mg

COOK'S NOTES

Chaat masala is available in Indian markets and online. Instead of the chaat masala, you can use ¼ tsp / 1.3 g ground cumin, ½ tsp / 2.5 g chili powder, and ⅛ tsp / 0.8 g salt. You can also add ¼ tsp / 1.3 g amchoor (mango) powder if you'd like.

CHAPTER 2
Appetizers, Snacks, and Street Food

Baked Spicy Kale Chaat Ⓥ ⓖⒻ

Chaat is a term for street snacks sold along the streets of India. Chaat originated in some parts of Uttar Pradesh in northern India, but now they are eaten all across the Indian subcontinent. There are many varieties of chaats. Some chaat recipes were influenced by colonizers of India.

SERVES: 8 • SERVING SIZE: 3 OZ / 85 G • PREP TIME: 10 MINUTES • COOKING TIME: 15 MINUTES

10 cups / 670 g **kale, torn into bite-size pieces, washed, and thoroughly dried**

2 Tbsp / 30 mL **extra-virgin olive oil**

1 tsp / 5 g **finely grated lemon zest**

¼ tsp / 1.7 g **coarse sea salt**

1 tsp / 5 g **chaat masala**

COOK'S NOTES

Instead of the chaat masala in this recipe, you can use ¼ tsp / 1.3 g cumin, ½ tsp / 2.5 g chili powder, and ⅛ tsp / 0.8 g salt. You can also add ¼ tsp / 1.3 g amchoor (mango) powder if you'd like.

CHOICES/EXCHANGES
1 Fat

Calories	40
Calories from Fat	30
Total Fat	3.5 g
Saturated Fat	0.5 g
Trans Fat	0.0 g
Cholesterol	0 mg
Sodium	75 mg
Potassium	100 mg
Total Carbohydrate	2 g
Dietary Fiber	1 g
Sugars	0 g
Protein	1 g
Phosphorus	20 mg

1 Heat oven to 350°F / 180°C.

2 In a large bowl, toss kale pieces with olive oil. Massage the oil onto each kale piece until oil is evenly distributed and the kale glistens. Spread kale out evenly on 2 (17 × 12–inch) jellyroll pans or regular sheet pans. Try not to let the kale overlap too much or it won't get crispy.

3 Take an additional 2 sheet pans of the same size, spray the bottom of the pans with cooking spray, and place them on top of the pans with kale chips. Press down.

4 Bake kale until the leaves look crisp and can be crumbled, about 15 minutes. If they are not crisp, bake for another 2–4 minutes.

5 Remove from the oven and cool kale to room temperature. Sprinkle with lemon zest, sea salt, and chaat masala.

COOK'S NOTES

Make sure the kale pieces are completely dry before baking; if not, they will steam rather than crisp in the oven.

You may need to bake the kale chips in 2 batches in order for the kale to crisp up well. Using the second baking sheet on top of the chips helps the chips to be flat rather than crinkled up.

Phal Ki Chaat (Mixed Fruit Salad)

The word *phal* means fruit in Hindi. Phal ki chaat is a very popular dish in the streets of India, especially during the hot summer days. This recipe features various seasonal mixed fruits and salty and spicy seasoning that will have your lips smacking.

SERVES: 8 • SERVING SIZE: 3 OZ / 85 G • PREP TIME: 5 MINUTES • COOKING TIME: NONE

1 cup / 150 g **cubed ripe papaya (½-inch / 13-mm cubes)**

1 cup / 150 g **cubed watermelon (½-inch / 13-mm cubes)**

1 cup / 150 g **halved green grapes**

½ cup / 75 g **pomegranate seeds**

Juice of ½ **lemon**

2 tsp / 10 g **chaat masala**

½ tsp / 3.3 g **sea salt**

7 **mint leaves, finely shredded**

1 In a large bowl, mix all the fruit together. Add lemon juice and mix well.

2 Sprinkle fruit with chaat masala and salt, and garnish with mint leaves.

CHOICES/EXCHANGES
½ Fruit

Calories	35
Calories from Fat	5
Total Fat	0.5 g
Saturated Fat	0.0 g
Trans Fat	0.0 g
Cholesterol	0 mg
Sodium	140 mg
Potassium	125 mg
Total Carbohydrate	9 g
Dietary Fiber	1 g
Sugars	7 g
Protein	1 g
Phosphorus	15 mg

COOK'S NOTES

You can mix a little amchoor (mango) powder, ground cumin, and chili powder together and sprinkle the mixture on the fruit instead of using the chaat masala, if desired. Use any fruit you'd like in this delicious snack recipe; try to look for fruit that is in season.

Roasted Chickpeas GF

SERVES: 8 • SERVING SIZE: 3 OZ / 85 G • PREP TIME: 10 MINUTES • COOKING TIME: 1 HOUR AND 30 MINUTES

2 (15-oz / 422-g) cans **chickpeas, rinsed and drained** OR
3 cups / 492 g **cooked chickpeas**
1 Tbsp / 15 mL **extra-virgin olive oil**

SPICE MASALA
1½ tsp / 7.5 g **mild curry powder**
¼ tsp / 1.3 g **smoked paprika**
¼ tsp / 1.3 g **ground black pepper**
1.2 tsp / 2.5 g **garlic powder**
½ tsp / 2.5 g **onion powder**
⅓ cup / 30 g **freshly grated parmesan cheese**

GARNISH
Juice of ½ **lemon**
¼ tsp / 1.7 g **sea salt**

1. Preheat oven to 400°F / 200°C. Line a baking sheet with parchment paper.

2. Once you have thoroughly rinsed and drained the chickpeas, place them on a clean dish towel. Wrap the towel around the chickpeas and rub them together to remove outer skins and to make sure they're fully dry.

3. Transfer chickpeas to a large bowl. Stir in olive oil and all spice masala ingredients. Toss to coat well.

4. Spread chickpeas evenly on a lined baking sheet and bake for 1 hour and 30 minutes, shaking the pan every 20 minutes to roast chickpeas evenly.

5. Remove chickpeas from the oven, top with lemon juice and salt, and serve.

CHOICES/EXCHANGES
1 Starch
1 Lean Protein
½ Fat

Calories	130
Calories from Fat	35
Total Fat	4.0 g
Saturated Fat	0.9 g
Trans Fat	0.0 g
Cholesterol	0 mg
Sodium	220 mg
Potassium	200 mg
Total Carbohydrate	18 g
Dietary Fiber	5 g
Sugars	3 g
Protein	7 g
Phosphorus	130 mg

COOK'S NOTES

Make sure the chickpeas are completely dry. If they're still wet when you bake them, they won't turn out crispy.

Sweet Potato Chaat Ⓥ ⒼⒻ

SERVES: 6 • SERVING SIZE: 3 OZ / 85 G • PREP TIME: 5 MINUTES • COOKING TIME: 1 HOUR AND 5 MINUTES

3 medium (5.25-oz / 148-g)
  **sweet potatoes, washed, dried,
  and pierced with a fork**
1 Tbsp / 15 mL **sunflower oil**

SPICE MASALA
1 tsp / 2 g **cumin seeds, toasted
and crushed**
1 tsp / 5 g **chili powder**
½ tsp / 2.5 mL **lemon juice**
1 tsp / 5 g **smoked paprika**
½ tsp / 3.3 g **salt**

GARNISH
Juice of ½ **lemon**

1 Preheat oven to 400°F / 200°C. Line a baking sheet with parchment paper.

2 Place sweet potatoes on baking sheet and bake (skin on) for 30 minutes.

3 Reduce the oven temperature to 375°F / 190°C. Remove sweet potatoes from oven and allow to cool.

4 Once they are cool enough to handle, peel and dice potatoes into ½-inch / 13-mm cubes. Place cubes in a bowl and mix with oil.

5 Bake potato cubes on lined baking sheet for about 25 minutes. Stir and bake for another 10 minutes, until crispy. Meanwhile, combine spice masala ingredients in a small bowl.

6 Remove potatoes from oven. While still hot, sprinkle with spice masala and garnish with lemon juice.

CHOICES/EXCHANGES
1 Starch

Calories	80
Calories from Fat	20
Total Fat	2.5 g
Saturated Fat	0.3 g
Trans Fat	0.0 g
Cholesterol	0 mg
Sodium	220 mg
Potassium	300 mg
Total Carbohydrate	13 g
Dietary Fiber	2 g
Sugars	4 g
Protein	1 g
Phosphorus	35 mg

COOK'S NOTES

Toasting the cumin seeds before use will give the spice an incredible flavor. The technique for toasting the cumin seeds can be found in Indain Cooking Techniques (p. 25). But if you don't have cumin seeds or don't want to toast your own, you can use ½ tsp / 2.5 g ground cumin instead.

Karela (Bitter Melon) Chips Ⓥ ⒼⒻ

Karela, or bitter melon, is a vegetable that is used extensively in Asian countries. It is widely grown and eaten in India, Southeast Asia, China, and East Africa, where it is appreciated for its nutritional value. In India it is considered to be a good vegetable option for people with diabetes. Bitter melon can be found in Indian and Asian markets.

SERVES: 4 • SERVING SIZE: ABOUT 7 CHIPS • PREP TIME: 35 MINUTES • COOKING TIME: 20 MINUTES

2 large (about 7 × 2 inches) or 3 medium **bitter melons, washed, trimmed, and sliced into ½-inch / 13-mm rounds**

1 tsp / 6.7 g **salt, divided**

1 tsp / 5 g **amchoor (mango) powder**

1 tsp / 5 g **ground coriander**

1 tsp / 5 g **cayenne pepper**

¼ tsp / 1.3 g **ground turmeric**

1 Tbsp / 7.5 g **chickpea flour**

1 Tbsp / 7.5 g **rice flour**

1 Tbsp / 15 mL **sunflower oil**

CHOICES/EXCHANGES
½ Carbohydrate
½ Fat

Calories	60
Calories from Fat	30
Total Fat	3.5 g
Saturated Fat	0.4 g
Trans Fat	0.0 g
Cholesterol	0 mg
Sodium	150 mg
Potassium	230 mg
Total Carbohydrate	6 g
Dietary Fiber	2 g
Sugars	1 g
Protein	1 g
Phosphorus	30 mg

1 Preheat oven to 400°F / 200 °C.

2 In a large bowl, combine the slices of the bitter melon and ¾ tsp / 5 g salt. Set aside at room temperature for 30 minutes. (This helps reduce the bitterness of the melon. After 30 minutes, the bitter melon will ooze out excess water.)

3 After 30 minutes, squeeze excess water out of the melon and pat dry with a paper towel.

4 In a medium bowl, combine the amchoor powder, coriander, cayenne, turmeric, chickpea flour, and rice flour; mix well.

5 Toss the spice mixture with melon pieces, making sure melon is evenly coated, and set aside.

6   Line a baking sheet with aluminum foil and place a wire cookie rack on top. Arrange the bitter melon slices on the rack, drizzle with oil, and bake for 15 minutes.

7   Turn melon slices and bake for another 5 minutes until golden brown.

8   Remove melon from the oven, sprinkle with remaining ¼ tsp / 1.7 g salt, and allow to cool before enjoying.

COOK'S NOTES

Instead of salting the bitter melon, you can soak the melon slices in some salt water, lemon water, or tamarind water (1 cup / 240 mL water and ½ tsp / 2.5 mL tamarind paste). Let sit for 30 minutes, then drain and pat dry. (Make sure you dry thoroughly; the melon needs to be very dry to get crispy in the oven.)

Golgappa
(Mini Pooris with Purple Potato Filling) 🄶🄵

The Indian snack *golgappa*, or *panipuri*, has various names depending on the region in which it is served. Golgappa is a popular street snack featuring poori—crispy puffed Indian bread—often filled with spiced liquid, sprouted chickpeas, or masala potatoes, served with a variety of chutneys. To keep this recipe quick and simple, I call for scoop-shaped chips instead of traditional poori.

SERVES: 8 • SERVING SIZE: 2 SCOOPS OR "POORIS" • PREP TIME: 5 MINUTES • COOKING TIME: 15–20 MINUTES

7 medium (1-oz / 28-g) **purple potatoes**

1 small **onion, finely minced**

1 **green chili, minced**

1 tsp / 0.3 g **finely chopped cilantro**

½ tsp / 3.3 g **sea salt**

1 tsp / 5 g **ground cumin**

½ tsp / 2.5 g **chili powder**

Juice of ½ **lemon**

16 **scoop-shaped tortilla chips** (Tostitos Scoops, for example)

4 Tbsp / 60 g **Green Mint and Coriander Chutney (p. 243)**

1. Fill a heavy-bottomed saucepan with cold water and add potatoes. Heat over medium-high heat and boil potatoes (skin on) for 15–20 minutes.

2. Once cooked, allow potatoes to cool and then peel them.

3. Add potatoes to a large bowl and break into bite-size pieces using a fork. Add the onion, chili, cilantro, salt, cumin, chili powder, and lemon juice and mix well to combine.

4. Divide the potato mixture evenly among the 16 chips. Top each stuffed "poori" with a dash of chutney and serve.

CHOICES/EXCHANGES
1 Starch

Calories	60
Calories from Fat	15
Total Fat	1.5 g
Saturated Fat	0.2 g
Trans Fat	0.0 g
Cholesterol	0 mg
Sodium	200 mg
Potassium	200 mg
Total Carbohydrate	11 g
Dietary Fiber	2 g
Sugars	1 g
Protein	1 g
Phosphorus	30 mg

Corn Bhutta (Roasted Corn on the Cob)

SERVES: 10 • SERVING SIZE: ½ EAR OF CORN • PREP TIME: 30 MINUTES • COOKING TIME: ABOUT 5 MINUTES

5 large (7¾–9-inch-long) **ears corn (husks on)**
1 tsp / 5 g **cayenne pepper**
¼ tsp / 1.3 g **ground cumin**
½ tsp / 3.3 g **sea salt**
3 **fresh limes, halved**

1 Soak the corn (husks on) in large bowl or pot of water for 30 minutes.

2 Remove the husks and silk from the corn. (Or you can roast corn with husks still on and remove the husks after roasting. This allows the corn to caramelize rather than char while roasting.)

3 Roast corn on a grill or over an open gas flame (gas stove) on medium-high heat. Rotate each ear every 30 seconds or so, so the corn gets roasted evenly. (You will hear some kernels pop while cooking.) Remove roasted ears from the grill or flame and set aside.

4 Mix cayenne, cumin, and salt in a bowl.

5 Carefully remove the husks and silk from corn if you have not done so already. Dip lime halves into the spice mix to pick up the spices and rub all over corn, making sure to squeeze lime juice while doing so. Serve.

COOK'S NOTES

Soaking the corn before cooking helps prevent it from burning.

CHOICES/EXCHANGES
1 Starch

Calories	60
Calories from Fat	10
Total Fat	1.0 g
Saturated Fat	0.1 g
Trans Fat	0.0 g
Cholesterol	0 mg
Sodium	110 mg
Potassium	140 mg
Total Carbohydrate	13 g
Dietary Fiber	2 g
Sugars	3 g
Protein	2 g
Phosphorus	45 mg

Beetroot Tikki Ⓥ 🅖🅕

SERVES: 8 • SERVING SIZE: 1 TIKKI • PREP TIME: 5 MINUTES • COOKING TIME: ABOUT 10 MINUTES

¾ cup / 146 g **boiled, peeled, and grated beetroot**

¼ cup / 21 g **finely grated carrot**

¼ cup /64 g **cooked and mashed potatoes** (about 1 medium potato)

½ tsp / 2.5 g **chaat masala**

½ tsp / 2.5 g **chili powder**

¼ tsp / 1.3 g **amchoor (mango) powder**

¼ tsp / 1.3 g **garam masala**

2 Tbsp / 2 g **finely chopped cilantro**

¾ tsp / 5 g **salt**

1 Tbsp / 7.5 g **corn flour**

2 Tbsp / 30 mL **sunflower oil**

1 Combine all ingredients except the corn flour and oil in a large bowl and mix well.

2 Divide the mixture into 8 equal portions and roll each portion into 1-inch / 2.5-cm round tikkis.

3 Add corn flour to a plate. Press tikkis into the corn flour until they are evenly coated on all sides.

4 Heat oil in a flat cast iron skillet over medium-high heat. Shallow fry the tikkis, a few at a time, until they turn golden brown on all sides.

5 Drain cooked tikkis on an absorbent paper towel. Serve immediately.

CHOICES/EXCHANGES
½ Starch
½ Fat

Calories	70
Calories from Fat	30
Total Fat	3.5 g
Saturated Fat	0.4 g
Trans Fat	0.0 g
Cholesterol	0 mg
Sodium	250 mg
Potassium	230 mg
Total Carbohydrate	10 g
Dietary Fiber	1 g
Sugars	3 g
Protein	1 g
Phosphorus	30 mg

COOK'S NOTES

This appetizer can be served with mint chutney (or any chutney recipe from this book). It also makes a delicious lunch. You can use ½ tsp / 2.5 mL lemon juice instead of the amchoor powder, if desired. The chaat masala can be replaced with ground cumin.

Spiced Beef Sliders

SERVES: 8 • SERVING SIZE: 1 SLIDER • PREP TIME: 5 MINUTES • COOKING TIME: 6 MINUTES

1 lb / 450 g **organic 95% lean ground beef**

2 medium **red onions, finely diced**
 (about 1 cup / 150 g)

1 **green chili, finely minced**

1 Tbsp / 15 g **ginger-garlic paste (p. 34)**

1 tsp / 5 g **garam masala**

1 tsp / 5 g **ground fennel**

½ tsp / 3.3 g **salt**

1 tsp / 5 g **ground black pepper**

1 Tbsp / 15 mL **Worcestershire sauce**

1 Tbsp / 15 mL **sunflower oil**

GARNISH

16–24 **baby spinach leaves**

1. In a large bowl, combine ground beef, red onions, chili, ginger-garlic paste, garam masala, fennel powder, salt, pepper, and Worcestershire sauce. Mix well.

2. Form mixture into eight 2-oz / 56-g patties (about ¼ packed cup per slider).

3. Heat oil on a cast iron griddle over medium-high. Once oil is hot, place patties onto the griddle and cook for 3 minutes per side, until they reach your desired doneness.

4. Serve each slider on 2–3 baby spinach leaves.

COOK'S NOTES

You can use grass-fed ground beef, if available; it's a healthy and delicious choice. If your meal plan allows, you can serve these sliders on small whole-wheat slider buns with the spinach leaves. Or the spinach leaves can be replaced by watercress (5 watercress leaves to replace 2–3 spinach leaves).

CHOICES/EXCHANGES
2 Lean Protein
½ Fat

Calories	110
Calories from Fat	45
Total Fat	5.0 g
Saturated Fat	1.5 g
Trans Fat	0.1 g
Cholesterol	35 mg
Sodium	200 mg
Potassium	280 mg
Total Carbohydrate	5 g
Dietary Fiber	1 g
Sugars	2 g
Protein	12 g
Phosphorus	120 mg

CHAPTER 3
Chicken and Vegetable Curries

Chicken Curry in a Hurry (GF)

The word curry comes from the Tamil word *kari*, which means "sauce." In the culinary world, curry is usually used to indicate a dish of vegetables and/or meat cooked with spices. Curry powder is generally a mixture of spices like turmeric, chili powder, ground coriander, ground cumin, ground ginger, and pepper, and it can be purchased in mild, medium, or hot strengths in many grocery stores. Many of these spices are used in this quick, delicious curry dish.

SERVES: 6 • SERVING SIZE: ½ CUP / 125 G • PREP TIME: 5 MINUTES • COOKING TIME: 30 MINUTES

2 lb / 900 g **boneless, skinless chicken thighs, cut into small pieces**

2 Tbsp / 30 mL **grapeseed oil**

1 tsp / 5 g **ginger paste (p. 34)**

1 tsp / 5 g **garlic paste (p. 34)**

¼ tsp / 1.3 g **ground turmeric**

1 tsp / 5 g **cayenne pepper**

3 tsp / 15 g **ground coriander**

1 tsp / 5 g **ground black pepper**

1 tsp / 5 mL **white vinegar**

2 medium **red or white onions, diced (1-inch /2.5-cm cubes)**

2 **green chilies, slit open**

1 **sprig curry leaves**

2 small (4-oz / 113-g) **sweet potatoes, diced (2-inch / 5-cm cubes)**

¼ cup / 60 mL **light coconut milk**

1¾ cup / 420 mL **water**

½ tsp / 3.3 g **salt**

GARNISH

1 Tbsp / 1 g **freshly chopped cilantro**

CHOICES/EXCHANGES
½ Starch
1 Nonstarchy Vegetable
3 Lean Protein
2 Fat

Calories	290
Calories from Fat	130
Total Fat	14.0 g
Saturated Fat	3.3 g
Trans Fat	0.0 g
Cholesterol	135 mg
Sodium	310 mg
Potassium	590 mg
Total Carbohydrate	15 g
Dietary Fiber	2 g
Sugars	5 g
Protein	26 g
Phosphorus	275 mg

1 Clean and dry chicken pieces. Set aside.

2 Heat the grapeseed oil in a heavy-bottomed pan over medium heat. Add the ginger and garlic paste and sauté for about 1 minute. In a small bowl, combine the turmeric, cayenne pepper, coriander, black pepper, and white vinegar to form a masala. Add the masala to the pan. (If the spice mixture seems dry, you can add a few drops of water to the pan to prevent it from burning.)

3 Add onions, green chilies, and curry leaves and sauté for about 3 minutes, or until brown.

4 Add chicken pieces and the sweet potatoes and sear them in the masala mixture. Reduce the heat to medium-low, cover with a lid, and cook the chicken for about 20 minutes.

5 Add coconut milk mixed with the water and simmer over low heat.

6 Turn off heat as soon the gravy starts to thicken. Remove green chilies and curry leaves. Season with salt, garnish with chopped cilantro, and serve hot.

COOK'S NOTES

This dish is often served with Indian bread or steamed brown basmati rice. You can remove the seeds of the green chili to reduce the heat level, but keep the skin for flavor.

Nilgiri Murgh Korma (Chicken Korma)

This Korma recipe originally comes from the Indian state of Tamil Nadu in southern India. The base of this dish consists of aromatic ingredients like coconut, mint, and coriander, and this recipe uses spices such as cinnamon, nutmeg, and white pepper to create a delicate flavor.

SERVES: 6 • SERVING SIZE: ABOUT ⅓ CUP / 85 G • PREP TIME: AT LEAST 2 HOURS • COOKING TIME: ABOUT 30 MINUTES

2 lb / 900 g **boneless, skinless chicken breast, cut into 1-inch / 2.5-cm cubes**

MARINADE

¼ cup / 61.3 g **plain fat-free Greek yogurt**

Juice of ½ **lemon**

1 tsp / 5 g **smoked paprika**

1 tsp /5 g **ground coriander**

½ tsp / 2.5 g **ground cinnamon**

¼ tsp / 1.3 g **ground nutmeg**

½ tsp / 2.5 g **ground white pepper**

1 Tbsp / 15 g **ginger-garlic paste (p. 34)**

½ tsp / 3.3 g **salt**

ONION MASALA

2 tsp / 10 mL **sunflower oil**

2 **white onions, chopped**

2 tsp /10 g **minced fresh ginger**

1 **green chili, seeds removed and finely chopped**

½ tsp / 2.5 g **ground white pepper**

1 Tbsp / 14 g **ground coriander**

½ tsp / 2.5 g **garam masala**

¼ tsp / 0.9 g **light brown sugar**

¼ tsp / 1.7 g **salt**

½ cup / 120 mL **light coconut milk**

GREEN MASALA

1 cup / 16 g **packed fresh cilantro leaves**

10 **mint leaves**

1 (1-inch / 2.5-cm) **piece fresh ginger, chopped**

1 **green chili, seeds removed**

Juice of 1 **lime**

1 Tbsp / 15 mL **sunflower oil**

2 Tbsp / 30 mL **light coconut milk**

CHOICES/EXCHANGES
½ Carbohydrate
5 Lean Protein

Calories	260
Calories from Fat	80
Total Fat	9.0 g
Saturated Fat	2.8 g
Trans Fat	0.0 g
Cholesterol	85 mg
Sodium	380 mg
Potassium	550 mg
Total Carbohydrate	10 g
Dietary Fiber	2 g
Sugars	4 g
Protein	34 g
Phosphorus	300 mg

1 Combine all of the marinade ingredients in a large bowl. Add the chicken and set aside in the refrigerator to marinate for at least 2 hours.

2 Once chicken is marinated, preheat oven to 400°F / 200°C.

3 Bake chicken for about 10 minutes, flip, and cook for an additional 10 minutes. Set chicken aside.

4 To make the onion masala: Heat the oil in a heavy-bottomed pan over medium heat and add the onions, ginger, and green chili. Sauté well for 1 minute. Add the white pepper, coriander, and garam masala and sauté for another minute. Then add the sugar, salt, and coconut milk and stir well. Simmer for 1 minute.

5 Remove onion masala from heat, add to a blender or food processor, and purée until smooth. Set aside.

6 Add all green masala ingredients to a blender or food processor and purée to form a smooth paste. Set aside.

7 Add cooked chicken and onion masala puree to the same pan you used to sauté the onion masala. Mix well and cook over medium heat for about 5 minutes.

8 Add the green masala and continue cooking for another minute over low heat. Add the coconut milk, stir, and turn off the heat. Serve hot.

Navratan Korma
(Mixed Fruit and Vegetable Braise) (GF)

SERVES: 4 • SERVING SIZE: ½ CUP / 113 G • PREP TIME: NONE • COOKING TIME: ABOUT 30 MINUTES

2 medium **white onions, cut into chunks**

¼ cup / 34.3 g **unsalted raw cashew nut, soaked in cold water**

2 cups / 320 g cubed **mixed spring fruits and vegetables** (¼ cup / 40 g each of **carrots, potatoes, radishes, Brussels sprouts, cauliflower, leeks, fava beans, and pineapple; all cut into 1-inch / 2.5-cm cubes**)

2 tsp / 10 mL **sunflower oil**

½ tsp / 1 g **cumin seeds**

5 **white peppercorns**

1 **cinnamon stick, broken**

3 **green cardamom pods**

3 **whole cloves**

2 tsp / 10 g **ginger-garlic paste (p. 34)**

1 **green chili, finely chopped**

¼ tsp / 1.3 g **ground turmeric**

⅓ tsp / 2.2 g **salt**

½ tsp / 2.5 g **Chinese five-spice powder**

1 Tbsp / 15 mL **heavy cream**

GARNISH

2 tsp / 6.7 g **pomegranate seeds**

1 Tbsp / 1 g **cilantro leaves**

CHOICES/EXCHANGES
½ Starch
3 Nonstarchy Vegetable
1½ Fat

Calories	180
Calories from Fat	70
Total Fat	8.0 g
Saturated Fat	2.0 g
Trans Fat	0.0 g
Cholesterol	8 mg
Sodium	210 mg
Potassium	470 mg
Total Carbohydrate	23 g
Dietary Fiber	5 g
Sugars	7 g
Protein	6 g
Phosphorus	145 mg

1   In a saucepan, boil onions and cashews in 1 cup / 240 mL water for about 10 mintues. Add the cashews, onions, and 1 Tbsp / 15 mL of the water from the saucepan to a blender or food processor. Purée to a fine paste and set aside.

2   Steam the vegetable mixture (except the leeks, fava beans, and pineapple) in a steamer for 2–3 minutes, until tender-crisp, and set aside.

3   Heat oil in a heavy-bottomed pan over medium-high heat and add the cumin seeds. When cumin seeds begin to splutter, add peppercorns, cinnamon, cardamom pods, and cloves. Sauté for 1 minute. Add the ginger-garlic paste, green chili, and turmeric and stir.

4   Add the white part of the leeks to the pan and stir well. Add the rest of the leeks, the fava beans, pineapple, salt, and Chinese five-spice powder. Stir-fry over medium heat until well coated with the spices.

5   Reduce heat to medium and add cashew-onion mixture, stirring a few times until the onion is translucent, about 10 minutes. Add cream and more water if needed (the consistency should be that of a thick gravy), reduce heat to low, and stir well until all ingredients are heated through.

6   Remove whole spices from the dish. Garnish the Korma with pomegranate seeds and cilantro before serving.

COOK'S NOTES

You can use any vegetables you'd like in this dish. Garam masala can be substituted for the Chinese five-spice powder.

Palak Tofu (Tofu in Spinach Sauce) Ⓥ

This recipe is a variation of the Indian dish *palak paneer*. Tofu is used in this recipe in place of the paneer (homemade cottage cheese) for a healthier twist. In traditional Indian preparations, palak—a large-leaf spinach—is used, but in this recipe I've used baby spinach.

SERVES: 4 • SERVING SIZE: 2 OZ / 56 G • PREP TIME: 5 MINUTES • COOKING TIME: 25 MINUTES

10 oz / 280 g **baby spinach, washed and cleaned**

2 Tbsp / 30 mL **sunflower oil, divided**

½ lb / 230 g **firm tofu, cut into ½-inch / 13-mm cubes**

1 tsp / 2 g **cumin seeds**

1 medium **onion, finely diced**

1 tsp / 1.7 g **grated fresh ginger**

3 **cloves garlic, minced**

1 **tomato, diced (¼-inch / 6-mm cubes)**

1 tsp / 5 g **smoked paprika**

1 tsp / 5 g **ground coriander**

1 **green chili, slit open (seeds removed if desired)**

¼ tsp / 1.7 g **salt**

2 tsp / 10 g **garam masala**

2 tsp / 10 mL **lemon juice**

KITCHEN TOOLS

Food processor

CHOICES/EXCHANGES
2 Nonstarchy Vegetable
1 Lean Protein
1½ Fat

Calories	150
Calories from Fat	90
Total Fat	10.0 g
Saturated Fat	1.3 g
Trans Fat	0.0 g
Cholesterol	0 mg
Sodium	210 mg
Potassium	680 mg
Total Carbohydrate	11 g
Dietary Fiber	4 g
Sugars	3 g
Protein	8 g
Phosphorus	135 mg

1 Bring a large saucepan of water to a boil. Cook spinach in the boiling water until wilted, about 2 minutes. Immediately shock the spinach in ice-cold water and set aside.

2 Transfer spinach to a food processor and purée to a smooth paste.

3 Heat 1 Tbsp / 15 mL oil in a large heavy-bottomed skillet over medium heat. Add tofu cubes and sauté, stirring constantly, until browned on all sides, about 5 minutes. Set aside.

4 Heat the remaining 1 Tbsp / 15 mL oil in the same skillet over medium-high heat. Add cumin seeds and cook until they begin to splutter, about 1 minute.

5 Add onion and cook, stirring often, until they begin to soften, about 4–5 minutes. Stir in ginger, garlic, tomato, paprika, coriander, and green chili. Cook, stirring frequently, until tomatoes break down, about 10 minutes.

6 Stir in spinach purée, tofu cubes, and salt and cook for 2 minutes, string gently. Add the garam masala and cook for 1 minute.

7 Add the lemon juice and stir. Remove green chili before serving.

COOK'S NOTES

Remove the seeds of the chili, if desired, to reduce the heat level. For a variation on this dish, replace the tofu with low-fat firm mozzarella cheese or paneer if it fits into your meal plan. This dish is often served with brown rice or an Indian bread.

Masala Okra (V) (GF)

SERVES: 6 • SERVING SIZE: 3 OZ / 84 G • PREP TIME: 5 MINUTES • COOKING TIME: 15 MINUTES

1 lb / 450 g **fresh okra, trimmed and cut into ¼-inch / 6-mm rounds**

2 Tbsp / 30 mL **sunflower oil, divided**

1 (1-inch / 2.5-cm) **piece ginger, peeled and minced**

1 **green chili, minced**

2 medium **red onions, finely minced**

1 tsp / 5 g **ground coriander**

½ tsp / 2.5 g **cayenne pepper**

½ tsp / 2.5 g **ground cumin**

½ tsp / 2.5 g **ground turmeric**

1 large **tomato, minced**

3 Tbsp / 45 mL **cold water**

½ tsp / 2.5 mL **lemon juice**

½ tsp / 3.3 g **salt**

2 Tbsp / 2 g **finely minced cilantro**

1 Wash the okra under cold water and set aside.

2 Heat a heavy-bottomed pan over medium-high heat with 1 Tbsp / 15 mL oil. Stir in the ginger, chili, and okra. Once in pan, turn up heat to high and cook for 3 minutes. Remove ingredients from the pan and set aside.

3 Place the remaining 1 Tbsp / 15 mL oil in the pan over medium-high heat and sauté onions until lightly brown. Add the coriander, cayenne, cumin, and turmeric and sauté for 2–3 minutes. Add tomatoes and cook for about 2–3 minutes.

4 Add okra mixture back to the pan, stir all ingredients together to coat okra in the masala, and sauté for 1 minute. Add 3 Tbsp / 45 mL water and combine well. Cover the pan with a lid and cook for another 3 minutes.

5 Stir in lemon juice, salt, and cilantro and remove from heat. Serve hot.

COOK'S NOTES

You can use any vegetables you'd like in this dish.

CHOICES/EXCHANGES
2 Nonstarchy Vegetable
1 Fat

Calories	100
Calories from Fat	45
Total Fat	5.0 g
Saturated Fat	0.5 g
Trans Fat	0.0 g
Cholesterol	0 mg
Sodium	200 mg
Potassium	390 mg
Total Carbohydrate	12 g
Dietary Fiber	3 g
Sugars	5 g
Protein	2 g
Phosphorus	70 mg

Adraki Gobi (Gingery Cauliflower)

1 lb / 450 g **cauliflower florets, broken into bite-size pieces**

1 Tbsp / 15 mL **sunflower oil**

2 Tbsp / 20 g **julienned ginger**

5 **garlic cloves, peeled and thinly sliced**

½ tsp / 3.3 g **salt**

1 tsp / 5 g **ground turmeric**

2 tsp / 10 g **ground black pepper**

1 Blanch cauliflower florets and set aside.

2 Heat oil in heavy-bottomed pan over medium-high heat and add ginger and garlic. Stir and cook for 1 minute. Add cauliflower and sauté for 1 minute, tossing constantly. Add about 1 Tbsp / 15 mL water to the pan and continue sautéing until cauliflower is tender-crisp. (Because you're cooking on medium-high heat it's important to keep tossing or stirring while cooking. Do not allow cauliflower to brown.)

3 Add salt, turmeric, and black pepper and mix well. Cook for 2 more minutes and remove from heat. Serve hot.

CHOICES/EXCHANGES
1 Nonstarchy Vegetable
½ Fat

Calories	45
Calories from Fat	20
Total Fat	2.5 g
Saturated Fat	0.4 g
Trans Fat	0.0 g
Cholesterol	0 mg
Sodium	220 mg
Potassium	260 mg
Total Carbohydrate	6 g
Dietary Fiber	2 g
Sugars	2 g
Protein	2 g
Phosphorus	40 mg

COOK'S NOTES

For extra color and flavor, you can add ½ tsp / 1 g crushed, toasted cumin seeds along with the rest of the spices. This recipe also tastes delicious using broccoli in place of the cauliflower.

Sweet Potato Aloo Gobi

Aloo Gobi is a popular dish in India. The word *aloo* means "potato" and *gobi* means "cauliflower." Those are the two main ingredients of a traditional aloo gobi. But in this recipe, I replace white potato with sweet potato and roast the cauliflower to create a healthy and flavorful side dish.

SERVES: 6 • SERVING SIZE: 2 OZ / 56 G • PREP TIME: 5 MINUTES • COOKING TIME: ABOUT 25 MINUTES

1 medium (2-lb / 900-g) head **cauliflower, separated into florets**

2 Tbsp / 30 mL **sunflower oil, divided**

2 tsp / 40 g **cumin seeds**

1 medium **onion, finely chopped**

1 Tbsp / 5.2 g **grated fresh ginger**

1 tsp / 5 g **garam masala**

2 tsp / 10 g **chili powder**

½ tsp / 3.3 g **salt**

3 medium **tomatoes, finely chopped**

1 large (8-oz / 230-g) **sweet potato, peeled and cut into ½-inch / 13-mm dice**

½ cup / 120 mL **water**

2 Tbsp / 2 g finely **minced cilantro**

CHOICES/EXCHANGES
½ Starch
2 Nonstarchy Vegetable
1 Fat

Calories	120
Calories from Fat	45
Total Fat	5.0 g
Saturated Fat	0.7 g
Trans Fat	0.0 g
Cholesterol	0 mg
Sodium	250 mg
Potassium	620 mg
Total Carbohydrate	17 g
Dietary Fiber	5 g
Sugars	7 g
Protein	4 g
Phosphorus	85 mg

1. Preheat oven to 425°F / 220°C.

2. Spread cauliflower out in a single layer on a baking sheet and drizzle with 1 Tbsp / 15 mL oil. Toss cauliflower with your hands to coat in oil. Roast for 10–15 minutes, until tender and golden on the bottoms and edges. Set aside.

3. Meanwhile, heat the remaining oil in a large, heavy-bottomed pan over medium-high heat. Add cumin seeds. When seeds begin to splutter, add the onion and cook for a few minutes, until it starts to soften. Add the ginger, garam masala, chili powder, and salt and cook for 1 minute.

4. Add tomatoes and sweet potato; stir to combine everything well. Pour ½ cup / 120 mL water into mixture, cover with a lid, reduce the heat to medium-low, and cook until the sweet potatoes are tender, approximately 8–10 mintues.

5. Add roasted cauliflower, sprinkle with cilantro, and stir to combine. Serve immediately.

COOK'S NOTES

Serve this recipe with brown rice or any Indian flatbread, if that works with your meal plan.

CHAPTER 4
Shorbas (Soups) and Dals

Butternut Squash Shorba (GF)

Shorba is a type of Indian soup. A spicy shorba is usually a formal course in Indian meals. Believed to have originated in Persia as a meat soup, vegetarian Indian cooks have reinvented shorba in a variety of forms using regional flavors and spices and seasonal vegetables.

SERVES: 8 • SERVING SIZE: 3 OZ / 90 ML • PREP TIME: 10 MINUTES • COOKING TIME: 55 MINUTES

1 Tbsp / 15 mL **extra-virgin cold-pressed olive oil**

2 medium **shallots, peeled and chopped**

1 Tbsp / 15 g **ginger-garlic paste (p. 34)**

2 large **butternut squash, cut into ¼-inch / 6-mm dice** (about 4 cups / 600 g)

1 **Granny Smith apple, peeled, cored, and chopped**

1 Tbsp / 14 g **mild curry powder**

½ tsp / 3.3 g **fine sea salt**

¼ cup / 60 mL **low-fat buttermilk**

4 cups / 950 mL **low-sodium chicken or vegetable stock**

Juice of ½ **lime** (about 1 Tbsp / 15 mL)

GARNISH

¼ cup / 40 g **julienned apple (skin on)**

1 tsp / 2 g **cumin seeds, toasted and crushed**

CHOICES/EXCHANGES
½ Starch
½ Carbohydrate
½ Fat

Calories	90
Calories from Fat	20
Total Fat	2.0 g
Saturated Fat	0.3 g
Trans Fat	0.0 g
Cholesterol	0 mg
Sodium	220 mg
Potassium	480 mg
Total Carbohydrate	17 g
Dietary Fiber	4 g
Sugars	6 g
Protein	4 g
Phosphorus	85 mg

1. Heat a large heavy-bottomed saucepan over medium-high heat and add oil. Once oil is hot, sauté the shallots for about 3–4 minutes or until translucent. Add ginger-garlic paste and sauté for another minute.

2. Add squash and cook for 10 minutes, or until it begins to soften. Add apples and cook for 5 minutes, or until slightly brown. Add curry and salt and sauté for another minute.

3. Add stock and bring to a boil. Once boiling, reduce to a simmer, cover, and cook for 30 minutes, or until squash and apples are tender.

4. Remove soup from heat and, using a submersion blender or food processor, purée soup until smooth. You can purée in batches if necessary.

5. Return puréed soup to the saucepan and reduce heat to low. Stir in buttermilk and lime juice.

6. Garnish soup with apple pieces and sprinkle with toasted and crushed cumin seeds before serving.

COOK'S NOTES

To toast the cumin seeds, add the seeds to a heavy-bottomed skillet over medium heat and stir for about 2 minutes. Make sure not to allow the seeds to turn dark brown or they will taste bitter.

Malabar Avocado and Cucumber Soup

The Malabar region in southwest India has its own distinctive cooking style and flavors influenced by the Arab traders who came to the Malabar coast. This refreshing summertime soup was inspired by traditional Malabar flavors like coconut, garlic, and green chilies. It also makes a great appetizer for a party.

SERVES: 6 • SERVING SIZE: 3 OZ / 90 ML • PREP TIME: 2 HOURS • COOKING TIME: NONE

½ large **ripe avocado, diced (other avocado half sliced and reserved for garnish)**

1 small **English cucumber, diced**

Juice of 1 **lime**

2 Tbsp / 30 mL **light coconut milk**

1 cup / 245 g **plain fat-free yogurt**

1 **green chili, seeds removed if desired**

2 **cloves garlic**

3 cups / 700 mL **water**

½ tsp / 3.3 g **sea salt**

2 tsp / 3.9 g **fennel seeds, toasted and crushed**

GARNISH

½ **avocado, cut into 6 thin slices**

1 **lime, cut into 6 wedges**

¼ cup / 4 g **finely chopped cilantro**

1 In a medium bowl, mix avocado and cucumber together and set aside.

2 Add the avocado and cucumber mixture, lime juice, coconut milk, yogurt, chili, garlic, water, salt, and crushed fennel seeds to a blender and purée to get a smooth consistency.

3 Chill the soup in the refrigerator for 1–2 hours and take out just before serving.

4 Serve the soup garnished with lime wedges, avocado slices, and cilantro.

CHOICES/EXCHANGES
1 Carbohydrate
1½ Fat

Calories	130
Calories from Fat	80
Total Fat	9.0 g
Saturated Fat	1.6 g
Trans Fat	0.0 g
Cholesterol	0 mg
Sodium	220 mg
Potassium	480 mg
Total Carbohydrate	11 g
Dietary Fiber	4 g
Sugars	4 g
Protein	4 g
Phosphorus	110 mg

Tamatar Dhaniya Shorba (Tomato Coriander Broth) Ⓥ ⒢⒡

This shorba is a light soup popular in the northern Indian regions. It is usually served in the winter.

SERVES: 6 • SERVING SIZE: 3 OZ / 90 ML • PREP TIME: 5 MINUTES • COOKING TIME: 37 MINUTES

1 Tbsp / 15 mL **sunflower oil**

1 **onion, finely chopped**

1 tsp / 1.8 g **coriander seeds**

2 **cloves garlic, finely minced**

1 (½-inch / 13-mm) **piece ginger, peeled and finely chopped**

3 **green cardamom pods**

3 **whole cloves**

1 **bay leaf**

2 lb / 900 g **ripe red tomatoes (preferably Italian plum), roughly chopped**

1 large **bunch cilantro, roughly chopped**

3 cups / 700 mL **cold water**

⅛ tsp / 0.5 g **sugar**

½ tsp / 3.3 g **salt**

2 Tbsp / 2 g **chopped cilantro leaves**

1 Heat the oil in a heavy-bottomed pan over medium-high heat. Add onions, coriander seeds, garlic, ginger, cardamom, cloves, and the bay leaf. Sauté until the onions are slightly brown, about 2 minutes.

2 Add tomatoes and sauté for another 2 minutes. Add the cilantro and cook until the tomatoes are pulpy and dry, about 3 minutes.

3 Add water and bring to a boil. Simmer for 30 minutes.

4 After 30 minutes, strain the soup, saving the thin broth and discarding the vegetables and spices (or save them to use as ingredients in another dish).

5 Stir in the sugar and salt and serve the soup garnished with chopped cilantro leaves.

COOK'S NOTES

This recipe pairs well with pappadums, crispy Indian lentil wafers.

CHOICES/EXCHANGES
½ Fat

Calories	30
Calories from Fat	20
Total Fat	2.5 g
Saturated Fat	0.2 g
Trans Fat	0.0 g
Cholesterol	0 mg
Sodium	200 mg
Potassium	85 mg
Total Carbohydrate	2 g
Dietary Fiber	0 g
Sugars	1 g
Protein	0 g
Phosphorus	10 mg

Mulakuthanni Soup (V) (GF)

Mulakuthanni is a soup featuring the traditional flavors of southern India. This light vegetarian spiced broth is lentil-based. There are many versions of Mulakuthanni that incorporate meat or chicken and were very popular as a first course during the British Era.

SERVES: 4 • SERVING SIZE: ABOUT 7 OZ / 210 ML • PREP TIME: 5 MINUTES • COOKING TIME: ABOUT 1 HOUR

½ cup / 96 g **dried lentils (preferably split mung dal)**
1 tsp / 5 g **ground coriander**
1 tsp / 5 g **ground cinnamon**
1 tsp / 5 g **ground cumin**
1 tsp / 5 g **ground fennel**
1 tsp / 5 g **ground turmeric**
1 Tbsp / 15 mL **sunflower oil**
2 medium **shallots, minced**
1 (½-inch / 13-mm) **piece ginger, peeled and finely chopped**
2 **cloves garlic, finely minced**
2 tsp / 6.7 g **crushed whole black peppercorns**
1 **stalk curry leaves**
1 medium **tomato, finely chopped**
1 cup / 240 mL **low-sodium vegetable stock**
3 cups / 700 mL **water**
¼ cup / 60 mL **light coconut milk**
⅛ tsp / 0.8 g **salt**

GARNISH
Juice of 1 **lemon**
1 stalk **curry leaves, stems removed**

CHOICES/EXCHANGES
½ Carbohydrate
1 Fat

Calories	80
Calories from Fat	40
Total Fat	4.5 g
Saturated Fat	1.2 g
Trans Fat	0.0 g
Cholesterol	0 mg
Sodium	125 mg
Potassium	230 mg
Total Carbohydrate	8 g
Dietary Fiber	3 g
Sugars	2 g
Protein	2 g
Phosphorus	75 mg

1. Rinse lentils under cold water until the water runs clear.

2. In a heavy-bottomed saucepan, combine the lentils with about 3 cups / 700 mL water. Bring the lentils to a boil and remove the foam from the pan. Lower the heat and simmer for about 20 minutes. Drain and set lentils aside when finished cooking.

3. Meanwhile, in a small heavy-bottomed pan, dry roast the coriander, cinnamon, cumin, fennel, and turmeric over medium-low heat until fragrant.

4. In another heavy-bottomed pan add oil, shallots, ginger, and garlic. Sauté until shallots are slightly brown, about 1–2 minutes. Add toasted spices, crushed pepper, and curry leaves and sauté for 2 more minutes.

5. Stir in tomatoes and sauté until soft. Add cooked lentils and mix well.

6. Add 1 cup / 240 mL vegetable stock and 3 cups / 700 mL water and bring to a boil. Reduce heat to simmer for 30 minutes.

7. Strain the soup, reserving the thin broth and discarding the solids.

8. Add coconut milk and salt, and mix well. Stir in lemon juice just serving and garnish with curry leaves.

COOK'S NOTES

You can serve this soup with pappadum, a crispy Indian lentil wafer. Or you can enjoy this light and healthy soup with brown rice on a cold winter day. You can substitute chicken for the lentils and use chicken stock instead of vegetable stock in this recipe, if desired.

Bhune Makai Ka Shorba
(Roasted Corn and Sweet Potato Soup) GF

This recipe was inspired by a roasted corn soup recipe from chef Hemant Oberoi's cookbook.

SERVES: 8 • SERVING SIZE: 3 OZ / 90 ML • PREP TIME: NONE • COOKING TIME: 35 MINUTES

2 Tbsp / 30 mL **sunflower oil**

1 **bay leaf**

3 **green cardamom pods**

½ cup / 75 g **white onion, thinly sliced**

1 **green chili, seeds removed**

1 small (3-oz / 84-g) **sweet potato, roasted, cut into 1-inch cubes**

2 small **tomatoes**

1 Tbsp / 5.2 g **grated ginger**

1 tsp / 5 g **good-quality curry powder**

4 **pieces corn on the cob, roasted and kernels cut from cob** (about 2½ cups / 412.5 g)

¼ cup / 57 g **roasted chana dal flour**

4 cups / 950 mL **water or vegetable or chicken stock**

¼ cup / 6 g **packed mint leaves**

¼ cup / 4 g **cilantro, finely chopped (including stalk)**

¾ tsp / 5 g **sea salt**

½ cup / 4 g **air-popped popcorn, without salt**

1 Tbsp / 1 g **chopped cilantro leaves**

KITCHEN TOOLS

Food processor

CHOICES/EXCHANGES
1 Starch
1 Fat

Calories	110
Calories from Fat	40
Total Fat	4.5 g
Saturated Fat	0.5 g
Trans Fat	0.0 g
Cholesterol	0 mg
Sodium	210 mg
Potassium	280 mg
Total Carbohydrate	17 g
Dietary Fiber	3 g
Sugars	4 g
Protein	3 g
Phosphorus	65 mg

1 Heat a heavy-bottomed pan over medium-high heat and add oil. Add the bay leaf and cardamom.

2 Add the onions, chili, roasted sweet potato, tomato, ginger, and curry powder and sauté well for 2 minutes.

3 Add roasted corn kernels and chana dal powder and mix well. Add water or stock, and bring to a boil. Once mixture is boiling, cook for 2 more minutes.

4 Add the mint and chopped cilantro and simmer over low heat for about 30 minutes. Remove bay leaf and cardamom pods.

5 Using a blender or food processor, purée the soup to smooth consistency, and strain. Add salt.

6 Serve the soup hot topped with popcorn and cilantro.

COOK'S NOTES

To roast the corn: Remove the husk and roast corn on charcoal grill or any other grill. Set it aside.

To roast the sweet potato: Preheat oven to 400°F / 200°C. Roast the whole sweet potato (with skin) for about 15 minutes. Cool the potato; when cool enough to handle, remove the skin and cut the sweet potato into 1-inch cubes. Set it aside. The sweet potato should only be halfway cooked.

Spinach and Pear Shorba (GF)

SERVES: 6 • SERVING SIZE: ½ CUP / 120 ML • PREP TIME: 5 MINUTES • COOKING TIME: 20 MINUTES

1 medium **onion, chopped** (about ½ cup / 75 g)

2 **ripe green Anjou pears, cored and chopped**

1 Tbsp / 15 mL **water**

½ tsp / 2.5 g **ground coriander**

4 cups / 950 mL **low-sodium vegetable or chicken stock**

6 oz / 168 g **baby spinach**

2 Tbsp / 2 g **chopped cilantro leaves**

1 tsp / 5 g **garam masala**

½ tsp / 2.5 g **ground black pepper**

¼ tsp / 1.7 g **sea salt**

1 In a heavy-bottomed pan over medium-low heat, add onions and chopped pears and cook for 3–5 minutes, or until they start to caramelize. Add 1 Tbsp / 15 mL water and cook until soft, about 2–5 minutes. (Do not let onions and pears burn. Add a little more water to the pan if they start to stick.)

2 Add coriander and cook for 2 minutes. Add vegetable stock and bring to a simmer. Simmer for 5 minutes or until pears are softened.

3 Add spinach and cilantro and simmer for 1 more minute, until spinach is completely wilted. Remove from heat.

4 Transfer soup to a blender or food processor, working in batches if necessary, and purée until smooth and creamy (use caution when blending hot liquids).

5 Serve hot and season with garam masala, black pepper, and sea salt.

COOK'S NOTES

This is vegetarian soup, but if your meal plan allows, you can stir 2 Tbsp / 24 g low-fat sour cream into this soup for a creamier texture and garnish with some crispy pancetta. To prepare the pancetta, heat a large saucepan or Dutch oven over medium-high heat. Add 1 oz / 28 g pancetta—cut into small cubes—and sauté for 5–7 minutes or until brown and crispy. Using a slotted spoon, transfer cooked pancetta to a paper towel-lined plate to rest before using.

If you don't like pancetta, another variation is to top the soup with air-popped popcorn.

CHOICES/EXCHANGES
½ Fruit
1 Nonstarchy Vegetable

Calories	60
Calories from Fat	5
Total Fat	0.5 g
Saturated Fat	0.1 g
Trans Fat	0.0 g
Cholesterol	0 mg
Sodium	210 mg
Potassium	350 mg
Total Carbohydrate	14 g
Dietary Fiber	4 g
Sugars	8 g
Protein	1 g
Phosphorus	80 mg

Dal Panchmel (V) (GF)

This dish is a popular dish from the northern Indian region Rajasthan. Dal panchmel is made of five different varieties of lentils, and it gets a nice smoky flavor from the spices used in the dish. In traditional versions of this dish, the spices are tempered in ghee but sunflower oil is used in this recipe.

SERVES: 4 • SERVING SIZE: 2 OZ / 56 G • PREP TIME: 2 HOURS • COOKING TIME: 50 MINUTES

1 cup / 192 g **mixed lentils (see Cook's Notes)**

1 tsp / 5 g **ground turmeric**

⅜ tsp / 2.4 g **salt, divided**

4 cups / 950 mL **water**

1 Tbsp / 15 mL **sunflower oil**

1 tsp / 2 g **cumin seeds**

3 **cloves garlic, finely minced**

1 **dried red chili, broken into pieces**

1 tsp / 5 g **smoked paprika**

2 medium **tomatoes, chopped into ½-inch / 13-mm cubes**

1 Tbsp / 1 g **finely chopped cilantro leaves**

CHOICES/EXCHANGES

1½ Starch
1 Nonstarchy Vegetable
1 Lean Protein
½ Fat

Calories	210
Calories from Fat	40
Total Fat	4.5 g
Saturated Fat	0.5 g
Trans Fat	0.0 g
Cholesterol	0 mg
Sodium	220 mg
Potassium	730 mg
Total Carbohydrate	32 g
Dietary Fiber	12 g
Sugars	5 g
Protein	13 g
Phosphorus	270 mg

1 Soak lentils in cold water for about 2 hours.

2 Drain lentils. Add to a large pot with turmeric, ⅛ tsp / 0.8 g salt, and 4 cups / 950 mL water. Bring to a boil.

3 Reduce heat to medium-low and bring lentils to a simmer and cook for about 45 minutes, or until lentils are soft. Remove from heat and set aside.

4 Take a heavy-bottomed pan over medium heat and heat oil. Add cumin seeds. When cumin seeds begin to splutter, add garlic, and red chili pieces and cook for 1–2 minutes. Add paprika, tomatoes, and remaining ¼ tsp / 1.7 g salt and cook for about 3 minutes until all of the ingredients come together.

5 Then add tomato mixture to the lentils and stir to combine. Garnish with cilantro and serve hot.

COOK'S NOTES

For the mixed lentils combine equal portions of the following varieties to get 1 cup / 192 g of mixed lentils:

- *chana dal (split chickpeas/split Bengal gram)*
- *mung dal (green gram dal/mung beans)*
- *masoor dal (split red/pink lentils)*
- *toor/tuvar/arhar dal (split pigeon peas)*
- *skinned urad dal (skinned black gram/black lentils)*

Dal Makhani

Dal makhani is a dish of whole black lentil and red kidney beans that comes from the Punjab region of India. It is recognized as a quintessentially Indian dish.

SERVES: 6 • SERVING SIZE: ⅓ CUP / 64 G • PREP TIME: 8 HOURS OR OVERNIGHT • COOKING TIME: ABOUT 1 HOUR

¾ cup / 144 g **urad dal (black lentils)**

¼ cup / 47 g **dried red kidney beans**

3 cups plus 3 Tbsp / 745 mL **cold water, divided**

1 Tbsp / 15 mL **sunflower oil**

½ tsp / 2.5 g **cumin seeds**

1 tsp / 5 g **ginger-garlic paste (p. 34)**

½ cup / 75 g **red onions, finely minced**

¾ cup / 187.5 g **salt-free tomato puree**

1 tsp / 5 g **smoked paprika**

2 tsp / 10 g **ground coriander**

¼ tsp / 1.3 g **ground turmeric**

1 tsp / 5 g **garam masala**

½ tsp / 3.3 g **salt**

GARNISH

1 tsp / 5 mL **heavy cream**

1 Tbsp / 1 g **chopped cilantro**

KITCHEN TOOL

Pressure cooker

CHOICES/EXCHANGES
1 Starch
1 Nonstarchy Vegetable
1 Lean Protein

Calories	150
Calories from Fat	25
Total Fat	3.0 g
Saturated Fat	0.5 g
Trans Fat	0.0 g
Cholesterol	0 mg
Sodium	210 mg
Potassium	520 mg
Total Carbohydrate	23 g
Dietary Fiber	8 g
Sugars	4 g
Protein	9 g
Phosphorus	170 mg

1. Soak lentils and kidney beans in separate bowls covered with cold water for 8 hours or overnight.

2. After lentils and beans have soaked, combine them with 3 cups / 700 mL of water in a pressure cooker and cook for about 6–7 whistles, or until soft. Take ¼ cup / 45 g of the cooked lentil and bean mixture, mash it, and set aside.

3. Heat oil in heavy-bottomed pan and add cumin seeds. When seeds begin to splutter, add ginger-garlic paste and onions and cook over medium heat until golden brown.

4. Add tomato puree, mix well, and cook over medium heat for 2–3 minutes, stirring occasionally.

5. Add smoked paprika, coriander, turmeric, garam masala, and 2 Tbsp / 30 mL water and mix well. Continue cooking mixture over medium heat for 2–3 minutes, stirring continuously.

6. Add 1 Tbsp / 15 mL water and the ¼ cup / 45 g of mashed lentils and beans and stir for few more minutes.

7. Add remaining lentil and bean mixture and salt, mix well, and cook over medium-low heat until it begins to bubble, stirring occasionally.

8. Garnish with a drizzle of cream and the cilantro and serve hot.

COOK'S NOTES

If you don't have a pressure cooker, cook the lentils and beans in a large pot, by adding 12 cups / 2.85 L of water. Bring the water to boil, cover with a lid, and simmer for about 40 minutes, until the lentils and beans are soft. Dal tastes great served with brown rice or whole-wheat Indian flatbread.

Dal Tadka

SERVES: 5 • SERVING SIZE: 1.6 OZ / 45 G • PREP TIME: 5 MINUTES • COOKING TIME: ABOUT 45 MINUTES

1 cup / 192 g **toor dal (split pigeon peas)**

1 medium **onion, finely chopped**

2 medium **tomatoes, finely chopped**

1 **green chili, finely minced**

1 (½-inch / 13-mm) **piece ginger, peeled and finely chopped or grated**

2½ cups / 595 mL **water**

1 tsp / 5 g **ground turmeric**

⅛ tsp / 0.6 g **asafoetida powder**

⅛ tsp / 0.6 g **garam masala**

1 Tbsp / 1 g **finely chopped cilantro leaves**

½ tsp / 3.3 g **salt**

1 Tbsp / 15 mL **sunflower oil**

1 tsp / 2 g **cumin seeds**

5 **cloves garlic, finely chopped**

1 **dried red chili, broken into small pieces**

GARNISH

1 Tbsp / 1 g **chopped cilantro**

KITCHEN TOOL

Pressure cooker

CHOICES/EXCHANGES

1½ Starch
1 Nonstarchy Vegetable
1 Lean Protein

Calories	180
Calories from Fat	30
Total Fat	3.5 g
Saturated Fat	0.4 g
Trans Fat	0.0 g
Cholesterol	0 mg
Sodium	240 mg
Potassium	650 mg
Total Carbohydrate	29 g
Dietary Fiber	10 g
Sugars	5 g
Protein	11 g
Phosphorus	230 mg

1 Rinse the split pigeon peas in a colander until water runs clear.

2 Add peas, onions, tomatoes, green chili, and ginger to a pressure cooker. Add 2½ cups / 595 mL water, turmeric, and asafoetida powder and stir well. Cook the lentil mixture for about 7–8 whistles, or longer if needed, until they become soft and creamy.

3 Stir in garam masala, cilantro, and salt, remove from heat, and set aside.

4 To make the tadka seasoning, heat oil in a heavy-bottomed pan over medium-high heat. Add cumin seeds. When cumin seeds begin to splutter add garlic and red chili and sauté until the ingredients release their aromas, about 1 minute. (Do not allow garlic to burn.)

5 Mix the garlic/chili tadka mixture into the lentil mixture and combine well. Serve hot garnished with cilantro.

COOK'S NOTES

If you don't have a pressure cooker, you can use a large pot. Soak the peas for 1–2 hours before cooking, then drain. Add peas and 4½ cups / 1.1 L cold water to a pot and bring to a boil. Once the water boils simmer and cook for about 45 minutes, or until peas are mushy.

CHAPTER 5
Elegant and Exotic Dinners

Chicken Piralen
(Traditional Keralan Roasted Chicken) GF

This is a traditional roasted chicken dish from the southern coast of the state of Kerala in India.

SERVES: 8 • SERVING SIZE: 2 OZ / 56 G • PREP TIME: 5 MINUTES • COOKING TIME: ABOUT 25 MINUTES

1 lb / 450 g **boneless, skinless organic chicken breasts (1-inch / 2.5-cm strips)**

½ lb / 230 g **boneless, skinless organic chicken thighs (1-inch / 2.5-cm strips)**

GROUND MASALA

1 tsp / 5 g **ground fennel**

1 Tbsp / 14 g **ground coriander**

1 Tbsp / 14 g **smoked paprika**

1 tsp / 5 g **cayenne pepper**

1 tsp / 5 g **ground black pepper**

½ tsp / 2.5 g **ground cinnamon**

½ tsp / 2.5 g **ground cardamom**

½ tsp / 2.5 g **ground cloves**

AROMATIC MASALA

2 tsp / 3.4 g **finely sliced garlic**

1 (2-inch / 5-cm) **piece ginger, peeled and julienned**

10 medium **shallots, sliced OR** 2 large **red onions, sliced**

2 **sprigs curry leaves**

GRAVY

¾ cup / 180 mL **hot water**

1 Tbsp / 15 mL **white vinegar**

1¼ tsp / 8.5 g **salt**

2 Tbsp / 30 mL **sunflower oil**

2 **sprigs curry leaves, stems removed**

CHOICES/EXCHANGES
1 Nonstarchy Vegetable
2 Lean Protein
1 Fat

Calories	160
Calories from Fat	60
Total Fat	7.0 g
Saturated Fat	1.2 g
Trans Fat	0.0 g
Cholesterol	60 mg
Sodium	410 mg
Potassium	310 mg
Total Carbohydrate	7 g
Dietary Fiber	2 g
Sugars	1 g
Protein	18 g
Phosphorus	155 mg

1 Wash chicken pieces and dry them well.

2 In a wide, heavy-bottomed pan, combine chicken pieces with all the ground masala ingredients. Mix well. Then add all the aromatic masala ingredients and mix well. Place pan over medium heat.

3 Add gravy ingredients to the pan and mix well. Cover and cook until chicken is tender and gravy has thickened, about 20 minutes.

4 Remove from heat. With a slotted spoon, remove chicken pieces from gravy and set both aside.

5 Heat another heavy-bottomed pan over medium-high heat. Add oil then add chicken pieces and fry until brown, about 2 minutes per side.

6 Remove curry leaf sprigs from gravy and discard. Pour gravy over chicken and cook until the chicken pieces are well coated with gravy. Serve hot garnished with curry leaves.

Malabar Mixed Seafood Curry ⓖⒻ

The Malabar coast in the southern state of Kerala served as a large trade post for the spice trade. The coast has its own cooking styles and flavors as well as an abundance of fresh seafood. A variety of spices are blended with coconut to form the base of traditional Malabar curries.

SERVES: 8 • SERVING SIZE: 3 OZ / 84 G • PREP TIME: 5 MINUTES • COOKING TIME: 25 MINUTES

1 Tbsp / 15 g **tamarind paste**

2 Tbsp / 30 mL **hot water**

2 lb / 900 g **mussels (with shells), cleaned and scrubbed**

2 Tbsp / 30 mL **sunflower oil**

½ tsp / 1.8 g **black mustard seeds**

12 **curry leaves**

1 **onion, chopped**

1 tsp / 1.7 g **grated fresh ginger**

1 tsp / 3.3 g **finely chopped garlic**

1 **green chili, slit open and seeds removed**

½ tsp / 2.5 g **red chili flakes**

½ tsp / 2.5 g **smoked paprika**

½ tsp / 2.5 g **ground turmeric**

1 tsp / 5 g **ground coriander**

½ tsp / 2.5 g **ground cumin**

¼ tsp / 1.3 g **ground cinnamon**

½ cup plus 2 Tbsp / 150 mL **water, divided**

2 **ripe Roma tomatoes, chopped**

¾ tsp / 5 g **sea salt**

1 cup / 240 mL **light coconut milk**

12 large **prawns, cleaned, shelled, and deveined**

2 **whole squid, cleaned and cut into rings**

GARNISH

¼ cup / 4 g **finely chopped cilantro**

CHOICES/EXCHANGES
½ Carbohydrate
4 Lean Protein

Calories	240
Calories from Fat	70
Total Fat	8.0 g
Saturated Fat	2.5 g
Trans Fat	0.0 g
Cholesterol	300 mg
Sodium	420 mg
Potassium	540 mg
Total Carbohydrate	10 g
Dietary Fiber	1 g
Sugars	5 g
Protein	33 g
Phosphorus	390 mg

1 In a small bowl, dissolve tamarind paste in 2 Tbsp / 30 mL hot water and set aside.

2 Place mussels in a large bowl of water to remove any remaining sand. Debeard mussels if necessary.

3 Heat oil in a large, heavy-bottomed saucepan over medium heat. Add mustard seeds and curry leaves and sauté until fragrant. When seeds begin to splutter, add chopped onions and cook for about 5 minutes, or until lightly browned.

4 Add ginger, garlic, green chili, and red chili flakes and sauté for 1 minute. Add the paprika, turmeric, coriander, cumin, cinnamon, and 2 Tbsp / 30 mL water and cook over medium heat for about 1 minute, or until spices are cooked. Add a little more water if the spices start to brown. Add chopped tomatoes, tamarind paste mixture, remaining ½ cup / 120 mL water, and salt. Simmer until tomatoes soften, about 5 minutes.

5 Add coconut milk and mussels. Cover and cook for about 8 minutes, or until shells start to open. Then add prawns and squid rings and cook until prawns are opaque and mussels have all opened, about 5 minutes. Remove green chili.

6 Serve garnished with cilantro.

Jaldi Kozhi Biryani (Quick Chicken Biryani) ⓖⓕ

Biryani was introduced during the Mughal rule in India. This one-pot meal, traditionally featuring lamb or chicken, incorporates a variety of spices and herbs. Vegetarian version of this dish can be found in many regions of India as well. Biryani offers both protein and other nutritients. The word jaldi, means fast and kozhi is the Tamil word for chicken; the pressure cooking method used in this recipe makes this dish quick and easy—perfect for a week night meal.

SERVES: 8 • SERVING SIZE: 2 OZ / 56 G • PREP TIME: ABOUT 4 HOURS • COOKING TIME: ABOUT 30 MINUTES

1 cup / 245 g **plain fat-free Greek yogurt**

1 Tbsp / 15 g **ginger-garlic paste (p. 34)**

1 tsp / 5 g **ground turmeric**

½ tsp / 2.5 g **ground black pepper**

½ tsp / 2.5 g **garam masala**

1 tsp / 6.7 g **sea salt**

2 lb / 900 g **boneless, skinless chicken thighs, cut into medium pieces**

2 cups / 380 g **brown basmati rice**

2 **green chilies**

5 **cloves garlic**

1 small **red onion, quartered**

1 (2-inch / 5-cm) **piece ginger**

1 bunch **cilantro**

1 small bunch **mint leaves**

1 Tbsp plus ½ tsp / 17.5 mL **sunflower oil, divided**

10 **raw unsalted cashews**

2 Tbsp / 20.6 g **raisins**

1 **bay leaf**

3 **green cardamom pods**

3 **cloves**

1 small **cinnamon stick**

3 **red onions, thinly sliced**

3¾ cups / 880 mL **water**

Juice of ½ **lemon**

KITCHEN TOOLS

Food processor (or blender)

Pressure cooker

CHOICES/EXCHANGES
2 ½ Starch
2 Nonstarchy Vegetable
2 Lean Protein
1 Fat

Calories	390
Calories from Fat	100
Total Fat	11.0 g
Saturated Fat	2.5 g
Trans Fat	0.0 g
Cholesterol	105 mg
Sodium	360 mg
Potassium	600 mg
Total Carbohydrate	47 g
Dietary Fiber	4 g
Sugars	7 g
Protein	27 g
Phosphorus	400 mg

1 In a large bowl, combine yogurt, ginger-garlic paste, turmeric, pepper, garam masala, and salt. Add the chicken, cover, and marinate in the refrigerator for 2–3 hours.

2 Soak brown basmasti rice in a bowl of water for about 1 hour. Rinse basmati rice until the water runs clear and drain the rice in a colander. Set aside.

3 In small blender or food processor, combine green chilies, garlic cloves, quartered onion, ginger, cilantro, and mint and blend to form a coarsely ground biryani masala. Set aside.

4 Heat ½ tsp / 2.5 mL oil in a pressure cooker over medium heat. Add cashews and raisins and sauté for about 2 minutes until the cashews turn golden brown. Remove from the pressure cooker and set aside to be used as garnish.

5 Now add the 1 Tbsp / 15 mL oil to the pressure cooker over medium heat. Add bay leaf, cardamom pods, cloves, cinnamon stick, and sliced onion and sauté.

6 When the onions start to brown, add the coarsely ground biryani masala and sauté for 2 minutes. Stir well.

7 Add chicken and mix well so that chicken is nicely coated with the masala and the moisture in the chicken is absorbed.

8 Add the water and bring mixture to a boil. Add lemon juice and mix well.

9 Add soaked basmati rice and stir. Close the pressure cooker and cook over medium-high for 1 whistle. Then reduce heat to low and simmer for 7 minutes.

10 Turn off the heat but do not open the pressure cooker. Let stand for 15–20 minutes.

11 After 15–20 minutes, open the pressure cooker, and remove whole spices. Garnish with cashews and raisins and serve.

COOK'S NOTES

After soaking the basmati rice, rinse gently so the grains don't break. Use the lowest pressure setting on your pressure cooker for cooking this dish.

Tandoori Lobster GF

SERVES: 6 • SERVING SIZE: 3 OZ / 84 G • PREP TIME: ABOUT 4 HOURS • COOKING TIME: 10 MINUTES

TANDOORI MARINADE

1 small **piece onion**

2 **cloves garlic**

$\frac{1}{16}$ tsp / 0.3 g **ground ginger**

1 Tbsp / 14 g **ground cumin**

1 Tbsp / 14 g **ground coriander**

1 Tbsp / 14 g **smoked paprika**

2 Tbsp / 30 mL **lime juice**

½ cup / 122.5 g **plain low-fat Greek yogurt**

¼ tsp / 1.3 g **ground black pepper**

¼ tsp / 1.3 g **ground turmeric**

½ tsp / 3.3 g **salt**

2 Tbsp / 2 g **minced cilantro leaves**

1 tsp / 0.5 g **minced mint leaves**

1 tsp / 7.1 g **honey**

2 **live lobsters** (1½ lb / 680 g each)

1 tsp / 5 mL **sunflower oil or ghee**

KITCHEN TOOLS

Blender or food processor

CHOICES/EXCHANGES
½ Carbohydrate
2 Lean Protein

Calories	100
Calories from Fat	20
Total Fat	2.0 g
Saturated Fat	0.8 g
Trans Fat	0.0 g
Cholesterol	45 mg
Sodium	430 mg
Potassium	310 mg
Total Carbohydrate	5 g
Dietary Fiber	1 g
Sugars	2 g
Protein	15 g
Phosphorus	150 mg

1 To prepare the marinade, place all of the Tandoori Marinade ingredients in a blender or food processor and process until smooth. Set aside.

2 Bring a large pot of salted water to a rapid boil. Place live lobsters into the boiling water, cover tightly, and let cook for 4–5 minutes, until lobster tails are curled and shells have turned bright red. Using tongs, carefully remove lobsters from water and place in an ice-water bath to stop the cooking.

3 Break off lobster claws and set aside. Separate the heads from the tails. Remove the meat from the tail in one piece by cutting along the soft underside of the tail shell to expose the flesh. With the back of a knife, lightly crack the claws and carefully remove the meat in one piece. Place the tail and claw meat in the marinade, cover, and refrigerate for 4 hours.

4 After 4 hours, preheat oven to 500°F / 260°C.

5 Place the marinated lobster meat on a baking sheet, brush with oil and cook for about 4 minutes, until the meat is opaque white and the marinade is slightly browned.

COOK'S NOTES

This entrée can be served with a flavorful pilaf, Indian flatbread, or with simple Kachumber Salad (see p. 209). Traditionally, Kashmiri chili powder is used in place of the smoked paprika in this recipe.

You can use jumbo prawns instead of lobster if you'd like. To clean the prawns use 1 Tbsp / 7.5 g chickpea flour or lemon juice mixed with water to rinse the prawns.

Masala Lamb Chops with Parsnips and Pears

This dish is popular in the northern regions of India and can be cooked on a tandoor (tandoori oven) or any outdoor grill.

SERVES: 8 • SERVING SIZE: 1 LAMB CHOP + ABOUT ¼ CUP / 40 G MIXTURE
PREP TIME: 8 HOURS OR OVERNIGHT • COOKING TIME: 37 MINUTES

8 **lamb rib chops, french cut**
(2½ lb / 1130 g)

4 medium **apples, sliced**

MARINADE

¾ cup / 184 g **plain fat-free Greek yogurt**

¼ cup / 48 g **fat-free sour cream**

3 Tbsp / 45 mL **fresh lemon juice**

1 (3-inch / 7.5-cm) **piece ginger, peeled and minced**

4 large **garlic cloves, minced**

1 Tbsp / 15 mL **malt vinegar**

1 Tbsp / 14 g **garam masala (a variety that contains nutmeg and mace)**

1 Tbsp / 14 g **ground cumin**

1 Tbsp / 14 g **smoked paprika**

½ tsp / 2.5 g **cayenne pepper**

1 tsp / 6.7 g **sea salt**

PARSNIP AND PEAR MIXTURE:

½ tsp / 2.5 mL **sunflower oil**

3 medium **parsnips, cubed**

1 **pear, cubed**

¼ tsp / 1.3 g **garam masala**

¼ tsp / 1.3 g **ground black pepper**

2 **shallots, diced**

¼ tsp / 1.7 g **sea salt**

1 tsp / 5 mL **sunflower oil**

Juice of ½ **lemon**

CHOICES/EXCHANGES
1 Carbohydrate
3 Lean Protein

Calories	210
Calories from Fat	60
Total Fat	7.0 g
Saturated Fat	2.3 g
Trans Fat	0.0 g
Cholesterol	60 mg
Sodium	480 mg
Potassium	490 mg
Total Carbohydrate	15 g
Dietary Fiber	3 g
Sugars	5 g
Protein	22 g
Phosphorus	215 mg

1 Using a paring knife, cut a few ¼-inch-deep slashes in each lamb chop.

2 In a large bowl, combine all marinade ingredients. Transfer lamb chops into the marinade and turn to coat. Cover and refrigerate 8 hours or overnight.

3 After marinating, toss lamb chops in the marinade again. Remove chops from the marinade (do not discard marinade) and let rest at room temperature for 30 minutes.

4 Meanwhile, preheat oven to 400°F / 200°C. Combine all parsnip and pear mixture ingredients in a large bowl and toss to combine. Add mixture to a baking sheet and bake for 25 minutes, stirring occasionally. Set aside when done cooking.

5 Light a tandoor, outdoor grill, or a cast iron griddle. Season chops with the remaining ¼ tsp / 1.7 g salt and grill over medium-high heat for 8 minutes, turning once, until browned.

6 Brush both sides of the chops with sunflower oil and grill for another 2 minutes per side for medium-rare. Trim fat from chops before serving with parsnip and pear mixture. Squeeze juice of ½ lemon over entire dish before serving.

COOK'S NOTES

You can replace the smoked paprika in this recipe with Kashmiri chili powder. If you use a garam masala that doesn't contain mace and nutmeg, please add ¼ tsp / 1.3 g mace and ¼ tsp / 1.3 g nutmeg to the marinade. If you don't have malt vinegar on hand, feel free to use any vinegar of your choice.

When I buy lamb, I look for New Zealand grass-fed lamb. The flavor is amazing!

Lamb Rogan Josh

Rogan josh is a staple dish in the Kashmir region of South Asia. It is one of the main dishes of the Kashmiri multi-course meal (called the "Wazwan"). Lamb rogan josh consists of braised lamb chunks cooked with gravy and aromatic spices. Traditionally, rogan josh is made with dried Kashmiri chilies that have been deseeded to reduce their heat and give the dish a mild chili flavor. These chilies give the dish its red color.

SERVES: 8 • SERVING SIZE: 2 OZ / 56 G LAMB MIXTURE + ⅓ CUP / 68 G RICE
PREP TIME: 2 HOURS • COOKING TIME: 40 MINUTES

CHOICES/EXCHANGES
1 Starch
2 Nonstarchy Vegetable
4 Lean Protein

Calories	340
Calories from Fat	90
Total Fat	10.0 g
Saturated Fat	3.3 g
Trans Fat	0.0 g
Cholesterol	75 mg
Sodium	450 mg
Potassium	550 mg
Total Carbohydrate	29 g
Dietary Fiber	4 g
Sugars	6 g
Protein	32 g
Phosphorus	315 mg

2 cups / 490 g **plain, low-fat Greek yogurt**

1 pinch **saffron**

1 Tbsp / 15 g **ginger-garlic paste (p. 34)**

1¼ tsp / 8.4 g **salt, divided**

2 **boneless lamb legs, fat trimmed and cut into cubes (about 2 lb / 900 g cubes)**

1 tsp / 2 g **cumin seeds, toasted**

5 **green cardamom pods**

1 (1-inch / 2.5-cm) **cinnamon stick**

5 **cloves**

1 **star anise**

1 Tbsp / 15 mL **sunflower oil**

2 large **onions, peeled and thinly sliced**

1 tsp / 5 g **ground nutmeg**

1 tsp / 5 g **ground black pepper**

1 Tbsp / 14 g **Kashmiri chili powder**

1½ Tbsp / 21 g **ground coriander**

1 tsp / 5 g **garam masala**

1 tsp / 5 g **ground turmeric**

4 Tbsp / 62.4 g **tomato purée**

1 bunch **cilantro, stems removed and leaves finely chopped**

1 (1-inch / 3-cm) piece **fresh ginger, peeled and julienned**

2⅔ cups / 546.6 g **cooked brown basmati rice**

1. In a medium bowl, whisk together yogurt, saffron, ginger-garlic paste, and ¼ tsp / 1.7 g salt. Pour mixture over lamb cubes in a large bowl. Cover and marinate in the refrigerator for 2 hours. Bring the lamb to room temperature before cooking.

2. Meanwhile, crush the toasted cumin seeds, cardamom pods, cinnamon stick, cloves, and star anise using a mortar and pestle or the bottom of a clean heavy pan to release the oils. Heat oil in a heavy-bottomed pan over medium-high heat, then add the crushed spices and cook for 1 minute, until they begin to splutter.

3. Reduce heat to medium-low and add onions. Cook, stirring frequently (to prevent them from burning), until the onions are golden brown, about 5 minutes.

4. Increase the heat to medium-high and add lamb with the marinade to the pan. Cook, stirring occasionally, until lamb is browned but not cooked through, about 2–4 minutes. The lamb might stick to the pan a bit, but don't worry. Keep stirring and scraping the pan to mix all the flavors together. You can add a splash of water if the mixture becomes too dry.

5. Reduce heat to medium-low, add nutmeg, pepper, chili powder, coriander, garam masala, turmeric, and remaining 1 tsp / 6.7 g salt and cook for another 5 minutes.

6. Add the tomato purée and stir. Cover, and cook until the lamb is cooked through, about 25 minutes.

7. Garnish lamb mixture with cilantro and ginger pieces, and serve each portion on top of ⅓ cup / 68.3 g basmati rice.

COOK'S NOTES

You can replace the Kashmiri chili powder in this recipe with smoked paprika. If you really want to make this recipe the authentic way, instead of using Kashmiri chili powder you can use 3 whole guajillo chilies; remove the seeds from the chilies, soak the chilies in warm water for 30 minutes, and crush into a fine paste.

Keralan Spice-Roasted Turkey 🟢GF

This special roast is served by Syrian Christians in Kerala during special occasions, especially for Easter and Christmas. Traditionally, this recipe is made using locally raised duck instead of turkey.

SERVES: 18 • SERVING SIZE: ABOUT 3 OZ / 84 G TURKEY + 1 POTATO
PREP TIME: 45 MINUTES • COOKING TIME: 1 HOUR AND 40 MINUTES

KERALAN MASALA

2 Tbsp / 30 g **ginger-garlic paste (p. 34)**

2 Tbsp / 28 g **ground black pepper**

1 tsp / 5 g **ground turmeric**

2 Tbsp / 30 mL **white vinegar**

2 tsp / 13.4 g **sea salt**

18 **fingerling potatoes** (about 1 oz / 28 g each as purchased)

1¼ tsp / 6.3 mL **sunflower oil, divided**

10 **shallots, peeled and halved**

½ tsp / 3.3 g **salt**

½ tsp / 2.5 g **ground black pepper**

1 (14-lb / 6300 g) **turkey, butterflied**

1 tsp / 5 g **ghee (p. 30)**

CHOICES/EXCHANGES
½ Starch
3 Lean Protein

Calories	190
Calories from Fat	45
Total Fat	5.0 g
Saturated Fat	1.6 g
Trans Fat	0.0 g
Cholesterol	65 mg
Sodium	370 mg
Potassium	430 mg
Total Carbohydrate	7 g
Dietary Fiber	1 g
Sugars	1 g
Protein	27 g
Phosphorus	210 mg

1 Preheat oven to 425°F /220°C.

2 In a small bowl, combine all Keralan masala ingredients and mix to form a smooth paste. Set aside.

3 Set a flat rack on a large rimmed baking sheet and spread the potatoes and the shallots on the rack and drizzle with ¼ tsp / 1.3 mL oil. Sprinkle with salt and pepper.

4 Run your fingers under the turkey breast and thigh skin to loosen it. Rub turkey skin with masala paste and massage well all over.

5 Brush turkey with ghee and remaining 1 tsp / 5 mL oil. Place turkey on the rack breast side up and let stand at room temperature for 45 minutes.

6 Roast the turkey for about 1 hour and 40 minutes, until an instant-read thermometer inserted in the thickest part of the breast registers 155°F / 68°C and in the thickest part of the thigh registers 165°F / 74°C.

7 Transfer turkey to a carving board and let it rest for about 10 minutes.

8 Carve turkey and garnish with potato and shallot mixture. Remove skin from the turkey before serving.

COOK'S NOTES

If you can't find small potatoes you can use 1 lb / 450 g large potatoes cut into 1½-inch / 3.8-cm cubes.

Chicken Tikka Masala ⒼⒻ

Chicken tikka masala is a very popular dish in Britain. It consists of roasted or grilled chunks of chicken in spicy tomato-cream sauce. This mild curry is not a traditional Indian dish; in fact it was tailored for a British palate. In 2001, British Foreign Secretary Robin Cook claimed that chicken tikka masala was a British national dish.

SERVES: 6 • SERVING SIZE: 3 OZ / 84 G • PREP TIME: 2 HOURS • COOKING TIME: 35 MINUTES

2 lb / 900 g **boneless, skinless chicken breasts**

MARINADE

¼ cup / 61.3 g **plain, low-fat Greek yogurt**

1 Tbsp / 14 g **smoked paprika**

½ tsp / 2.5 g **cayenne pepper**

1 tsp / 5 g **ground coriander**

½ tsp / 2.5 g **ground cinnamon**

¼ tsp / 1.3 g **ground cardamom**

½ tsp / 2.5 g **ground white pepper**

1 Tbsp / 15 g **ginger-garlic paste (p. 34)**

Juice of 1 **lemon**

¼ tsp / 1.7 g **salt**

1 tsp / 5 mL **sunflower oil**

TIKKA MASALA

2 Tbsp / 30 mL **sunflower oil**

1 cup / 150 g **diced onions**

1 Tbsp / 15 g **ginger-garlic paste (p. 34)**

1 Tbsp / 14 g **smoked paprika**

¼ tsp / 1.3 g **ground black pepper**

1 cup / 242 g **canned crushed tomatoes**

1 Tbsp / 15 mL **heavy cream**

½ cup / 122.5 g **plain, low-fat Greek yogurt**

1 tsp / 7.1 g **honey**

¼ tsp / 1.7 g **salt**

¼ tsp / 1.3 g **garam masala**

CHOICES/EXCHANGES
1 Carbohydrate
5 Lean Protein

Calories	290
Calories from Fat	100
Total Fat	11.0 g
Saturated Fat	2.6 g
Trans Fat	0.0 g
Cholesterol	90 mg
Sodium	340 mg
Potassium	560 mg
Total Carbohydrate	12 g
Dietary Fiber	2 g
Sugars	6 g
Protein	37 g
Phosphorus	310 mg

1 Cut chicken breasts into 1-inch / 2.5-cm cubes. Place in a large bowl and set aside.

2 In a small bowl, combine all the marinade ingredients (except the sunflower oil). Add marinade to chicken and stir to coat. Marinate the chicken in the refrigerator for at least 2 hours.

3 Heat 1 tsp / 5 mL oil in a heavy-bottomed pan over medium-high. Add chicken and sear for 2 minutes per side. Set aside.

4 To make tikka masala, heat 2 Tbsp / 30 mL oil in the same pan over medium-high heat. Add onions and sauté for about 6 minutes, or until translucent. Add ginger-garlic paste and sauté for another 2 minutes. Reduce heat to medium and add paprika and black pepper and sauté for 1 minute.

5 Add tomatoes, bring mixture to a boil, then reduce heat and simmer for about 15 minutes.

6 In a small bowl, mix together heavy cream and yogurt. Add this mixture, honey, salt, and garam masala to the tomatoes. Turn heat back up to bring mixture to a boil, then reduce heat and simmer for 3 minutes.

7 Add chicken to pan and cook for another 3 minutes, or until the chicken cubes are fully cooked. Serve hot.

COOK'S NOTES

Traditionally, ½ tsp / 0.9 g crushed dried fenugreek leaves is mixed into the sauce just before serving, but this is optional. If you decide to add fenureek leaves, crush them in your hand before adding to release the flavor.

Chicken tikka doesn't need to be eaten with the sauce. Marinate the chicken acoording to the recipe instructions above. Then add 1 tsp / 5 mL oil to a heavy-bottomed pan over medium-high heat and cook the chicken for 3–4 minutes per side, or until cooked through. You can saute it with grilled onions or peppers for a light meal or delicious appetizer.

Hara Adrak Chops with Pickled Salad

These lamb chops are traditionally cooked in a tandoori (though you can use an outdoor grill, grill pan, or cast iron griddle). In Hindi, the word *hara* means "green" and *adrak* means "ginger." Spinach and cilantro form the base of the green sauce in this dish. You'll love the bright flavors of these chops!

SERVES: 8 • SERVING SIZE: 1 CHOP + ⅓ CUP / 50 G SALAD
PREP TIME: 6 HOURS OR OVERNIGHT • COOKING TIME: 12 MINUTES

8 **lamb rib chops** (weighing 2½ lb / 1130 g total)
1 cup / 150 g **fresh spinach, blanched**
2 **green chilies, seeds removed**
1 Tbsp / 1 g **chopped cilantro**
¼ cup / 36.3 g **cubed raw papaya**
1 cup / 245 g **plain fat-free Greek yogurt**
2 Tbsp / 10.4 g **grated fresh ginger**
3 tsp / 15 mL **sunflower oil, divided**
1 tsp / 6.7 g **salt**

SALAD

2 cups / 300 g **julienned radish (skin on)**
2 small **red onions, thinly sliced**
1 **green chili, julienned**
¼ tsp / 1.7 g **salt**
Juice of 1 **lemon**

KITCHEN TOOLS

Food processor

CHOICES/EXCHANGES
1 Nonstarchy Vegetable
3 Lean Protein
½ Fat

Calories	190
Calories from Fat	70
Total Fat	8.0 g
Saturated Fat	2.3 g
Trans Fat	0.0 g
Cholesterol	60 mg
Sodium	440 mg
Potassium	470 mg
Total Carbohydrate	7 g
Dietary Fiber	1 g
Sugars	4 g
Protein	22 g
Phosphorus	200 mg

1 Using a paring knife, cut a few ¼-inch / 6-mm-deep slashes in each lamb chop.

2 Add blanched spinach to a food processor along with green chilies, cilantro, and papaya cubes. Purée to reach a smooth consistency.

3 Add yogurt and grated ginger to the purée and mix well. Add 1 tsp / 5 mL sunflower oil to the marinade.

4 In a large bowl or deep pan, toss the masala with lamb chops and marinate, covered, for 6 hours (or overnight) in the refrigerator.

5 After marinating, remove chops from the marinade and let stand at room temperature for 30 minutes.

6 Light an outdoor grill or cast iron griddle. Season the chops with salt and grill over medium-high heat for 8 minutes, turning once.

7 Brush both sides of the chops with the remaining 2 tsp / 10 mL sunflower oil and grill for another 2 minutes per side, until chops are medium-rare. Remove visible fat from chops.

8 In a small bowl, combine all salad ingredients and toss. Serve each chop with ⅓ cup / 50 g salad.

COOK'S NOTES

The salt should be added to the chops just before grilling, otherwise it will toughen the meat. The papaya in this recipe acts as a tenderizer. Papaya is often used in meat marinades in India; it is a natural tenderizer. You can replace the papaya with juice of 1 lemon, if desired.

CHAPTER 6
Fish and Seafood Delicacies

Roasted Masala Branzino

The coastal state of Kerala is the largest fishing state in the India peninsula. Naturally, seafood is vital part of Keralan cuisine. While branzino is typically found in Europe, it is common in seafood markets around the globe. You can replace the branzino in this recipe with any mild white fish such as red snapper or striped bass. The masala blend in this dish is the perfect complement for mild fish.

SERVES: 2 • SERVING SIZE: 4 OZ / 113 G • PREP TIME: 10 MINUTES • COOKING TIME: 16 MINUTES

MASALA
Juice of ½ **lemon**
2 tsp / 10 g **ginger paste (p. 34)**
2 tsp / 10 g **garlic paste (p. 34)**
1 tsp / 5 g **ground black pepper**
1 Tbsp / 14 g **smoked paprika**
1 tsp / 5 g **ground turmeric**
1 Tbsp / 15 mL **white vinegar**

1 (1¼-lb / 563 g) **whole branzino or striped bass, scaled and gutted**
¼ tsp / 1.7 g **salt**
1 **lemon, sliced into 8 rounds**
3 sprigs **curry leaves**
1 Tbsp / 15 mL **extra-virgin olive oil**

CHOICES/EXCHANGES
1 Carbohydrate
3 Lean Protein
1 Fat

Calories	240
Calories from Fat	100
Total Fat	11.0 g
Saturated Fat	1.8 g
Trans Fat	0.0 g
Cholesterol	50 mg
Sodium	390 mg
Potassium	630 mg
Total Carbohydrate	15 g
Dietary Fiber	5 g
Sugars	3 g
Protein	26 g
Phosphorus	285 mg

1 Preheat oven to 425°F / 220°C.

2 In a medium bowl, combine all masala ingredients. Set mixture aside.

3 Season branzino with salt and the masala mixture. Stuff the fish with lemon rounds and curry leaf sprigs. Score the outer flesh of the fish on a slant so that the masala flavors the flesh.

4 Heat olive oil in a large cast iron skillet. Add branzino and cook over high heat until the skin is browned and crisp, about 3 minutes per side.

5 Transfer fish to a large rimmed baking sheet, or leave in the skillet if it is ovenproof. Roast the fish in the oven for about 10 more minutes, until just cooked through.

6 Remove skin from the fish (it should come off easily). Serve fish whole or serve the fillets separately with the lemon rings.

COOK'S NOTES

If you're short on time, you can skip browning the fish on the stovetop and put it directly in the oven instead. Drizzle it with olive oil and bake in an oven preheated to 400° F / 200°C for about 20 minutes. Then you can broil it for 5 minutes to get a nice color on the fish (be careful not to let the fish burn). For a deeper flavor, you can marinate the fish for 30 minutes at room temperature before cooking on the stovetop or in the oven. Any white fish can be used in this recipe; look for what is fresh and seasonal.

Goan-Style Shrimp Curry GF

Portuguese colonists, who used to control the western part of the Indian state of Goa, influenced the development of this dish. The main ingredients (seafood and coconut) are naturally abundant in this part of the country, and Portuguese traders incorporated chilies (introduced to India through the spice trade) into the dish.

SERVES: 6 • SERVING SIZE: 2 OZ / 56 G • PREP TIME: 2 HOURS • COOKING TIME: 18 MINUTES

1 Tbsp / 15 mL **white vinegar**

1 Tbsp / 15 mL **water**

2 **dried guajillo chilies, seeds removed**

1 tsp / 2 g **cumin seeds**

2 small **ripe tomatoes, finely minced**

¼ cup / 20.8 g **freshly grated coconut**

¼ tsp / 0.9 g **yellow mustard seeds**

2 lb / 900 g **cleaned and deveined medium shrimp, divided**

1 Tbsp / 15 mL **sunflower oil**

1 medium **red onion, finely minced**

¾ tsp / 5 g **salt**

1 Tbsp / 15 g **ginger-garlic paste (p. 34)**

½ tsp / 2.5 g **ground turmeric**

1 Tbsp / 14 g **ground coriander**

¼ tsp / 1.3 g **ground black pepper**

½ cup / 120 mL **water**

½ tsp / 2.5 g **garam masala**

$\frac{1}{16}$ tsp / 0.3 g **sugar**

1 Tbsp / 1 g **freshly chopped cilantro leaves**

KITCHEN TOOL

Food processor

CHOICES/EXCHANGES
1 Nonstarchy Vegetable
3 Lean Protein

Calories	150
Calories from Fat	35
Total Fat	4.0 g
Saturated Fat	1.3 g
Trans Fat	0.0 g
Cholesterol	180 mg
Sodium	400 mg
Potassium	420 mg
Total Carbohydrate	6 g
Dietary Fiber	1 g
Sugars	2 g
Protein	24 g
Phosphorus	255 mg

1 Combine vinegar and water in a small bowl or saucepot and heat the mixture on the stove or in the microwave (about 1 minute). Soak red chilies and cumin seeds in the warm vinegar and water mixture for 2 hours.

2 Add chili and cumin mixture (including soaking liquid), tomatoes, grated coconut, mustard seeds, and two raw shrimp to a food processor and grind to a fine paste. Set aside.

3 Heat oil in a heavy-bottomed pan over medium-high. Add chopped onions and salt and cook until onions are golden brown.

4 Add ginger-garlic paste, turmeric, coriander, pepper, and the ground shrimp mixture and stir. Reduce heat to medium and cook, stirring constantly, for 2–3 minutes, or until the ingredients come together.

5 Add water to the pan, little by little, until mixture reaches a thick gravy-like consistency. Add shrimp and cook for about 10 minutes.

6 Add garam masala and sugar. Cook for 1 minute then remove from heat.

7 Garnish with cilantro and serve.

COOK'S NOTES

This dish can be served with brown rice or any whole-grain Indian bread.

Meen Molee (Keralan Fish Stew) 🄶🄵

This traditional fish stew was influenced by British rule in India. It has a light coconut sauce that features flavors from the southern coast of India. It is a specialty in Kerala where seafood is abundant.

SERVES: 4 • SERVING SIZE: 1 (4-OZ / 113-G) FILLET + ¼ CUP / 59 G GRAVY
PREP TIME: 15 MINUTES • COOKING TIME: 20 MINUTES

MARINADE

1 tsp / 5 g **ground turmeric**

¼ tsp / 1.3 g **ground black pepper**

2 tsp /10 mL **white vinegar**

4 (4-oz / 113-g) **salmon fillets**

1 Tbsp /15 mL **sunflower oil**

7 **shallots, quartered**

5 **cloves garlic, thinly sliced**

1 (3-inch / 7.5-cm) **piece ginger, peeled and julienned**

1 **green chili, slit open**

½ tsp / 1.2 g **black peppercorns**

6 **cherry tomatoes** OR 2 medium **ripe Roma tomatoes, halved crosswise**

3 Tbsp / 45 mL **light coconut milk, divided**

½ cup / 120 mL **water**

½ tsp / 3.3 g **kosher salt**

2 tsp / 10 mL **white vinegar**

⅔ cup / 160 mL **fat-free evaporated milk**

CHOICES/EXCHANGES
½ Fat-Free Milk
2 Nonstarchy Vegetable
3 Lean Protein
1½ Fat

Calories	290
Calories from Fat	120
Total Fat	13.0 g
Saturated Fat	2.9 g
Trans Fat	0.0 g
Cholesterol	65 mg
Sodium	360 mg
Potassium	810 mg
Total Carbohydrate	16 g
Dietary Fiber	2 g
Sugars	7 g
Protein	27 g
Phosphorus	425 mg

1   In a small bowl, combine marinade ingredients. Add salmon fillets to a bowl or pan and marinate fillets for 15 minutes.

2   In a large, flat heavy-bottomed pan or on a cast iron griddle, carefully sear salmon, 2 at a time, and set fillets aside.

3   In the same pan heat oil over medium heat. Sauté the shallots, garlic, ginger, chili, black peppercorns, and tomatoes over medium heat for 3 minutes.

4   Meanwhile, mix 2 Tbsp / 30 mL of the coconut milk with the water and salt in a medium bowl. Set aside.

5   Reduce heat under pan to medium-low and place fillets back in pan. When fillets begin to release their juices, add coconut milk mixture and vinegar. Cook for about 10 minutes.

6   In a separate bowl, combine the remaining 1 Tbsp / 15 mL coconut milk, and evaporated milk. Add this milk mixture to the pan and cook for 2 minutes.

7   Remove pan from heat. Remove the green chili before serving. Place fillets in a rimmed serving tray or a large shallow bowl and pour stew over the salmon.

COOK'S NOTES

Traditionally, coconut oil is used in this recipe instead of sunflower oil. The coconut milk can be replaced with same amount of fat-free evaporated milk, if desired. A souring agent known as kokum is used in traditional versions of this recipe instead of the vinegar. If you're interested in using kokum, the root can be found in Indian markets.

Country-Style Keralan Crab and Mango Curry (GF)

The state of Kerala is geographically located in one of the best places for fresh seafood, including crab. The Keralan seafood industry exports to many counties in the world including Japan. This country-style crab preparation from Kerala is usually eaten with a spiced yucca mash. This dish can be prepared with shrimp or any of your favorite seafood instead of the crab.

SERVES: 4 • SERVING SIZE: 4 OZ / 113 G • PREP TIME: ABOUT 5 MINUTES • COOKING TIME: 15 MINUTES

MASALA

1 tsp / 5 g **ground turmeric**

1 tsp / 5 g **cayenne pepper**

1 **green chili, seeds removed**

1 (1-inch / 2.5-cm) **piece fresh ginger, finely chopped**

2 Tbsp / 10.4 g **freshly grated coconut**

3 medium **shallots**

¼ tsp / 0.9 g **fenugreek seeds**

¼ cup / 60 mL **water**

1 Tbsp / 15 mL **sunflower oil**

1 cup / 150 g **thinly sliced raw green mango**

1 **green chili, slit open and seeds removed**

1 **sprig curry leaves**

2 lb / 900 g **fresh blue crab, outer shell removed, cleaned, and claws separated**

1 cup / 240 mL **water**

KITCHEN TOOLS

Food processor

CHOICES/EXCHANGES
1 Carbohydrate
3 Lean Protein

Calories	190
Calories from Fat	50
Total Fat	6.0 g
Saturated Fat	14 g
Trans Fat	0.0 g
Cholesterol	115 mg
Sodium	480 mg
Potassium	600 mg
Total Carbohydrate	13 g
Dietary Fiber	2 g
Sugars	8 g
Protein	23 g
Phosphorus	315 mg

1 Combine all the masala ingredients in a food processor and grind to a fine paste. Set aside.

2 Heat oil in a heavy-bottomed pan over medium heat and add the masala and cook for 2–3 minutes. Once the mixture starts to bubble, add mango, chili, and curry leaves. Mix well and cook for another minute.

3 Now add the crab, including claws (crack claws slightly before adding), and water and simmer for 10 minutes. Remove from heat, remove curry leaves and green chili, and serve hot.

COOK'S NOTES

This is one of my favorite recipes! It's a special dish that my mom used to make for my family.

I love serving this dish with a delicious yucca mash, but it also tastes great with roasted sweet potatoes. This recipe does not have any added salt because crab is higher in sodium than some other types of seafood, such as fish. But the mango, coconut, and spices in this dish give it a pure taste and more than enough flavor.

Looking for even more flavor? You can make a tadka with 1 Tbsp / 15 mL sunflower oil, ¼ tsp / 0.9 g fenugreek seeds, 1 tsp / 3.5 g black mustard seeds, 1 bunch of fresh curry leaves, and 2 minced shallots. In a small heavy-bottomed pan, heat the oil over medium heat. When the pan is hot, add the fenugreek and mustard seeds and curry leaves. When the seeds begin to splutter, add the shallots and sauté for about 3 minutes, until brown. Pour the tadka over the crab curry before serving.

Mussel Curry with Aromatic Herbs

SERVES: 4 • SERVING SIZE: 4 OZ / 113 G • PREP TIME: ABOUT 5 MINUTES • COOKING TIME: 20 MINUTES

1 Tbsp / 15 mL **sunflower oil or coconut oil**

1 cup / 150 g **sliced shallots**

1 tsp / 5 g **ginger paste (p. 34)**

1 tsp / 5 g **garlic paste (p. 34)**

2 **green chilies, slit open and seeds removed**

2 Tbsp / 28 g **ground coriander**

½ tsp / 2.5 g **ground turmeric**

½ tsp / 2.5 g **ground cumin**

2 lb / 900 g **fresh mussels, scrubbed and debearded**

3½ cups / 820 mL **water, divided**

6 Tbsp / 90 mL **light coconut milk**

1 tsp / 5.2 g **tamarind paste**

¼ cup / 4 g **cilantro leaves, finely minced**

2 **bunches curry leaves, cleaned and leaves separated**

¼ tsp / 1.7 g **kosher salt**

CHOICES/EXCHANGES
½ Carbohydrate
1 Nonstarchy Vegetable
2 Lean Protein
½ Fat

Calories	190
Calories from Fat	70
Total Fat	8.0 g
Saturated Fat	2 g
Trans Fat	0.0 g
Cholesterol	30 mg
Sodium	340 mg
Potassium	460 mg
Total Carbohydrate	16 g
Dietary Fiber	3 g
Sugars	6 g
Protein	15 g
Phosphorus	220 mg

1. In a wide heavy-bottomed saucepan (preferably cast iron), heat oil over medium-high heat. Add shallots and sauté until brown.

2. Add ginger paste, garlic paste, and green chilies and sauté over medium heat for about 1 minute. Add coriander, turmeric, and cumin and reduce heat to medium low. Cook, stirring, for 1 minute or until flavors are blended.

3. Add mussels and sauté for 1–2 minutes. Add 3 cups / 700 mL water, cover saucepan with lid, and cook for about 10 minutes until all the mussels have opened.

4. Meanwhile, mix coconut milk, remaining ½ cup / 120 mL water, and tamarind paste in a small bowl. Add coconut mixture to the pan and continue cooking, uncovered, over medium heat for 2 minutes.

5. Remove green chilies and discard any unopened mussels. Stir in cilantro and curry leaves and remove from heat. Sprinkle with salt. Allow to cool slightly before serving.

COOK'S NOTES

Any mussels that remain closed after cooking need to be discarded; they are bad. The tamarind paste in this recipe can be replaced with the juice of 1 lime.

If you can't find light coconut milk, you can make fresh light coconut milk by taking a 1 cup / 83.3 g fresh or frozen grated coconut, adding the coconut to a bowl, and adding 1 cup / 240 mL hot water. Drain and discard the water, squeezing the coconut to remove the excess moisture. Then add another 1 cup / 240 mL hot water to the coconut, and use a strainer to drain the water into a cup, squeezing all the moisture from the coconut. Use this water in place of store-bought light coconut milk.

Patrani Machi (Fish in Banana Leaves)

This dish has its roots in western India, where Parsis—Persian Zoroastrian immigrants—settled around the 7th–9th century CE. Parsi cuisine is a unique regional Indian cuisine with ancient Persian influence.

SERVES: 4 • SERVING SIZE: 4 OZ / 113 G • PREP TIME: 5 MINUTES • COOKING TIME: 15 MINUTES

GREEN CHUTNEY MASALA

1 **green chili, seeds removed**

3 **cloves garlic**

2 oz / 56 g **raw mango**

½ cup / 8 g **cilantro leaves**

2 Tbsp / 10.4 g **grated fresh coconut**

½ tsp / 3.3 g **salt**

1½ lb / 680 g **sea bass, scaled and cleaned** OR 4 (4-oz / 113-g) **fillets**

4 **pieces banana leaf** or 4 **Swiss chard leaves**

1 Tbsp / 15 mL **sunflower oil**

KITCHEN TOOLS

Steamer (any kind)

1 Combine all green chutney masala ingredients in a blender and blend to a fine paste.

2 Evenly apply the paste to each fillet or the whole fish, and then wrap tightly in the banana or Swiss chard leaves. Brush the tops of the leaves with sunflower oil. Place the wrapped fish in a steamer and cook for 15 minutes.

3 Cutting away from your face, cut open the leaf wrapping and carefully release the steam before serving.

COOK'S NOTES

You can replace the mango in the masala with the juice of ½ lemon, if desired. You can usually find banana leaves in Asian markets; they are often available frozen. If you can't find banana leaf pieces or Swiss chard to use for this recipe, you can use parchment paper instead.

CHOICES/EXCHANGES
½ Carbohydrate
3 Lean Protein

Calories	170
Calories from Fat	60
Total Fat	7.0 g
Saturated Fat	1.7 g
Trans Fat	0.0 g
Cholesterol	45 mg
Sodium	400 mg
Potassium	560 mg
Total Carbohydrate	6 g
Dietary Fiber	1 g
Sugars	3 g
Protein	22 g
Phosphorus	255 mg

Tuna-Parsnip Tikki

Tikki is similar to savory cakes such as crab cakes. It incorporates spices and herbs for great flavor. Tikki is quite popular in the northern Indian states. You can form the tikkis ahead of time, refrigerate, and then shallow fry them just before serving.

SERVES: 4 • SERVING SIZE: 2 TIKKIS + 1 TSP / 5 G CHUTNEY • PREP TIME: 10 MINUTES • COOKING TIME: 6 MINUTES

1½ (5-oz / 141-g) cans **water-packed tuna, drained**

1 large **parsnip, boiled and mashed**

1 **egg, lightly beaten**

1 **green chili, finely diced**

3 **cloves garlic, finely mined**

¼ tsp / 0.4 g **grated fresh ginger**

2 **green onions, green and white parts, finely minced**

2 Tbsp / 2 g **finely chopped cilantro**

½ tsp / 2.5 g **garam masala**

1 tsp / 5 g **red chili powder**

1 tsp / 5 mL **lemon juice**

¼ tsp / 1.7 g **salt**

2 Tbsp / 20 g **bread crumbs**

2 Tbsp / 30 mL **sunflower oil**

4 tsp / 20 g **Green Mint and Coriander Chutney (p. 243)**

1. In a large mixing bowl, combine tuna, mashed parsnip, and egg. Add chili (remove seeds to reduce heat), garlic, and ginger to the tuna-parsnip mixture and mix well.

2. Add the green onion, cilantro, garam masala, chili powder, lemon juice, salt, and the bread crumbs and mix well.

3. Using your hands, take handfuls of the tuna mixture and make 8 (2-inch / 5-cm) balls. Flatten the balls a bit to form the tikkis.

4. Preheat a flat cast iron skillet over medium-high heat and add the oil.

5. Shallow fry the tikkis, a few at a time, for about 3 minutes per side, or until they are golden brown. Garnish each with a dab of chutney and serve hot.

CHOICES/EXCHANGES
1 Carbohydrate
1 Lean Protein
1½ Fat

Calories	170
Calories from Fat	90
Total Fat	10.0 g
Saturated Fat	1.3 g
Trans Fat	0.0 g
Cholesterol	60 mg
Sodium	360 mg
Potassium	370 mg
Total Carbohydrate	13 g
Dietary Fiber	3 g
Sugars	3 g
Protein	11 g
Phosphorus	145 mg

COOK'S NOTES

You can remove the seeds from the chili to reduce the heat level, but keep the skin for flavor. You can use 5 oz / 141 g fresh tuna instead of the canned tuna for this recipe if you'd like. I recommend buying sushi-grade tuna, cooking over low heat with 1 Tbsp / 15 mL water, and then finely shred it with a fork before mixing with the other ingredients.

CHAPTER 7
Regional Delicacies

Gobi Musallam (Baked Spiced Cauliflower)

The diverse history of this dish is evident in its name; *gobi* is Hindi for "cauliflower," and the word *musallam* comes from Urdu—the language associated with the Muslims of Hindustan—and means "whole" or "complete." The word musallam comes from the same root as the words Islam and Muslim. The Islamic Mughal dynasty of northern India introduced this dish to India, and it is now enjoyed throughout the country.

SERVES: 4 • SERVING SIZE: 4.5 OZ / 127 G CAULIFLOWER + 1 TBSP / 15 ML SAUCE
PREP TIME: ABOUT 5 MINUTES • COOKING TIME: 55 MINUTES

GOBI MUSALLAM

1 medium **cauliflower, leaves removed and stem on**

½ tsp / 3.3 g **salt, divided**

1 tsp / 5 g **ground turmeric**

1 Tbsp plus 1 tsp / 20 mL **sunflower oil, divided**

1 **onion, peeled and roughly chopped**

2 **green chilies**

12 **raw, unsalted cashews**

1 **clove garlic, peeled**

1 (1-inch / 2.5-cm) **piece ginger, peeled**

1 tsp / 5 g **ground cinnamon**

2 **cloves**

½ tsp / 2.5 g **ground nutmeg**

6 **green cardamom pods, husks removed and crushed**

4 Tbsp / 61.2 g **plain, low-fat Greek yogurt**

1 tsp / 5 g **ghee (p. 30)**

⅔ cup / 100 g **chopped fresh tomatoes, puréed**

1 Tbsp / 15.6 g **concentrated tomato paste**

1 cup / 240 mL **low-fat milk**

1 cup / 135 g **frozen peas**

1 Tbsp / 1 g **finely chopped cilantro leaves**

KITCHEN TOOLS

Food processor

CHOICES/EXCHANGES
½ Carbohydrate
3 Nonstarchy Vegetable
1 Lean Protein
1 Fat

Calories	210
Calories from Fat	80
Total Fat	9.0 g
Saturated Fat	2.4 g
Trans Fat	0.0 g
Cholesterol	5 mg
Sodium	430 mg
Potassium	890 mg
Total Carbohydrate	26 g
Dietary Fiber	7 g
Sugars	12 g
Protein	10 g
Phosphorus	225 mg

1 Preheat oven to 375°F / 190°C.

2 Rub cauliflower with ¼ tsp / 1.7 g salt, turmeric, and 1 tsp / 5 mL oil. Place the spiced cauliflower on an ovenproof tray and roast for 25 minutes, or until tender. Remove tray from the oven and set aside.

3 Using a food processor, grind onion, chilies, cashews, garlic, ginger, cinnamon, cloves, nutmeg, cardamom pods, yogurt, and remaining ¼ tsp / 1.7 g salt into a smooth paste.

4 In a large, deep heavy-bottomed pan over medium-high heat, combine ghee, remaining 1 Tbsp / 15 mL oil, and the spice paste. Cook, stirring constantly, until paste turns a light golden brown.

5 Stir in puréed tomatoes, tomato paste, and milk. Continue stirring until well mixed. Reduce heat to low and allow spices and tomatoes to simmer for 8 minutes. Add peas and stir well.

6 Gently add the whole cauliflower to the pan and baste with the prepared sauce. Cover the pan with a lid and cook for 5 minutes. (If cauliflower begins to stick to the pan, add a little water to prevent it from sticking and burning.)

7 Remove lid and baste again. Cook, uncovered, for 10 more minutes. Serve in a large bowl or platter garnished with cilantro.

COOK'S NOTES

Gobi Musallam makes a stunning centerpiece for the dinner table and is perfect for sharing. Give everyone a large spoon and dig in, being sure to break the tender morsels of cauliflower off their stem. This dish is best accompanied with either a paratha or a cucumber raita. You can substitute for the cauliflower with a whole head of broccoli and cook it in the same way, if desired. You can replace the cinnamon, cloves, nutmeg, and cardamom pods with 1 tsp / 5 g good-quality garam masala. You can also substitute light coconut milk for the low-fat milk in this recipe.

Slow-Roasted Salmon in Red Masala

SERVES: 6 • SERVING SIZE: 5.3-OZ / 150-G FILLET • PREP TIME: ABOUT 2 HOURS • COOKING TIME: 25 MINUTES

2 lb / 900 g **salmon, divided into 6 fillets**
Juice of ½ **lemon**
½ tsp / 3.3 g **salt**

RED MASALA

1 tsp / 5 g **smoked paprika**
2 tsp / 10 g **mild paprika**
1 tsp / 5 g **ground black pepper**
2 tsp / 10.4 g **tomato paste**

½ tsp / 2.5 g **ground turmeric**
½ tsp / 2.5 g **ground mustard**
1 tsp / 5 g **ginger paste (p. 34)**
1 tsp / 5 g **garlic paste (p. 34)**
¼ tsp / 1.7 g **kosher salt**
Juice of ½ **lemon**

1 tsp / 5 mL **grapeseed oil**
1 **lemon, cut into thin slices**

1 Lightly score the salmon fillets. In a large bowl or baking dish, combine salmon with lemon juice and salt and marinate in the refrigerator for 30 minutes.

2 Meanwhile, combine all red masala ingredients in a food processor and grind to form a smooth paste.

3 After 30 minutes of marinating, add the red masala to salmon. Cover and refrigerate for another 1–2 hours.

4 Preheat oven to 350°F / 180°C.

5 Remove the marinated salmon from refrigerator and brush with grapeseed oil. Place lemon slices on the top of fillets and bake for 25 minutes.

COOK'S NOTES

When prepared correctly, the red masala should be a good consistency for spreading; you can add a few drops of water if necessary to reach the right consistency. You can use any fish of your choice in this recipe.

CHOICES/EXCHANGES
½ Carbohydrate
4 Lean Protein
1 Fat

Calories	250
Calories from Fat	110
Total Fat	12.0 g
Saturated Fat	2.6 g
Trans Fat	0.0 g
Cholesterol	80 mg
Sodium	380 mg
Potassium	640 mg
Total Carbohydrate	5 g
Dietary Fiber	2 g
Sugars	1 g
Protein	30 g
Phosphorus	400 mg

Peppery Shrimp with Curry Leaves ⒼⒻ

This dish highlights traditional flavors of southern India. Combining black pepper with turmeric is said to help the body absorb the nutrients in turmeric.

SERVES: 4 • SERVING SIZE: 2 OZ / 56 G • PREP TIME: 30 MINUTES • COOKING TIME: 35 MINUTES

1 Tbsp / 6.9 g **black peppercorns**

1 tsp / 5 g **ground turmeric**

1 tsp / 5 g **lemon zest**

3 **sprigs curry leaves**

½ tsp / 3.3 g **salt**

1 lb / 450 g large **peeled, deveined shrimp**

1 tsp / 5 mL **sunflower oil**

Juice of ½ **lemon**

KITCHEN TOOLS:

Spice grinder

1 Coarsely grind peppercorns in a spice grinder or food processor. In a small bowl, combine pepper, turmeric, lemon zest, curry leaves, and salt.

2 Add shrimp to the spice mixture. Toss to coat thoroughly and marinate in the refrigerator for 30 minutes.

3 After 30 minutes, discard curry leaves and preheat a cast iron griddle over medium-high heat. Add oil.

4 Once griddle is hot add shrimp and cook for 2 minutes per side. Add lemon juice and serve.

COOK'S NOTES

If you can't find curry leaves, you can replace them with 3 sprigs of thyme.

CHOICES/EXCHANGES

3 Lean Protein

Calories	120
Calories from Fat	15
Total Fat	1.5 g
Saturated Fat	0.2 g
Trans Fat	0.0 g
Cholesterol	190 mg
Sodium	400 mg
Potassium	310 mg
Total Carbohydrate	2 g
Dietary Fiber	1 g
Sugars	0 g
Protein	24 g
Phosphorus	240 mg

Spicy Calamari GF

The southwest coast of India is known for its high-quality shellfish. You'll taste the flavors of that region when you bite into this delicious calamari dish.

SERVES: 4 • SERVING SIZE: 8 OZ / 230 G • PREP TIME: NONE • COOKING TIME: 25 MINUTES

2 lb / 900 g **fresh calamari, cleaned and cut into 1-inch / 2.5-cm pieces**

1 tsp / 5 g **sweet paprika**

1 tsp / 5 g **cayenne pepper**

½ tsp / 2.5 g **ground turmeric**

1 Tbsp / 15 mL **sunflower oil or coconut oil**

3 medium **red onions, thinly sliced**

1 **sprig curry leaves**

¾ tsp / 5 g **kosher salt**

1 Heat a heavy-bottomed pan over medium heat. Add calamari and cook until the water released from the calamari evaporates, about 5 minutes.

2 Add the paprika, cayenne pepper, and turmeric and sauté for 2 minutes, stirring well.

3 Add oil, sliced onions, and curry leaf sprig and stir well. Cover pan and cook over medium-low heat for about 12 minutes, stirring occasionally to prevent burning.

4 Remove lid, stir, and cook for 2 more minutes. Remove curry sprig and sprinkle with salt before serving.

COOK'S NOTES

This dish tastes great over steamed rice or served with Indian flatbread.

CHOICES/EXCHANGES
½ Carbohydrate
2 Nonstarchy Vegetable
4 Lean Protein

Calories	270
Calories from Fat	50
Total Fat	6.0 g
Saturated Fat	1.1 g
Trans Fat	0.0 g
Cholesterol	470 mg
Sodium	430 mg
Potassium	590 mg
Total Carbohydrate	18 g
Dietary Fiber	2 g
Sugars	5 g
Protein	33 g
Phosphorus	390 mg

90 • Bhune Makai Ka Shorba (Roasted Corn and Sweet Potato Soup)

76 • Chana (Chickpea) Masala | 160 • Whole-Wheat Spinach Parathas

63 • Corn Bhutta (Roasted Corn on the Cob)

194 • Jewel Roasted Root Vegetables with Panch Phoran

193 • Masala Baingan (Grilled Eggplant)

120 • Roasted Masala Branzino

49 • Masala Omelette with Mixed Veggies

146 • Roasted Chicken Tandoori | 209 • Kachumber Salad (Onion and Tomato Salad)

218 • Shrikhand (Sweetened Hung Curd) with Poached Peaches

148 • Spiced Turkey Meatballs | 207 • Carrot and Beet Slaw

Vindaloo-Style Roasted Pork Tenderloin

This dish is popular among Anglo-Indian cooks in Goa in southwestern India. The term *vindaloo* is derived from the Portuguese dish *carne de vinha d'alhos*, a dish of meat (usually pork) marinated in wine and garlic. Vindaloo recipes modify the Portuguese dish by substituting vinegar (usually palm vinegar) for the red wine. Kashmiri chili peppers and other spices were added during the evolution of vindaloo.

SERVES: 6 • SERVING SIZE: 3 OZ / 84 G • PREP TIME: ABOUT 7 HOURS • COOKING TIME: 30 MINUTES

2 tsp / 10 g **Kashmiri chili powder**
1 tsp / 2.3 g **black peppercorns**
1 Tbsp / 6 g **cumin seeds, toasted**
1 tsp / 3.5 g **yellow mustard seeds**
¼ tsp / 1.3 g **ground cinnamon**
3 **cloves**
7 **garlic cloves, chopped**
1 (2-inch / 5-cm) **piece fresh ginger**
½ cup / 120 mL **apple cider vinegar**
1¼ tsp / 8.4 g **sea salt**
2 (¾-lb / 340-g) **pork tenderloins, silver skin removed**

KITCHEN TOOLS
Food processor

CHOICES/EXCHANGES
3 Lean Protein

Calories	140
Calories from Fat	30
Total Fat	3.5 g
Saturated Fat	1.1 g
Trans Fat	0.0 g
Cholesterol	60 mg
Sodium	430 mg
Potassium	440 mg
Total Carbohydrate	4 g
Dietary Fiber	1 g
Sugars	0 g
Protein	23 g
Phosphorus	220 mg

1. In a food processor, combine chili powder, peppercorns, cumin seeds, mustard seeds, cinnamon, cloves, garlic, ginger, and vinegar, and grind to a fine paste. Add salt and mix thoroughly.

2. Add paste to pork tenderloins, cover, and refrigerate for at least 6 hours.

3. After 6 hours, transfer pork to a plate, cover, and let stand at room temperature for 1 hour.

4. Preheat oven to 425°F / 220°C.

5. Place pork in a heavy roasting pan, and cook on the middle rack of the oven for 30 minutes, or until an instant-read thermometer inserted into the thickest part of a tenderloin registers 140°F / 60°C.

6. Remove from oven, transfer pork to a carving board, and tent with aluminum foil. Let pork rest for 10 minutes before serving.

COOK'S NOTES

You can replace the Kashmiri chili powder with smoked paprika, if desired. Cut each tenderloin crosswise into thick slices. Arrange the slices on a platter or individual plates.

Nadan Tharavu Roast
(Traditional Keralan Roasted Duck) GF

This festive dish originated from Syrian Christian cooks in southern India. This dish is a must for Christmas and Easter celebrations. You can get locally raised duck from small farmers in the state of Kerala, and fresh duck is a delicacy in the southern region of India.

SERVES: 6 • SERVING SIZE: 3 OZ / 84 G MIXTURE + 1 POTATO
PREP TIME: ABOUT 5 MINUTES • COOKING TIME: 1 HOUR AND 5 MINUTES

6 small **whole potatoes**

2 medium **red onions, thinly sliced**

2¾ tsp / 13.8 mL **sunflower oil, divided**

2 Tbsp / 28 g **ground black pepper**

½ tsp / 2.5 g **ground turmeric**

1 Tbsp / 15 g **ginger-garlic paste (p. 34)**

¾ tsp / 5 g **salt**

4 **shallots**

1 Tbsp / 15 mL **white vinegar**

1 (5–6-lb / 2250–2700 g) **fresh Pekin duck, boned, skinned, visible fat removed, and cut into 2-inch / 5-cm cubes**

KITCHEN TOOLS

Food processor

CHOICES/EXCHANGES
1½ Starch
2 Nonstarchy Vegetable
2 Lean Protein
1½ Fat

Calories	320
Calories from Fat	110
Total Fat	12.0 g
Saturated Fat	3.6 g
Trans Fat	0.0 g
Cholesterol	75 mg
Sodium	370 mg
Potassium	780 mg
Total Carbohydrate	30 g
Dietary Fiber	4 g
Sugars	3 g
Protein	23 g
Phosphorus	245 mg

1 Preheat oven to 400°F / 200°C. Add potatoes and onions to a baking sheet or dish and drizzle with 1 tsp / 5 mL oil. Bake for about 30 minutes. Set aside.

2 Using a food processor, grind the black pepper, turmeric, ginger-garlic paste, salt, shallots, and vinegar to a smooth paste.

3 In a large bowl, combine masala paste and duck pieces and mix well.

4 Heat a deep, heavy-bottomed pan over medium-high heat. Add duck mixture and cook until it starts to bubble. Reduce heat to medium and cook covered for about 30 minutes, or until the duck is cooked through.

5 Separate the cooked duck pieces from the gravy (leaving gravy in the pan) and set duck aside.

6 Add 1¾ tsp / 8.8 mL oil to the gravy and reduce until gravy thickens, about 2–3 minutes. Now add duck back into the gravy and mix everything well, until duck is coated with gravy.

7 Garnish with roasted potatoes and serve.

COOK'S NOTES

For variations on this recipe, try replacing the duck with chicken or goose. Adjust the cooking time as needed. Pekin duck (not to be confused with the dish peking duck) is an American breed of duck raised for meat and eggs. This breed is also known as Long Island duck. I prefer to use Pekin duck in my kitchen, but it's not a requirement; just make sure you use good-quality duck meat for this recipe.

CHAPTER 8
Kebabs and Grilled Dishes

Grilled Fish Trio

SERVES: 8 • SERVING SIZE: 3 OZ / 84 G • PREP TIME: 2 HOURS • COOKING TIME: 12 MINUTES

MARINADE

1 Tbsp / 15 mL **smoked paprika**

1 cup / 245 g **plain, low-fat Greek yogurt**

Juice of 1 **lemon**

2 tsp / 3.4 g **finely grated ginger**

1 tsp / 2.2 g **ajwain seeds or caraway seeds**

1 tsp / 6.7 g **sea salt**

1 Tbsp / 15.6 g **tomato paste**

¼ tsp / 1.8 g **honey**

1 Tbsp / 15.5 g **Dijon mustard**

½ lb / 230 g **salmon, cut into 1-inch / 2.5-cm cubes**

½ lb / 230 g **tuna, cut into 1-inch / 2.5-cm cubes**

½ lb / 230 g **swordfish, cut into 1-inch / 2.5-cm cubes**

1 medium **red onion, cut into 1-inch / 2.5-cm wedges and separate the layers**

1 **green bell pepper, cut into 1-inch / 2.5-cm pieces**

1 **red bell pepper, cut into 1-inch / 2.5-cm pieces**

1 Tbsp / 15 mL **sunflower oil or ghee**

2 Tbsp / 2 g **chopped cilantro leaves**

KITCHEN TOOLS

8 wooden skewers

CHOICES/EXCHANGES
1 Nonstarchy Vegetable
3 Lean Protein
½ Fat

Calories	180
Calories from Fat	60
Total Fat	7.0 g
Saturated Fat	1.7 g
Trans Fat	0.0 g
Cholesterol	40 mg
Sodium	400 mg
Potassium	450 mg
Total Carbohydrate	7 g
Dietary Fiber	2 g
Sugars	4 g
Protein	22 g
Phosphorus	280 mg

1 Soak wooden skewers in cold water for at least 10 minutes.

2 In a large bowl, combine all marinade ingredients. Add salmon, tuna, swordfish, onion, and bell peppers to the bowl, mix well, and marinate in the refrigerator for 2 hours.

3 Preheat a grill or cast iron griddle over medium-high heat. Thread fish and vegetables, alternating, onto 8 skewers and brush with oil or ghee. Grill skewers for about 6 minutes per side. If any marinade is left over, brush onto the skewers while cooking.

4 Garnish with chopped cilantro and serve.

COOK'S NOTES

This dish pairs well with Carrot and Beet Slaw (p. 207) or can be served wrapped in Whole-Wheat Roti (p. 158). If you can't find ajwain seeds, you can use caraway seeds or leave the seeds out of the dish completely. You can use any firm fish of your choice.

Keralan Masala Scallops GF

MARINADE

1 Tbsp / 14 g **medium-heat curry powder**

1 tsp / 5 g **garlic paste (p. 34)**

1 **sprig curry leaves**

⅓ tsp / 2.2 g **salt**

8 large **scallops** (1.6 oz / 44.8 g each), **coral removed and patted dry**

2 tsp / 10 mL **sunflower oil**

1 **lemon, cut into wedges**

1   In a medium bowl, combine all marinade ingredients. Add scallops, mix well, and marinate in the refrigerator for 30 minutes. Discard curry leaf sprig after marinating.

2   Heat oil in a large cast iron frying pan over medium-high heat.

3   Add scallops and fry for 2 minutes. Turn scallops and cook for another minute.

4   Serve scallops with lemon wedges so juice can be squeezed over top.

COOK'S NOTES

Keralan curry is a blend of earthy spices, including coriander, nutmeg, cardamom, smoked paprika, black pepper, etc. It gives these scallops amazing flavor. You want to use a good-quality (organic, if possible) curry powder for this recipe. You can replace the scallops with shrimp or any seafood of your choice.

CHOICES/EXCHANGES

½ Carbohydrate
1 Lean Protein

Calories	90
Calories from Fat	25
Total Fat	3.0 g
Saturated Fat	0.4 g
Trans Fat	0.0 g
Cholesterol	25 mg
Sodium	350 mg
Potassium	230 mg
Total Carbohydrate	5 g
Dietary Fiber	1 g
Sugars	0 g
Protein	12 g
Phosphorus	255 mg

Roasted Chicken Tandoori

The tandoori oven originated in ancient India under Persian rule. Tandoori ovens (or tandoors) provide wraparound heat, due to the unique design of the dome-shaped clay apparatus. Tandoori-style cooking is popular in the north Indian regions and is used to cook both naan breads and vegetarian and non-vegetarian delicacies that are marinated in traditional spices and souring agents like lemon and yogurt.

SERVES: 6 • SERVING SIZE: 3 OZ / 84 G • PREP TIME: ABOUT 6 HOURS OR OVERNIGHT • COOKING TIME: 55 MINUTES

1 whole **organic chicken** (about 3–3½ lb / 1350–1580 g)
1 Tbsp / 15 mL **lemon juice**
1 tsp / 6.7 g **kosher salt**

TANDOORI MASALA
½ cup / 122.5 g **plain low-fat organic yogurt**
1 tsp / 5 g **garam masala**
1 tsp / 5 g **cayenne pepper**
3 tsp / 15 g **Punjabi red tandoori or smoked paprika**
½ tsp / 2.5 g **ground black pepper**
½ tsp / 5 g **ground turmeric**
½ tsp / 2.5 g **ginger paste (p. 34)**
½ tsp / 2.5 g **garlic paste (p. 34)**
1 tsp / 6.7 g **kosher salt**
1 Tbsp / 15 mL **lemon juice**
¼ cup / 48 g **reduced-fat sour cream**

2 tsp / 10 mL **sunflower oil**

CHOICES/EXCHANGES
4 Lean Protein

Calories	180
Calories from Fat	70
Total Fat	8.0 g
Saturated Fat	2.2 g
Trans Fat	0.0 g
Cholesterol	75 mg
Sodium	390 mg
Potassium	280 mg
Total Carbohydrate	3 g
Dietary Fiber	1 g
Sugars	1 g
Protein	24 g
Phosphorus	285 mg

Indian Cuisine Diabetes Cookbook

1 Transfer chicken to a large rimmed baking sheet, poke holes in the chicken with a fork.

2 In a small bowl, combine the lemon juice and salt. Rub chicken with lemon/salt mixture until thoroughly coated, and set aside for 30 minutes.

3 Combine all tandoori masala ingredients in a large bowl. Rub chicken with the masala and massage into the skin. Cover and refrigerate for 5–6 hours or overnight.

4 When chicken is done marinating remove from the refrigerator and allow to rest until it reaches room temperature. Preheat oven to 425°F / 220°C.

5 Brush chicken with sunflower oil and place chicken in a cast iron skillet or any roasting pan.

6 Bake chicken for about 30 minutes, then reduce oven temperature to 350°F / 180°C and bake for another 25 minutes, or until juices from the chicken run clear. Remove chicken skin before serving.

COOK'S NOTES

The chicken has to be refrigerated while marinating. It can be kept in the refrigerator for up to 2 days, but must be brought to room temperature before roasting. You can roast the chicken using an outdoor grill, preferably on a rotisserie so the chicken cooks evenly. Any remaining marinade can be used for basting the chicken; this will prevent it from drying out.

Spiced Turkey Meatballs

This is a dish I often make for dinner during the week. It's easy and delicious! Traditional Indian meatball recipes use lamb or goat, but these turkey meatballs have great flavor and are a healthier verison of the traditional dish.

SERVES: 6 • SERVING SIZE: 3 MEATBALLS • PREP TIME: ABOUT 5 MINUTES • COOKING TIME: 20 MINUTES

AROMATICS

2 medium **red onions**

1 **green chili**

1 (2-inch / 5-cm) **piece fresh ginger**

5 **sprigs cilantro, stems removed**

1 lb / 450 g **lean ground turkey meat**

1 tsp / 5 mL **lemon juice**

1 tsp / 5 mL **Worcestershire sauce**

1 tsp / 6.7 g **salt**

2 tsp / 10 mL **sunflower oil**

KITCHEN TOOLS

Food processor

Bamboo steamer

CHOICES/EXCHANGES

1 Nonstarchy Vegetable
2 Lean Protein
1 Fat

Calories	160
Calories from Fat	60
Total Fat	7.0 g
Saturated Fat	1.8 g
Trans Fat	0.1 g
Cholesterol	55 mg
Sodium	450 mg
Potassium	290 mg
Total Carbohydrate	6 g
Dietary Fiber	1 g
Sugars	3 g
Protein	15 g
Phosphorus	160 mg

1 Using a food processor, mince the aromatics (onions, green chilies, ginger, and cilantro leaves) by pulsing until the ingredients reach a finely minced consistency.

2 In a large bowl, combine turkey, lemon juice, Worcestershire, and salt with the minced vegetables. Form mixture into 18 balls with your hands.

3 Steam meatballs in a bamboo basket steamer (baskets can be stacked, if necessary; but meatballs should be in a single layer in each basket) or in a wide pan for 7 minutes, or until all the water is absorbed.

4 Add sunflower oil to a heavy-bottomed frying pan over medium-high heat and fry meatballs for about 4 minutes per side, until they're brown on all sides. (Or you can place meatballs on a baking sheet, drizzle with the oil, and bake them in a 400°F / 200°C oven for 7–8 minutes or until they are brown.) Serve hot.

COOK'S NOTES

You can grill the meatballs on an outdoor grill as well. You could serve this as an appetizer with Green Mint and Coriander Chutney (p. 243) or you can fill pita bread or any flatbread with the meatballs and top them with Cucumber Raita (p. 245). This is a great dish to prepare ahead of time and keep on hand for weeknights. Just steam the meatballs and keep them in the fridge for up to a week. Brown them in a pan or the oven when you're ready to eat them! You can replace the ground turkey in this recipe with ground chicken or even lamb if you prefer.

Beef Boti Kebabs GF

This boti kebabs recipe takes its inspiration from a kebab recipe popular during Nizam rule in Hyderabad. Back then this prominent dish consisted of tender pieces of boneless mutton dipped in spices and egg wash, rolled in crumbs, and deep fried.

SERVES: 6 • SERVING SIZE: 1 KEBAB (5–6 PIECES BEEF) • PREP TIME: ABOUT 4 HOURS • COOKING TIME: 8 MINUTES

MARINADE

1 Tbsp / 10 g **minced garlic cloves**

½ tsp / 2.5 g **ground turmeric**

2 tsp / 10 g **ground coriander**

1 tsp / 5 g **crushed fennel seeds**

½ tsp / 2.5 g **crushed red chili flakes**

1 **green chili, finely chopped**

1 tsp / 5 g **garam masala**

½ tsp / 3.3 g **salt**

1 Tbsp / 15 mL **lime juice**

1 lb 2 oz / 506 g **lean sirloin steak, all visible fat removed and cut into 1-inch / 2.5-cm cubes**

2 tsp / 10 mL **sunflower oil, divided**

½ tsp / 3.3 g **salt**

1 **lime, cut into wedges**

1 **bunch cilantro, stems removed and leaves chopped**

KITCHEN TOOLS

6 wooden skewers

CHOICES/EXCHANGES
3 Lean Protein

Calories	130
Calories from Fat	45
Total Fat	5.0 g
Saturated Fat	1.4 g
Trans Fat	0.1 g
Cholesterol	30 mg
Sodium	430 mg
Potassium	310 mg
Total Carbohydrate	3 g
Dietary Fiber	1 g
Sugars	1 g
Protein	17 g
Phosphorus	150 mg

1 Soak wooden skewers in cold water for at least 10 minutes.

2 Mix all marinade ingredients in a bowl until well combined. Add steak cubes, stir to coat, and marinate in the refrigerator for 2–3 hours (or up to 6 hours). Remove from refrigerator and let stand at room temperature for 30 minutes before grilling.

3 After steak has marinated and rested at room temperature, preheat a cast iron griddle over medium-high heat or an outdoor grill. Brush griddle or grill lightly with ½ tsp / 2.5 mL oil to prevent kebabs from sticking.

4 Skewer steak onto wooden skewers (about 5–6 pieces of steak per skewer), leaving some space between each piece, and brush with remaining 1½ tsp / 7.5 mL oil. Sprinkle with salt.

5 Place kebabs on the griddle or grill and cook for about 4 minutes per side (8 minutes total). Serve hot, garnished with lime wedges (for squeezing over kebabs) and cilantro.

COOK'S NOTES

You can replace the beef in this recipe with lamb or chicken (also see Murgh Bukni Kebabs on p. 152 and Murgh Malai Kebabs on p. 154), just make sure you adjust the cooking time accordingly. When using wooden skewers for kebabs, make sure to soak them before grilling. You can also wrap the ends in aluminum foil so they don't burn on the grill or griddle.

In India, kebab meat is often served wrapped in a flatbread and topped with about 1 Tbsp / 15 g Cucumber Raita (p. 245) and a little bit of Green Mint and Coriander Chutney (p. 243).

Murgh Bukni Kebabs
(Pounded Chili–Spiced Kebabs) GF

This kebab recipe comes from the northern region of India. It's a spicier variety of Indian kebab. The chilies in this recipe give it a beautiful red color.

SERVES: 8 • SERVING SIZE: 2 KEBABS • PREP TIME: 4 HOURS • COOKING TIME: 13 MINUTES

2 **dried guajillo chilies, seeds removed**

1 lb / 450 g **lean ground chicken**

1 tsp / 5 g **ginger paste (p. 34)**

1 Tbsp plus 1 tsp / 20 mL **sunflower oil, divided**

1 Tbsp / 14 g **smoked paprika**

⅓ tsp plus ¼ tsp / 3.9 g **sea salt, divided**

1 Tbsp / 12 g **roasted chana dal (split chickpeas)**

1 Tbsp / 5.2 g **finely grated ginger**

1 **onion, minced**

1 Tbsp / 1 g **chopped cilantro leaves**

1 **egg**

⅓ cup / 40 g **roasted chana dal flour**

1 **red onion, sliced into rings**

2 **lemons, cut into wedges**

KITCHEN TOOLS:

Food processor

16 wooden skewers

CHOICES/EXCHANGES
1 Nonstarchy Vegetable
1 Lean Protein
1½ Fat

Calories	150
Calories from Fat	70
Total Fat	8.0 g
Saturated Fat	1.7 g
Trans Fat	0.0 g
Cholesterol	65 mg
Sodium	210 mg
Potassium	450 mg
Total Carbohydrate	9 g
Dietary Fiber	2 g
Sugars	3 g
Protein	12 g
Phosphorus	140 mg

1. Soak 16 wooden skewers in cold water for at least 10 minutes.

2. In a cast iron skillet over medium heat, toast chilies for 2 minutes and then pound into fine pieces using a small food processor or a mortar and pestle.

3. In a large bowl, mix ground chicken with pounded chilies, ginger paste, 1 tsp / 5 mL sunflower oil, paprika, and ⅓ tsp / 2.2 g salt. Marinate in the refrigerator for 3 hours.

4. After 3 hours, grind chana dal, grated ginger, minced onion, and cilantro into a fine paste using a food processor.

5. Add chana dal mixture to ground chicken mixture, stir to combine, and refrigerate for 1 hour to allow flavors to marry.

6. After 1 hour, beat egg with chana dal flour and remaining ¼ tsp / 1.7 g salt in a bowl until well mixed. Add egg mixture to ground chicken mixture and combine to reach a smooth texture. (The mixture should not be too loose; if it is too loose to mold over the skewer, you can add a tiny bit more flour.) Oil the skewers and form the chicken mixture around each skewer to form 16 sausage-shaped kebabs.

7. Preheat an outdoor grill or cast iron griddle over medium-high heat. Grill kebabs, basting with the remaining 1 Tbsp / 15 mL oil, for about 6 minutes per side to get a charred flavor. Serve kebabs with raw red onion rings and lemon wedges (for squeezing over chicken).

COOK'S NOTES

No skewers? No problem. You can simply form the chicken into 8 sausage-like shapes and grill without the skewers.

You can add 1 Tbsp / 15.6 g raw papaya paste or 1 Tbsp / 15 mL lemon juice to the first marinade (chilies/ginger mixture) to help tenderize the chicken. If you can't find roasted chana dal flour, use chickpea flour instead.

You can sometimes find roasted chana dal in the grocery store, but if you can't find the roasted variety, you can buy plain chana dal and roast it yourself in a heavy-bottomed pan over medium heat for 2–3 minutes.

Murgh Malai Kebabs (Chicken Kebabs)

In Hindi, *murgh* means "chicken" and *malai* means "cream." This dish is traditionally made in a tandoori oven, but this easy recipe uses a grill or griddle.

SERVES: 6 • SERVING SIZE: 2 KEBABS • PREP TIME: ABOUT 2 HOURS OR OVERNIGHT • COOKING TIME: 8 MINUTES

5 strands **saffron**

2 lb / 900 g **boneless, skinless chicken breasts,
   cut into 1-inch / 2.5 cm cubes**

1 tsp / 5 g **ground cardamom**

1 Tbsp / 15 g **ginger-garlic paste (p. 34)**

1 tsp / 5 g **ground white pepper**

1 cup / 245 g **plain low-fat Greek yogurt**

1 Tbsp / 12 g **reduced-fat sour cream**

¾ tsp / 5 g **sea salt**

1 Tbsp / 15 mL **lemon juice**

3 **bell peppers (different colors), cut into
   1-inch / 2.5-cm cubes**

2 **red onions, cut into 1-inch / 2.5-cm wedges
   and layers separated**

1 tsp / 5 mL **sunflower oil**

1 tsp / 5 g **ghee (p. 30)**

1 **lemon, cut into wedges**

KITCHEN TOOLS

12 wooden skewers

CHOICES/EXCHANGES
2 Nonstarchy Vegetable
5 Lean Protein

Calories	260
Calories from Fat	50
Total Fat	6.0 g
Saturated Fat	2.2 g
Trans Fat	0.0 g
Cholesterol	90 mg
Sodium	370 mg
Potassium	560 mg
Total Carbohydrate	13 g
Dietary Fiber	2 g
Sugars	6 g
Protein	37 g
Phosphorus	320 mg

1   Soak 12 wooden skewers in cold water for at least 10 minutes. Soak saffron in ½ tsp / 2.5 mL lukewarm water for about 10 minutes.

2   In a large bowl, combine chicken, cardamom, ginger-garlic paste, white pepper, yogurt, sour cream, salt, lemon juice, and saffron water, and mix well. Marinate in the refrigerator for at least 2 hours (or overnight).

3   After 2 hours, thread 2–3 pieces chicken onto skewers, alternating with onion and pepper pieces. In a small bowl, combine oil and ghee and brush chicken with this mixture.

4   Heat a grill or cast iron griddle over medium-high heat. Cook skewers for about 3 minutes, then turn, reduce the heat to medium (if possible), and cook for 5 more minutes. Brush any remaining marinade on kebabs while cooking.

5   Serve with lemon wedges (to squeeze over kebabs).

CHAPTER 9
Indian Flatbreads

Whole-Wheat Roti (Indian Flatbread)

Roti (also called chapati) is a staple of Indian meals, especially in the northern and western parts of India. The word *chapat* in Hindi means "slap" and traditionally roti is formed by slapping rounds of thin dough between wet palms. With each slap, the round of dough is rotated and flattened. Rotis are one of the most common forms in which wheat—a staple of northern and western India—is consumed. Evidence of the cultivation of wheat dates back to the ancient Indus Valley civilization, which extended into part of modern-day northern India. Roti is made of whole-wheat flour and is traditionally cooked on a tava (a cast iron skillet). In India, rotis are often made fresh while meals are being eaten.

SERVES: 6 • SERVING SIZE: 1 ROTI • PREP TIME: ABOUT 35 MINUTES • COOKING TIME: 7 MINUTES PER ROTI

1 cup /110 g **whole-wheat pastry flour, divided**
⅓ cup / 80 mL **warm water (100°F / 38°C)**
1 Tbsp plus 1 tsp / 20 mL **sunflower oil, divided**
⅛ tsp / 0.8 g **salt**
1 Tbsp / 7.5 g **whole-wheat flour**

COOK'S NOTES

You can also make the roti dough in a food processor using a dough hook, but you need to double or triple the recipe in order for this to work. Mix the pastry dough, sunflower oil, and salt together, then add the water little by little. Keep processing the dough until you get a smooth, not sticky, consistency.

You could use whole-wheat flour instead of the whole-wheat pastry flour in this recipe, but you may need to add more water for the dough to reach the right consistency.

CHOICES/EXCHANGES
1 Starch
½ Fat

Calories	100
Calories from Fat	30
Total Fat	3.5 g
Saturated Fat	0.4 g
Trans Fat	0.0 g
Cholesterol	0 mg
Sodium	45 mg
Potassium	85 mg
Total Carbohydrate	16 g
Dietary Fiber	3 g
Sugars	0 g
Protein	2 g
Phosphorus	75 mg

1 In a shallow bowl, combine all but 1 tsp / 2.2 g pastry flour with 1 tsp / 5 mL sunflower oil, and salt and mix well.

2 Now stir with one hand as you pour warm water, little by little, into the dry mixture. Mix dough until it reaches a consistency similar to pizza dough. Knead well to get a smooth dough consistency. Cover dough with a damp cloth and set aside for 30 minutes.

3 After 30 minutes, divide dough into 6 round balls and flatten each ball. Dust flattened disks with remaining 1 tsp / 2.2 g flour and, using a rolling pin, gently roll the dough into 6-inch-diameter / 15-cm-diameter rounds.

4 Preheat a cast iron griddle or flat skillet over medium-high heat. Place a piece of dough in the skillet and roast about 1 minute, or until it begins to bubble.

5 Turn the roti. Add ½ tsp / 2.5 mL of the remaining oil, spread oil all around, and continue to turn and roast the roti until it has brown edges on both sides, about 3 minutes. Using a flat spatula, press the middle of the roti as it's cooking so it cooks evenly.

6 Repeat the cooking process with the remaining pieces of dough. Serve hot.

Whole-Wheat Spinach Parathas

Paratha is a type of flatbread that originated in the northern part of India, where it is still popular. Wheat is a staple in this part of the country. The term *paratha* is an amalgamation of the Hindi words *parat* and *atta*, which roughly translate to "layers of cooked dough."

SERVES: 8 • SERVING SIZE: 1 PARATHA • PREP TIME: 1 HOUR • COOKING TIME: 7–9 MINUTES PER PARATHA

3 tsp / 15 mL **sunflower oil, divided**

1 tsp / 2.2 g **ajwain seeds**

1 tsp / 1.7 g **finely grated ginger**

1 **green chili, finely minced (seeds removed)**

1 cup / 150 g (tightly packed) **organic baby spinach, chopped**

½ tsp / 3.3 g **fine sea salt, divided**

½ tsp / 2.5 g **amchoor (mango) powder**

1 tsp / 5 g **ground cumin**

2 cups plus 1 Tbsp / 226.5 g **whole-wheat pastry flour, divided**

⅔ cup / 160 mL **water**

COOK'S NOTES

Make sure to add the right amount of water; do not add too much. Water should be added slowly and you should take into account any moisture from the spinach. You can also make this paratha dough in a food processor using a dough hook.

If you can't find ajwain seeds you can use caraway seeds or celery seeds. If you don't have amchoor powder, it is fine to leave this out of the recipe.

CHOICES/EXCHANGES
1½ Starch

Calories	130
Calories from Fat	20
Total Fat	2.0 g
Saturated Fat	0.2 g
Trans Fat	0.0 g
Cholesterol	0 mg
Sodium	150 mg
Potassium	180 mg
Total Carbohydrate	25 g
Dietary Fiber	4 g
Sugars	0 g
Protein	3 g
Phosphorus	115 mg

1 In a heavy-bottomed pan, heat 1 tsp / 5 mL sunflower oil over medium-high heat. Add ajwain seeds, ginger, and green chili and cook for about 1 minute.

2 Add spinach and ¼ tsp / 1.7 g sea salt and cook until moisture released from the spinach is absorbed and the base becomes dry, about 3 minutes. Add the amchoor powder and cumin, mix well, and remove from heat. Set aside to cool.

3 To make the dough for the paratha: mix 2 cups / 220 g pastry flour and remaining salt in a shallow dish. Add spinach mixture to the flour mixture, then add water, little by little, to form a smooth dough (similar to a pizza dough consistency).

4 Knead dough to get a smooth consistency. Place dough in a glass bowl, cover with a damp towel, and set aside at room temperature for 30 minutes to 1 hour.

5 After 30 minutes to 1 hour, knead dough once again and form into 8 balls. Lightly dust your work surface with remaining flour and flatten each dough ball using a rolling pin into a 6-inch-diameter / 15-cm-diameter round.

6 Preheat a cast iron griddle or flat skillet over medium-high heat. Place one piece dough in the skillet and cook for about 1 minute, or until it begins to bubble.

7 Turn the paratha. Brush with ¼ tsp / 1.3 mL of the remaining sunflower oil. Continue cooking for about 3–4 minutes per side, turning as necessary, until it has brown edges on both sides. Using a flat spatula, press the middle of the paratha as it's cooking so it cooks evenly.

8 Remove from skillet. Repeat the cooking process with the remaining pieces of dough. Serve hot.

Jowar Ki Bhakri (Sorghum Flatbread)

Jowar ki Bhakri is a type of flatbread commonly prepared in the Maharashtra region of western India. This simple, nutritious bread is made with sorghum flour. Jowar ki bhakri is a staple in western and central Indian cuisine. Jowar—sorghum—is also known by various other names, including *durra*, Egyptian millet, *jwari* (in Marathi), *cholam* (in Tamil), and *jola* (in Kannada). Sorghum is native to regions of Africa, Asia, and Mexico, where it has been an important staple in the diets of rural people because it is a source of carbohydrate, protein, and vitamins and minerals. Sorghum contains phytochemicals and essential nutrients such as iron, calcium, potassium, and phosphorous, and phytochemicals.

SERVES: 8 • SERVING SIZE: 1 BHAKRI • PREP TIME: ABOUT 35 MINUTES • COOKING TIME: ABOUT 5 MINUTES PER BHAKRI

2 cups / 240 g **sorghum flour**
⅔ cup / 160 mL **hot water**
¼ tsp / 1.7 g **salt**

KITCHEN TOOLS
Parchment paper

CHOICES/EXCHANGES
1½ Starch

Calories	120
Calories from Fat	10
Total Fat	1.0 g
Saturated Fat	0.2 g
Trans Fat	0.0 g
Cholesterol	0 mg
Sodium	75 mg
Potassium	120 mg
Total Carbohydrate	25 g
Dietary Fiber	3 g
Sugars	1 g
Protein	4 g
Phosphorus	100 mg

1 In a shallow bowl, combine flour and salt and mix well. Add hot water, little by little, while mixing until a soft dough (dumpling-like consistency) forms. Cover dough with a clean kitchen towel and set dough aside for 30 minutes at room temperature.

2 After dough has rested, form the dough into 8 balls. Place dough balls, one by one, in between two sheets of parchment paper and roll into a thin flat round using a rolling pin.

3 Preheat a cast iron griddle over medium-high heat.

4 Place 1 flat piece of dough on the griddle. When the bhakri begins to puff up, turn and continue cooking until it has brown edges on both sides. Using a flat spatula, press the middle of the bhakri while cooking so it cooks evenly.

5 Repeat the cooking process with the remaining pieces of dough and serve.

COOK'S NOTES

You can also use a food processor with a dough hook to prepare the dough for this recipe.

Amaranth Ki Bhakri (Amaranth Flatbread)

Amaranth is a small seed with a rich history dating back to when it was first cultivated in Mesoamerica. This seed was a staple food in the diet of the ancient Aztecs. Amaranth also has a special place in Indian cuisine. In many regions of India, amaranth leaves are cooked like spinach leaves and the seeds are ground to make dough for breads like this hearty flatbread.

SERVES: 6 • SERVING SIZE: 1 BHAKRI • PREP TIME: ABOUT 5 MINUTES • COOKING TIME: 6 MINUTES PER BHAKRI

1 cup / 120 g **amaranth flour**

5 tsp / 25 mL **sunflower oil, divided**

¼ cup / 60 mL **low-fat milk, warmed**

KITCHEN TOOLS

Parchment paper

CHOICES/EXCHANGES
1 Starch
1 Fat

Calories	110
Calories from Fat	45
Total Fat	5.0 g
Saturated Fat	0.7 g
Trans Fat	0.0 g
Cholesterol	0 mg
Sodium	10 mg
Potassium	115 mg
Total Carbohydrate	14 g
Dietary Fiber	2 g
Sugars	1 g
Protein	3 g
Phosphorus	120 mg

1 In a shallow bowl, combine amaranth flour with 2 tsp / 10 mL oil and mix well. The mixture should be a bread crumb–like consistency. Add warm milk and mix well to form a sticky dough.

2 Roll dough into 6 olive-sized balls.

3 Place dough balls, one by one, in between two sheets of parchment paper and roll into ¼-inch-thick / 6-mm-thick flatbreads using a rolling pin. Preheat a heavy cast iron griddle over low heat. Place 1 rolled-out bhakri on the griddle and cook for 1 minute per side.

4 Brush about ½ tsp / 2.5 mL oil or ghee on each bhakri (brush both sides) and continue cooking over low heat for 4 minutes, or until light golden brown.

5 Repeat the cooking process with the remaining bhakris. Transfer to a serving platter and cover with a towel to keep them warm until ready to serve.

COOK'S NOTES

You can also use a food processor with a dough hook to prepare the dough for this recipe, but you will need to double or triple the recipe.

Whole-Wheat Zucchini Thepla (Griddle Bread) Ⓥ

SERVES: 5 • SERVING SIZE: 1 THEPLA • PREP TIME: ABOUT 10 MINUTES • COOKING TIME: ABOUT 15 MINUTES PER THEPLA

1½ cups / 180 g **whole-wheat flour**
½ tsp / 1 g **cumin seeds**
1 medium **zucchini, finely grated** (1 cup / 83 g)
½ tsp / 2.5 g **ground turmeric**
½ tsp / 3.3 g **kosher salt**
½ tsp / 2.5 g **cayenne pepper**
1 **green chili, finely minced (remove seeds if desired)**
3 Tbsp / 45 mL **extra-virgin olive oil, divided**
1 cup / 240 mL **room temperature water**

COOK'S NOTES

You can cut thepla into wedges and serve as an appetizer or alongside any of the vegetarian or meat dishes in this book. Make sure the skillet is not too hot when you add the dough; if it's very hot, carefully sprinkle some cold water on the skillet to cool it down. This recipe also tastes great with yellow squash instead of zucchini.

CHOICES/EXCHANGES

2 Starch
1 Fat

Calories	210
Calories from Fat	80
Total Fat	9.0 g
Saturated Fat	1.3 g
Trans Fat	0.0 g
Cholesterol	0 mg
Sodium	190 mg
Potassium	290 mg
Total Carbohydrate	29 g
Dietary Fiber	5 g
Sugars	1 g
Protein	6 g
Phosphorus	145 mg

1 Place flour in a large bowl. Crush cumin seeds by rubbing between the palms of your hands to release the oils inside. Add crushed seeds to the flour, then add the turmeric, salt, and cayenne pepper and mix well.

2 Mix grated zucchini, green chili, and 1 Tbsp / 15 mL oil into the flour mixture. Mix well and add water, little by little as needed, to form a wet dough. Form the dough into 5 equal-size balls.

3 Preheat 1 tsp / 5 mL oil in a cast iron skillet over medium-high heat.

4 Using your fingers, press and stretch 1 ball of dough into an even circle about ½ inch / 13 mm thick. (If the dough sticks to your hands, put a small amount of oil on your fingers.)

5 Place 1 thepla on the skillet for about 1 minute. Turn thepla, reduce heat to medium-low and, using your fingers, very carefully make holes or indents in the dough, spaced about 1 inch / 2.5 cm apart. Fill these holes with 1 tsp / 5 mL oil, cover the skillet, and cook for about 5 minutes. Carefully turn the thepla and cook, uncovered, for another 7 minutes. Using a flat spatula, press the middle of the thepla while cooking so it cooks evenly.

6 Remove from pan when it is lightly brown. Repeat the cooking process with the remaining pieces of dough.

Stuffed Mooli Parathas (Radish-Stuffed Parathas) ⓥ

SERVES: 12 • SERVING SIZE: 1 PARATHA • PREP TIME: 35 MINUTES • COOKING TIME: 7–9 MINUTES PER PARATHA

2 cups / 220 g **whole-wheat pastry flour**

⅔ cup / 160 mL **water**

1 Tbsp plus 1 tsp / 20 mL **sunflower oil, divided**

½ tsp / 3.3 g **salt, divided**

2 cup / 167 g **finely grated radish**

2 **green chilies, seeds removed**

1 small **bunch cilantro, stems removed, leaves finely chopped**

Juice of ½ **lemon**

CHOICES/EXCHANGES
1 Starch
½ Fat

Calories	90
Calories from Fat	20
Total Fat	2.0 g
Saturated Fat	0.2 g
Trans Fat	0.0 g
Cholesterol	0 mg
Sodium	110 mg
Potassium	180 mg
Total Carbohydrate	17 g
Dietary Fiber	3 g
Sugars	1 g
Protein	2 g
Phosphorus	80 mg

1 In a large mixing bowl, mix the pastry flour, water, 1 tsp / 5 mL sunflower oil, and ¼ tsp / 1.7 g salt and knead to make a smooth dough. Cover with a clean wet kitchen towel and set aside at room temperature for 30 minutes.

2 Meanwhile, place grated radish in a clean tea towel and squeeze out any excess water to make the radish as dry as possible. Mix radish, chilies, cilantro, lemon juice, and remaining ¼ tsp / 1.7 g salt together in a bowl and set aside.

3 Form paratha dough into 12 small balls. Take each ball in your hands, flatten it, and place 1 tsp / 2 g radish mixture into each paratha. Seal the edges well, making a round stuffed ball.

4 Carefully roll each stuffed paratha using a rolling pin, taking care not to tear the seal or spill the filling. Roll into 5-inch-diameter / 12.5-cm-diameter rounds.

5 Heat a cast iron griddle or skillet over medium-high heat. Place 1 paratha on the griddle. When it begins to slowly puff up, flip it. Brush paratha with ⅛ tsp / 0.6 mL of the remaining oil, reduce heat to low, and cook for 3 minutes and flip again. Brush with another ⅛ tsp / 0.6 mL oil and cook for 3 more minutes. Using a flat spatula, press the middle of the paratha while cooking so it cooks evenly.

6 Repeat the cooking process with the remaining pieces of stuffed dough, and serve.

Stuffed Paneer Parathas

SERVES: 10 • SERVING SIZE: 1 PARATHA • PREP TIME: 35 MINUTES • COOKING TIME: ABOUT 10 MINUTES PER PARATHA

2 cups / 220 g **whole-wheat pastry flour, divided**

½ tsp / 3.3 g **salt, divided**

⅔ cup / 160 mL **water**

1 Tbsp plus 1 tsp / 20 mL **sunflower oil, divided**

1 cup / 122 g **crumbled paneer (p. 32)**

1 **sprig curry leaves, stems removed
and leaves finely minced**

2 **green chilies, seeds removed and finely minced**

¼ tsp / 1.3 g **amchoor (mango) powder**

CHOICES/EXCHANGES
1½ Starch
1 Lean Protein

Calories	130
Calories from Fat	20
Total Fat	2.5 g
Saturated Fat	0.3 g
Trans Fat	0.0 g
Cholesterol	0 mg
Sodium	120 mg
Potassium	190 mg
Total Carbohydrate	20 g
Dietary Fiber	3 g
Sugars	1 g
Protein	8 g
Phosphorus	150 mg

1 In a large mixing bowl, combine all but 1 Tbsp / 6.5 g flour with ¼ tsp / 1.7 g salt. Add water, little by little, and knead to make a soft, smooth dough. Once all the flour has come together into the dough, drizzle 1 tsp / 5 mL oil on the dough and knead for another 2–3 minutes. Cover dough and set aside for 30 minutes.

2 Meanwhile, in a large bowl, combine paneer, curry leaves, chilies, amchoor powder, and remaining ¼ tsp / 1.7 g salt and mix together to reach a smooth, dough-like consistency. Set aside.

3 Divide dough into 10 medium balls. Take each dough ball and dust it with some of the remaining flour. Roll out dough into a 5-inch-diameter / 12.5-cm-diameter round using a rolling pin.

4 Spoon about 1½ Tbsp / 11.5 g filling into the center of each round. Gather the edges and bring dough together over the filling to form a bundle. Seal the edges and dust parathas lightly with flour again. Roll gently to remove any air pockets, making sure filling does not ooze out.

5 Preheat a skillet over medium-high heat and place 1 paratha on the skillet. Cook on both sides, turning occasionally, until you see small air pockets forming, about 1 minute. Brush paratha with ⅛ tsp / 0.6 mL of the remaining oil, reduce heat to medium-low, and cook for 3 minutes and flip again. Brush with another ⅛ tsp / 0.6 mL oil and cook for 3 more minutes until both sides are golden brown. Using a flat spatula, press the middle of the paratha while cooking so it cooks evenly.

6 Repeat the cooking process with the remaining pieces of stuffed dough. Transfer cooked parathas to a platter and cover with a clean tea towel to keep warm until serving.

Stuffed Gobi Parathas (Cauliflower-Stuffed Parathas) Ⓥ

SERVES: 12 • SERVING SIZE: 1 PARATHA • PREP TIME: 35 MINUTES • COOKING TIME: ABOUT 10 MINUTES PER PARATHA

2 cups plus 1 Tbsp / 226.5 g **whole-wheat pastry flour, divided**

½ tsp / 3.3 g **salt, divided**

⅔ cup / 160 mL **water**

1 Tbsp plus 2 tsp / 25 mL **sunflower oil, divided**

1 large **cauliflower, cut into florets**

1 **onion, quartered**

2 **green chilies, seeds removed**

1 (1-inch / 2.5-cm) **piece ginger, peeled**

1 small **bunch cilantro, stems removed**

1 tsp / 5 g **ground cumin**

½ tsp / 2.5 g **ground turmeric**

KITCHEN TOOLS

Food processor

CHOICES/EXCHANGES
1 Starch
1 Nonstarchy Vegetable
½ Fat

Calories	120
Calories from Fat	20
Total Fat	2.5 g
Saturated Fat	0.3 g
Trans Fat	0.0 g
Cholesterol	0 mg
Sodium	115 mg
Potassium	300 mg
Total Carbohydrate	21 g
Dietary Fiber	4 g
Sugars	2 g
Protein	3 g
Phosphorus	105 mg

COOK'S NOTES

You can serve this stuffed paratha with any kind of raita or even plain yogurt. These are so filling that they are often considered a full meal for vegetarians.

1 In a large mixing bowl, combine 2 cups / 220 g flour and ¼ tsp / 1.7 g salt. Add water, little by little, and knead to make a soft, smooth dough. Once all the flour has come together into the dough, drizzle 1 tsp / 5 mL oil on the dough and knead for another 2–3 minutes. Cover dough and set aside for 30 minutes.

2 Meanwhile, add cauliflower, onion, chilies, ginger, cilantro, cumin, ¼ tsp / 1.7 g salt, turmeric, and 1 tsp / 5 mL oil into a food processor. Pulse to a fine mince consistency. Transfer the stuffing to a bowl, mix well, and set aside.

3 Divide dough into 12 medium balls. Flatten each ball with your hands and dust dough and rolling surface with some of the remaining flour. Roll out dough into 5-inch-diameter / 12.5-cm-diameter rounds using a rolling pin.

4 Spoon a large portion (about 1 Tbsp / about 10 g) of the filling onto half of each round. Spread filling evenly on half of each round and cover with the other half to form a half-moon shape. Seal the edges (using a little water to

help them stick, if necessary) and dust parathas lightly with flour again. Roll gently with a rolling pin to remove any air pockets, making sure filling does not ooze out.

5 Preheat cast iron griddle or skillet over medium-high heat and place 1 paratha on the skillet. Cook on both sides, turning occasionally, until you see small air pockets forming, about 1 minute. Brush paratha with ⅛ tsp / 0.6 mL of the remaining oil, reduce heat to low, and cook for 3 minutes and flip again. Brush with another ⅛ tsp / 0.6 mL oil and cook for 3 more minutes until both sides are golden brown. Using a flat spatula, press the middle of the paratha while cooking so it cooks evenly.

6 Repeat the cooking process with the remaining pieces of stuffed dough. Transfer cooked parathas to a platter and cover with a clean tea towel to keep warm until serving.

Stuffed Keema Parathas (Chicken-Stuffed Parathas)

Keema is a traditional southern Asian minced meat dish, often used as a filling for samosas or naan. Any type of meat can be used to make keema, including lamb, goat, or beef.

SERVES: 12 • SERVING SIZE: 1 PARATHA • PREP TIME: 35 MINUTES • COOKING TIME: ABOUT 10 MINUTES PER PARATHA

2 cups plus 2 Tbsp / 233 g **whole-wheat pastry flour, divided**

¾ tsp / 5 g **salt, divided**

⅔ cup / 160 mL **water**

1½ Tbsp plus 1 tsp / 27.5 mL **sunflower oil, divided**

1 tsp / 5 g **ginger-garlic paste (p. 34)**

1 small **onion, minced**

1 **green chili, minced**

½ tsp / 2.5 g **ground turmeric**

¼ tsp / 1.3 g **cayenne pepper**

½ lb / 230 g **minced chicken meat**

1 **sprig cilantro, stems removed and leaves minced**

CHOICES/EXCHANGES
1 Starch
1 Lean Protein

Calories	120
Calories from Fat	25
Total Fat	3.0 g
Saturated Fat	0.4 g
Trans Fat	0.0 g
Cholesterol	15 mg
Sodium	160 mg
Potassium	160 mg
Total Carbohydrate	18 g
Dietary Fiber	3 g
Sugars	1 g
Protein	6 g
Phosphorus	110 mg

COOK'S NOTES

You can use any kind of meat in this recipe, but you may need to adjust the meat cooking time accordingly. Whatever meat you use, make sure that the meat mixture is dry before stuffing into the dough, otherwise moisture from the filling will leak out during the cooking process.

1. In a large mixing bowl, combine 2 cups / 220 g flour and ¼ tsp / 1.7 g salt. Add water, little by little, and knead to make a soft, smooth dough. Once all the flour has come together into the dough, drizzle 1 tsp / 5 mL oil on the dough and knead for another 2–3 minutes. Cover dough and set aside for 30 minutes.

2. Meanwhile, heat a heavy-bottomed skillet over medium-high heat and add ½ Tbsp / 7.5 mL oil. Add ginger-garlic paste and sauté for 1 minute, then add onion and sauté until translucent, about 1–2 minutes. Add chili, turmeric, and cayenne pepper, and stir. Add chicken and remaining ½ tsp / 3.3 g salt and cook until chicken is cooked through, about 8 minutes. (The chicken mixture should be dry.) Remove from heat and add cilantro. Transfer mixture to a bowl and set aside to cool.

3. Divide dough into 12 medium balls. Flatten each ball with your hands and dust dough and rolling surface with some of the remaining 2 Tbsp / 13 g flour. Roll out dough into 5-inch-diameter / 12.5-cm-diameter rounds using rolling pin.

4. Spoon 1 Tbsp / about 11 g keema filling into the middle of each round. Gather the edges and fold dough around the filling to make a bundle. Seal the edges (using a little water to help them stick, if necessary) and dust parathas lightly with flour again. Roll gently with a rolling pin to remove any air pockets, making sure filling does not ooze out.

5. Preheat the skillet over medium-high heat and place 1 paratha on the skillet. Cook on both sides, turning occasionally, until you see small air pockets forming, about 1 minute. Brush paratha with ⅛ tsp / 0.6 mL of the remaining oil, reduce heat to low, and cook for 4 minutes and flip again. Brush with another ⅛ tsp / 0.6 mL oil and cook for 4 more minutes until both sides are golden brown. Using a flat spatula, press the middle of the paratha while cooking so it cooks evenly. Repeat the cooking process with the remaining pieces of stuffed dough. Transfer cooked parathas to a platter and cover with a clean tea towel to keep warm until serving.

CHAPTER 10
Whole-Grain One-Pot Meals

Basic Khichdi (V) (GF)

Khichdi is an Indian one-pot meal made from rice and dal (lentils). In some regions, khichdi is one of the first solid foods that babies eat. This popular dish can be made with vegetables such as cauliflower, potatoes, tomatoes, and/or green peas. One popular variant of this recipe in the western region, like along the coast of Maharashtra, is made with prawns as well. This is a comfort food in India and it's gentle on the stomach.

SERVES: 6 • SERVING SIZE: 3 OZ / 84 G • PREP TIME: 30 MINUTES • COOKING TIME: ABOUT 35 MINUTES

½ cup / 96 g **mung dal (yellow split lentils), husks removed**

½ cup / 95 g **brown basmati rice**

1 Tbsp / 15 mL **sunflower oil**

¾ tsp / 1.5 g **cumin seeds**

1 small **onion, finely chopped**

1 medium **tomato, finely chopped**

1 small **green chili, finely chopped**

1 (½-inch / 13-mm) **piece ginger, peeled and finely grated**

¼ tsp / 1.3 g **ground turmeric**

4 cups / 950 mL **water**

¼ cup / 4 g **cilantro, finely chopped**

KITCHEN TOOLS

Pressure cooker

CHOICES/EXCHANGES
1½ Starch
½ Fat

Calories	140
Calories from Fat	25
Total Fat	3.0 g
Saturated Fat	0.4 g
Trans Fat	0.0 g
Cholesterol	0 mg
Sodium	0 mg
Potassium	310 mg
Total Carbohydrate	24 g
Dietary Fiber	5 g
Sugars	3 g
Protein	6 g
Phosphorus	135 mg

1   Rinse dal and rice and add both to a large bowl. Cover with cold water and soak them together for 30 minutes.

2   Meanwhile, heat a pressure cooker over medium heat, and add 1 Tbsp / 15 mL oil and the cumin seeds. When cumin seeds begin to splutter, add onion and sauté until translucent, about 1 minute.

3   Add tomatoes, green chili, and ginger. Sauté for 1 minute. Add turmeric and sauté until tomatoes soften, about 1 more minute.

4   Drain the dal and rice and add them to the pressure cooker. Stir for 1 minute then add water. Lightly season with salt, if desired.

5   Close the pressure cooker lid tightly and cook the khichdi for 6 whistles. Serve khichdi in a bowl garnished with cilantro.

COOK'S NOTES

This dish can also be cooked in a large heavy-bottomed pot or Dutch oven, instead of a pressure cooker. Simply follow steps 1–3 of this recipe, and then add the dal and rice to the pot and cook over medium-low heat for about 40 minutes. The khichdi will have the consistency of a risotto.

This is a great dish to make ahead and store in the refrigerator overnight. The flavors taste even better the next day. You can even save leftover khichdi and serve the next day with some grilled prawns. Delicious!

Farro Tahiri ⓥ

Tahiri is a traditional Indian one-pot meal from the Uttar Pradesh in northern India. It is aromatic, rice-based, and usually prepared using a cooking method called *dum* (see p. 26). Farro is a whole grain with a complex nutty taste. It looks similar to a grain of brown rice. The Italian word *farro* is derived from the Latin word for "wheat."

SERVES: 10 • SERVING SIZE: ABOUT ½ CUP / 75 G • PREP TIME: 5 MINUTES • COOKING TIME: 1 HOUR AND 10 MINUTES

1 Tbsp plus 1 tsp / 20 mL **sunflower oil, divided**

1½ tsp / 10 g **salt, divided**

1 tsp / 5 g **ground black pepper**

2 lb / 900 g **sweet potatoes (about 2), peeled and cut into ½-inch / 13-mm cubes**

2 **red onions, thinly sliced** (about 1 cup / 150 g)

1 Tbsp / 15 g **ginger-garlic paste (p. 34)**

2 medium **tomatoes, diced** (about ½ cup / 75 g)

1 **green chili, slit open and seeds removed**

1 tsp / 5 g **cayenne pepper**

1 tsp / 5 g **ground coriander**

½ tsp / 2.5 g **ground turmeric**

2 cups / 380 g **farro, rinsed and drained**

2 cups / 475 mL **warm water**

2 cups / 475 mL **low-sodium vegetable stock**

3 Tbsp / 3 g **finely chopped cilantro leaves**

1 Tbsp / 1.5 g **finely chopped mint leaves**

½ Tbsp / 7.5 mL **lemon juice**

CHOICES/EXCHANGES
2½ Starch
1 Nonstarchy Vegetable
½ Fat

Calories	240
Calories from Fat	30
Total Fat	3.5 g
Saturated Fat	0.4 g
Trans Fat	0.0 g
Cholesterol	0 mg
Sodium	400 mg
Potassium	540 mg
Total Carbohydrate	45 g
Dietary Fiber	8 g
Sugars	5 g
Protein	7 g
Phosphorus	225 mg

1 Preheat oven to 375°F / 190°C and position an oven rack in the center.

2 In a large bowl, combine 1 tsp / 5 mL oil, ¼ tsp / 1.7 g salt, black pepper, and sweet potatoes. Toss until well combined. Transfer mixture onto a rimmed baking sheet, spreading evenly. Roast potatoes for about 30 minutes or until fork tender, stirring every 15 minutes. Remove from oven and set aside.

3 Preheat a Dutch oven over medium-high heat and add remaining 1 Tbsp / 15 mL oil. Add onions and ¼ tsp / 1.7 g salt and sauté until onions become golden, about 3 minutes.

4 Reduce the heat to medium. Add ginger-garlic paste and sauté for about 2 minutes. Add tomatoes and sauté for another 2 minutes. Add chili, cayenne, coriander, and turmeric and sauté for 1 minute.

5 Add farro and remaining 1 tsp / 6.7 g salt and sauté for 1 minute. Then add water and vegetable stock and bring to a boil over medium-high heat. Once liquid is boiling, cover the Dutch oven and very carefully cover the lid with aluminum foil to prevent steam from escaping. Reduce heat to low and cook for another 30 minutes.

6 Remove lid and add roasted sweet potatoes, cilantro, mint, and lemon juice. Remove green chili. Fluff the farro and serve.

COOK'S NOTES

If the farro is not fully cooked after 30 minutes, close the lid, turn off the heat, and let it rest for another 2 minutes.

Hara Freekeh Tahiri

Freekeh (pronounced free-kah) is a grain food made from young green wheat that is roasted. Freekeh is prepared by harvesting wheat while the grains are green and the seeds are still soft. The wheat is sun-dried and roasted using a special technique. The wheat is then rubbed, and sometimes cracked. The word freekeh comes from the Arabic word *farīk*, meaning "rubbed." Hara Freekeh Tahiri is a fresh, healthy one-pot meal. Hara means green in Hindi. In this recipe, the green comes from the spinach, peas, and cilantro.

SERVES: 8 • SERVING SIZE: ¼ CUP / 40 G • PREP TIME: 5 MINUTES • COOKING TIME: 1 HOUR

1 Tbsp / 1 g **chopped cilantro**

12 oz / 340 g **fresh baby spinach, washed and blanched**

12 oz / 340 g **frozen petite peas, cooked in boiling salted water for 3 minutes**

2 Tbsp / 30 mL **cold water**

1 tsp / 5 mL **sunflower oil**

1 tsp / 5 g **ghee (p. 30)**

1 cup / 150 g **finely diced red onions**

2 tsp / 10 g **finely minced ginger**

2 tsp / 10 g **finely minced garlic**

½ cup / 75 g **diced fresh tomatoes**

1 Tbsp / 14 g **mild curry powder**

2 pieces **star anise**

2 **cinnamon sticks**

2 cups / 380 g **whole-grain freekeh, soaked for 30 minutes, rinsed, and drained**

3½ cups / 820 g **low-sodium vegetable or chicken stock**

1 tsp / 6.7 g **salt**

½ tsp / 2.5 g **ground black pepper**

½ tsp / 2.5 g **garam masala**

CHOICES/EXCHANGES
2½ Starch
1 Nonstarchy Vegetable
½ Fat

Calories	240
Calories from Fat	25
Total Fat	3.0 g
Saturated Fat	0.8 g
Trans Fat	0.0 g
Cholesterol	0 mg
Sodium	420 mg
Potassium	620 mg
Total Carbohydrate	44 g
Dietary Fiber	12 g
Sugars	5 g
Protein	11 g
Phosphorus	330 mg

1. Place cilantro, spinach, peas, and cold water into a blender and blend until very smooth. Set aside.

2. Combine sunflower oil and ghee in a small bowl, then add mixture to a heavy-bottomed Dutch oven over medium-high heat. Add onions and sauté for 6 minutes, or until transparent.

3. Add ginger and garlic and sauté for 1 minute. Add tomatoes and sauté for 1 minute.

4. Add curry powder, star anise, and cinnamon sticks. Sauté for 1 minute.

5. Add freekeh and toast, stirring occasionally, for 5 minutes, or until it becomes aromatic.

6. Add stock and bring up to a boil. Then reduce heat to medium-low and bring mixture to a simmer. Cook, covered, for 45 minutes.

7. Turn off heat, remove the whole spices, and gently stir in spinach and pea purée. Let stand, uncovered, for 5 minutes.

8. Add salt, pepper, and garam masala; stir well and serve hot.

COOK'S NOTES

You can replace the freekeh in this recipe with brown rice if you prefer. Make sure you use good-quality curry powder in this recipe. Try to select a product that does not contain too much salt or too many artificial ingredients; try to find an organic version if you can.

To blanch the spinach, add to boiling water for 2 minutes, then remove spinach immediately with a slotted spoon and add to a bowl of ice water to stop the cooking. This will give the spinach a beautiful color.

Forbidden Rice Kedgeree

Kedgeree is a one-pot Indian meal made of flaked fish—such as haddock or cod—cooked rice, hard-boiled eggs, curry powder, butter/ghee, herbs, and sultanas (golden raisins). Black rice (forbidden rice) is used in this version of the recipe. It is a kind of sticky rice with many nutrients. The word *kedgeree* comes from the Hindi word *khichrī*, which refers to a rice-and-lentil Indian dish. The history of this dish is controversial. Some say that kedgeree was introduced to the U.K. by returning British colonists who had enjoyed the dish in India. Others say this dish originated in Scotland and was taken to India by Scottish troops during the British Raj, where it was adapted and incorporated into Indian cuisine and later reintroduced to the U.K.

SERVES: 6 • SERVING SIZE: ABOUT ½ CUP / 113 G • PREP TIME: 20 MINUTES • COOKING TIME: ABOUT 1 HOUR

CHOICES/EXCHANGES
2 Carbohydrate
2 Lean Protein
½ Fat

Calories	240
Calories from Fat	70
Total Fat	8.0 g
Saturated Fat	1.5 g
Trans Fat	0.0 g
Cholesterol	95 mg
Sodium	260 mg
Potassium	470 mg
Total Carbohydrate	26 g
Dietary Fiber	2 g
Sugars	10 g
Protein	17 g
Phosphorus	245 mg

1 cup / 190 g **black rice (forbidden rice)**

2 cups / 475 mL **water**

8 oz / 230 g **smoked haddock or other flaky white fish** (2 fillets)

1 **bay leaf**

2 cups / 475 mL **1% milk**

1 Tbsp / 15 mL **sunflower oil**

1 tsp / 3.5 g **mustard seeds**

2 **cloves garlic, peeled and finely chopped**

1 (1-inch / 2.5-cm) **piece ginger, peeled and finely minced**

1 **small yellow onion, finely chopped**

2 tsp / 10 g **curry powder**

½ tsp / 2.5 g **ground turmeric**

Juice of ½ **lemon, divided**

2 **stalks green onions, finely chopped**

⅓ cup / 50 g **golden raisins**

⅓ cup / 50 g **sliced almonds**

¼ cup / 4 g **minced cilantro, divided**

1 Tbsp / 1.5 g **roughly chopped mint leaves, divided**

2 large **eggs, hard boiled**

½ cup / 122.5 g **organic, plain low-fat yogurt**

½ **lemon, cut into 6 wedges**

1 Combine rice and 2 cups / 475 mL water in a large pot and bring to a boil. Cover with a tight-fitting lid, reduce heat to low, and simmer for 40 minutes. Remove from heat, but leave lid on and let stand for 10 minutes. Fluff rice with a fork and set aside.

2 Place fish fillets in a large skillet with bay leaf. Pour enough milk into the skillet to just cover the fish. Cover skillet and simmer for 4–5 minutes. Remove from heat and let stand for 10 minutes to finish cooking the fish. Discard bay leaf and remaining milk and set fish aside.

3 Heat a heavy-bottomed pan over medium-high heat and add oil. Add mustard seeds and cook until they begin to splutter.

4 Lower heat to medium and add garlic and ginger. Sauté for 1 minute. Add yellow onions and sauté for about 5 minutes. Add curry powder, turmeric, ½ of the lemon juice, and green onions and cook for another 2–3 minutes.

5 Add cooked rice, fish, and golden raisins to the pan and stir gently until heated through, about 2–3 minutes. Add almonds and most of the cilantro and mint to the pot (reserve a little cilantro and mint to mix with the yogurt). Gently stir.

6 Quarter the hard-boiled eggs, and add to the pan. Transfer the mixture onto a warm serving dish.

7 In a small bowl, mix yogurt with remaining cilantro and mint and remaining half of the lemon juice. Mix and serve with the kedgeree with a lemon wedge on top of each serving.

COOK'S NOTES

Kedgeree is traditionally eaten as a breakfast dish, but you can enjoy it any time! It makes a satisfying brunch or lunch dish or a light, tasty evening meal. It's a great way to use leftover fish or rice.

In the state of Manipur, in northeastern India, black rice is used in community feasts and for ceremonial purposes.

CHAPTER 11
Healthy Sides

Cabbage and Peas Sabzi Ⓥ ᴳᶠ

The word *sabzi* comes from a Persian word (*sabzī*) and refers to leafy green vegetables or herbs. Traditionally this verdant side dish consists of a mixture of seasonal green leafy vegetables and legumes cooked together with spices and herbs. Sabzi is often served with Indian flatbread and is a staple of northern India.

SERVES: 8 • SERVING SIZE: ⅓ CUP / 48 G • PREP TIME: NONE • COOKING TIME: 15 MINUTES

1 Tbsp / 15 mL **sunflower oil**

1 Tbsp / 6 g **cumin seeds**

1 tsp / 5 g **finely chopped ginger**

1 **green chili, finely minced**

1 Tbsp / 10 g **finely minced red onions**

2 medium (2-oz / 56-g) **new potatoes (skin on), cut into ½-inch / 13-mm cubes**

½ tsp / 3.3 g **salt**

½ tsp / 2.5 g **ground turmeric**

1 tsp / 5 g **ground cumin**

1 tsp / 5 g **ground black pepper**

¼ cup / 34 g **shelled fresh or frozen green peas**

2 medium **tomatoes, diced into 1-inch / 2.5-cm pieces**

1 medium (2½-lb / 1130-g) **cabbage, chopped into ½-inch / 13-mm chunks**

COOK'S NOTES

If the vegetables stick to the bottom of the pan, sprinkle some water into the pan as needed. You can use any combination of seasonal vegetables in this dish.

CHOICES/EXCHANGES

2 Nonstarchy Vegetable
½ Fat

Calories	70
Calories from Fat	20
Total Fat	2.0 g
Saturated Fat	0.3 g
Trans Fat	0.0 g
Cholesterol	0 mg
Sodium	170 mg
Potassium	410 mg
Total Carbohydrate	13 g
Dietary Fiber	4 g
Sugars	5 g
Protein	3 g
Phosphorus	60 mg

1 Heat a heavy-bottomed pan over medium-high heat and add oil. Add cumin seeds and cook until they begin to splutter. Then add ginger, green chili, and onions and sauté for 1 minute.

2 Add potatoes, salt, and turmeric and stir-fry over medium-low heat until potatoes are about halfway cooked, about 3–4 minutes. (If the potatoes get too dry, add a few drops of water to prevent them from sticking to the pan.)

3 Add ground cumin, black pepper, and peas and mix well. Cook for 2–3 minutes until you see the peas begin to shrivel. Add tomatoes and cook, covered, until tomatoes get mushy, about 3 minutes.

4 Add cabbage, mix well, and cook, covered, until cabbage gets limp and looks translucent. (The cabbage should not be overcooked; it should still be a little crunchy for this dish.) Serve hot.

Indian Cuisine Diabetes Cookbook

Beans Ulathu (Stir-Fried Beans) Ⓥ 🄶🄵

SERVES: 7 • SERVING SIZE: ¼ CUP / 45 G • PREP TIME: ABOUT 5 MINUTES • COOKING TIME: 6 MINUTES

1 Tbsp / 15 mL **safflower oil**

1 medium **onion** or 2 **shallots,**
  diced into ½-inch / 13-mm pieces

2 **cloves garlic**

1 **dried red chili, seeds removed**

30 oz / 845 g **haricot vert beans, cut
  into 2-inch-long/ 5-cm-long pieces**

1 Tbsp / 15 mL **cold water**

¾ tsp / 5 g **salt**

1 Heat oil in a wide heavy-bottomed pan over medium-high heat.

2 Add onions and sauté until they are translucent, about 2 minutes. Using a mortar and pestle or the bottom of a clean heavy pan, crush the garlic cloves and dried chili together. Add garlic and crushed chili and sauté for 1 minute.

3 Add beans and mix everything well. Stir to keep ingredients from sticking to the bottom of the pan. Add water, reduce heat to low, close the lid on the pan, and cook for 3 minutes to steam the beans.

4 Open the lid and stir well, making sure beans are tender but not mushy. Sprinkle with salt and serve hot.

CHOICES/EXCHANGES
2 Nonstarchy Vegetable
½ Fat

Calories	60
Calories from Fat	20
Total Fat	2.5 g
Saturated Fat	0.3 g
Trans Fat	0.0 g
Cholesterol	0 mg
Sodium	250 mg
Potassium	190 mg
Total Carbohydrate	11 g
Dietary Fiber	4 g
Sugars	3 g
Protein	2 g
Phosphorus	40 mg

COOK'S NOTES

This side dish goes great with grilled fish or meat, steamed rice, or Indian whole-wheat bread. You can replace the beans with any vegetable you like. For extra flavor, you can add 2 sprigs of curry leaves to the pan along with the beans; just be sure to remove the sprigs before serving.

If you don't have a mortar and pestle to crush the garlic and chili, you can place them on a cutting board and crush them together using the bottom of a clean heavy pan.

Thoran (Trio of Mixed Vegetables)

This traditional southern Indian dish is a staple of everyday cooking in that region, and is a great way to use seasonal vegetables. It is usually served with plain rice or an Indian flatbread.

SERVES: 4 • SERVING SIZE: ½ CUP / 90 G • PREP TIME: 5 MINUTES • COOKING TIME: 10 MINUTES

2 Tbsp / 10.4 g **fresh or frozen grated unsweetened coconut**

¼ tsp / 1.3 g **ground turmeric**

1 Tbsp / 15 mL **sunflower oil**

1 tsp / 2 g **cumin seeds**

1 tsp / 3.5 g **black mustard seeds**

1 **dried red chili**

1 medium **red onion, finely minced**

2 **carrots, finely minced** (about 1 cup / 150 g)

3 **asparagus stalks, cleaned and minced** (about 1 cup / 150 g)

1 **yellow squash, minced** (about 1 cup / 150 g)

¼ tsp / 1.7 g **salt**

KITCHEN TOOLS

Food processor

CHOICES/EXCHANGES
2 Nonstarchy Vegetable
1 Fat

Calories	90
Calories from Fat	45
Total Fat	5.0 g
Saturated Fat	1.2 g
Trans Fat	0.0 g
Cholesterol	0 mg
Sodium	170 mg
Potassium	320 mg
Total Carbohydrate	10 g
Dietary Fiber	3 g
Sugars	5 g
Protein	2 g
Phosphorus	65 mg

1 In a small bowl, combine the coconut and turmeric together and mix well. Set aside.

2 Heat oil in a wide heavy-bottomed pan over medium-high heat. Add cumin seeds, mustard seeds, and red chili. When seeds start spluttering, add minced onion and sauté well, about 1 minute. Then add coconut mixture and sauté for 1 minute.

3 Add minced carrots, asparagus, and squash and stir well. Close the lid, reduce heat to medium, and cook for about 5 minutes.

4 Open the lid and stir to mix everything together. Check to make sure vegetables are cooked through. Remove red chili. Sprinkle with salt and serve.

COOK'S NOTES

You can mince the carrots, asparagus, and squash easily using a food processer with a chopping blade. Finely mince the vegetables but don't let them get mushy. Set aside until ready to use. Finely mince onions as well and set aside in a separate bowl. If you don't have a food processor, you can finely mince the vegetables manually. Sprinkle some water into the pan if the vegetables start to stick to the bottom while cooking.

This recipe calls for carrots, asparagus, and squash, but you can use any three vegetables for this trio. If you don't have mustard seeds on hand when making this recipe, you can leave them out.

Corn Tikki (V) (GF)

2½ cups / 412.5 g **fresh or frozen corn**

2½ Tbsp / 37.5 mL **safflower oil, divided**

½ Tbsp / 7.5 g **minced ginger**

1 Tbsp / 7.5 g **finely minced garlic**

2 Tbsp / 2 g **minced cilantro leaves**

½ tsp / 3.3 g **salt**

½ tsp / 2.5 g **ground white pepper**

2 Tbsp / 15 g **rice flour**

CHILI-MINT CHUTNEY

1 cup / 25 g **packed mint leaves**

1 **serrano chili**

⅛ tsp / 2.1 g **sugar**

¼ tsp / 1.7 g **salt**

1 tsp / 5 mL **lemon juice**

½ tsp / 2.5 g **ground cumin**

¼ cup / 60 mL **water**

KITCHEN TOOLS

Food processor

CHOICES/EXCHANGES
1 Starch
½ Fat

Calories	100
Calories from Fat	45
Total Fat	5.0 g
Saturated Fat	0.4 g
Trans Fat	0.0 g
Cholesterol	0 mg
Sodium	250 mg
Potassium	170 mg
Total Carbohydrate	13 g
Dietary Fiber	2 g
Sugars	2 g
Protein	2 g
Phosphorus	50 mg

1 Blanch frozen corn in boiling water for 2 minutes, then drain and set aside.

2 In a medium heavy-bottomed skillet, heat ½ Tbsp / 7.5 mL oil over medium heat. Add ginger and garlic and cook, stirring, until fragrant, about 2 minutes. Add the corn and cook, stirring, for 2 more minutes.

3 Transfer corn mixture to a food processor and purée to a coarse consistency. Scrape mixture into a medium bowl. Stir in cilantro, salt, and pepper. Form into 7 patties (2 inches / 5 cm around) and refrigerate for at least 20 minutes.

4 Meanwhile, combine all Chili-Mint Chutney ingredients in a food processor and puree until smooth. Set aside.

5 In a large cast iron skillet, heat remaining 2 Tbsp / 30 mL oil over medium-high heat until shimmering. Dust the tikkis with rice flour and tap off the excess. Add half the tikkis to the skillet and cook until browned and crisp, about 2 minutes per side. Repeat with the remaining tikkis.

6 Drain cooked tikkis on an absorbent paper towel. Serve on a platter and top each with a small dollop of the chutney.

COOK'S NOTES

You can remove the seeds from the serrano chili to reduce the heat level, but keep the skin for flavor. If you're not ready to serve this dish right away, you can keep it warm in a 325°F / 165°C oven and serve when needed.

Curried Mixed Lentils and Butternut Squash (V) (GF)

SERVES: 4 • SERVING SIZE: 2 OZ / 56 G • PREP TIME: ABOUT 5 MINUTES • COOKING TIME: 1 HOUR AND 25 MINUTES

1 cup / 192 g **masoor dal (split pink lentils)**

5 cups / 1.2 L **water**

1 Tbsp plus 1 tsp / 20 mL **grapeseed oil, divided**

1 tsp /5 g **ground turmeric**

1 lb / 450 g **butternut squash, cleaned, peeled, and cubed (1-inch / cubes)**

2 medium **onions, cubed (½-inch / 13-mm cubes)**

3 **cloves garlic, thinly sliced**

1 tsp / 5 g **mild curry powder**

¾ tsp / 5 g **kosher salt**

¼ tsp / 1.3 g **ground black pepper**

Juice of ½ **lime**

GARNISH

1 Tbsp / 1 g **chopped cilantro leaves**

CHOICES/EXCHANGES
2½ Starch
1 Nonstarchy Vegetable
1 Lean Protein

Calories	260
Calories from Fat	45
Total Fat	5.0 g
Saturated Fat	0.6 g
Trans Fat	0.0 g
Cholesterol	0 mg
Sodium	360 mg
Potassium	830 mg
Total Carbohydrate	43 g
Dietary Fiber	14 g
Sugars	7 g
Protein	14 g
Phosphorus	290 mg

1 Wash and drain lentils. Add lentils and 5 cups / 1.2 L water to a large pot and bring to a boil. Once boiling, remove the foam from top. Reduce the heat to bring to a simmer. Add 1 tsp / 5 mL oil and turmeric to the lentils and cook until lentils become tender, about 35–40 minutes. Set aside.

2 Meanwhile, preheat oven to 400°F / 200°C. In a large bowl, mix butternut squash, onions, garlic, curry powder, and the remaining 1 Tbsp / 15 mL oil. Mix well, transfer to a baking sheet, and roast squash mixture for about 30 minutes.

3 Remove squash mixture from the oven and add to pot with cooked lentils. Cook over medium heat for about 12 minutes, or until squash is soft.

4 Add the salt, black pepper, and the lime juice and stir well to combine. Remove from heat, garnish with cilantro, and serve hot.

Masala Baingan (Grilled Eggplant) Ⓥ Ⓖ🇫

SERVES: 6 • SERVING SIZE: 3 OZ / 84 G • PREP TIME: 1 HOUR • COOKING TIME: 6 MINUTES

2 medium **eggplants, sliced into ½-inch-thick / 13-mm-thick rounds**

1 tsp / 6.7 g **salt**

1 tsp / 5 g **hot paprika**

3 Tbsp / 42 g **ground coriander**

1 tsp / 5 g **ground black pepper**

½ tsp / 2.5 g **ground turmeric**

¾ tsp / 5 g **kosher salt**

2 Tbsp / 30 mL **white vinegar**

1 Tbsp / 15 mL **grapeseed oil**

1 In a large bowl or baking dish, combine eggplant slices and 1 tsp / 6.7 g salt and set aside for about 30 minutes. (The salt will draw moisture from the eggplant.)

2 Rinse and drain eggplant in a colander and dry the slices. Place in a dry bowl or pan.

3 In a small bowl, combine paprika, coriander, pepper, turmeric, salt, and vinegar and whisk to make the marinade. Add eggplant slices to marinade and set aside for 30 minutes to marinate.

4 Brush marinated eggplant slices with oil. Preheat a cast iron griddle over high heat and place the eggplant slices on griddle. Cook for 3 minutes per side.

CHOICES/EXCHANGES
2 Nonstarchy Vegetable
½ Fat

Calories	70
Calories from Fat	20
Total Fat	2.5 g
Saturated Fat	0.3 g
Trans Fat	0.0 g
Cholesterol	0 mg
Sodium	240 mg
Potassium	480 mg
Total Carbohydrate	11 g
Dietary Fiber	7 g
Sugars	4 g
Protein	2 g
Phosphorus	50 mg

COOK'S NOTES

This dish also makes a delicious appetizer that can be served with a dollop of yogurt or mint chutney. Salting eliminates the acid in the eggplant and draws out excess moisture to prevent it from getting soggy. Be sure to rinse the eggplant and then pat it dry after salting.

Jewel Roasted Root Vegetables with Panch Phoran (V) (GF)

Panch phoran or "five-spice mix" is a spice blend used in eastern Indian food. Panch phoran has a distinct flavor and is made up of green fennel seeds, black mustard and nigella seeds, golden fenugreek seeds, and brown cumin seeds. These ingredients are usually added in equal proportions, but this can be adjusted to suit your personal tastes. Panch phoran is typically added to hot cooking oil or ghee, which causes the seeds to start popping immediately. To learn more about this technique of tempering the spices, see Indian Cooking Techniques on p. 26.

SERVES: 12 • SERVING SIZE: 2 OZ / 56 G • PREP TIME: ABOUT 5 MINUTES • COOKING TIME: 1 HOUR AND 45 MINUTES

2 medium (4-oz / 113-g) **red beets**

2 medium (4-oz / 113-g) **golden beets**

1 Tbsp plus 1 tsp / 20 mL **sunflower oil, divided**

1½ lb / 680 g **carrots, peeled and cut into 1-inch / 2.5-cm cubes**

1½ lb / 680 g **Brussels sprouts, halved lengthwise**

8 large **cloves garlic, unpeeled**

½ tsp / 3.3 g **salt**

½ tsp / 2.5 g **ground black pepper**

PANCH PHORAN

½ tsp / 1.8 g **black mustard seeds**

½ tsp / 1.8 g **fenugreek seeds**

½ tsp / 1 g **fennel seeds**

½ tsp / 1.8 g **nigella seeds**

½ tsp / 1 g **cumin seeds**

1 tsp / 5 mL **sunflower oil**

CHOICES/EXCHANGES
3 Nonstarchy Vegetable
½ Fat

Calories	80
Calories from Fat	20
Total Fat	2.5 g
Saturated Fat	0.3 g
Trans Fat	0.0 g
Cholesterol	0 mg
Sodium	170 mg
Potassium	460 mg
Total Carbohydrate	14 g
Dietary Fiber	4 g
Sugars	6 g
Protein	3 g
Phosphorus	70 mg

1. Preheat oven to 375°F / 190°C.

2. Rub all 4 beets with 1 tsp / 5 mL sunflower oil and put them in a small baking dish. Cover the dish with aluminum foil and roast for 30 minutes. (Make sure there is space in your oven for a second baking dish.)

3. While beets are roasting, toss carrots, Brussels sprouts, and garlic cloves with the remaining 1 Tbsp / 15 mL oil in a medium bowl. Transfer vegetables to a large baking dish and sprinkle with salt and pepper.

4. After beets have been cooking for 30 minutes, place the baking dish with the other vegetables in the oven next to the beets. Cook both the beets and the other vegetables for 1 hour, making sure to stir the vegetable medley once or twice.

5. Meanwhile, prepare the panch phoran: Mix black mustard, fenugreek, fennel, nigella, and cumin seeds in a small bowl. Take a small, heavy-bottomed pan and heat 1 tsp sunflower oil over medium-high heat. Add seeds to the hot pan and cook until they begin to splutter. As the seeds start to pop, turn off the heat immediately, put seeds back into the small bowl. Set aside.

6. After 1 hour, remove the baking dish with beets from the oven and transfer beets to a cutting board to cool for about 5 minutes. Stir the carrot/Brussels sprout mixture and continue to cook in the oven for another 10 minutes.

7. Once beets are cool enough to handle, peel and cut them into 1-inch / 2.5-cm chunks and set aside. Remove other vegetables from the oven and add to a large serving bowl. Add the beets and toss. Sprinkle with the panch phoran spice blend and serve.

COOK'S NOTES

If you cannot find nigella seeds, you may use onion seeds instead. You may also use ghee instead of sunflower oil when heating the spices for a nuttier flavor. While panch phoran is best made fresh, you can buy a premade blend at any Indian market and use 1 Tbsp / 14 g of the blend instead.

Khandvi (Chickpea Rolls) GF

This dish comes from the west coast of India, where it's a traditional snack. Chickpea flour (also called besan flour) is made of hulled chickpeas that are ground to a powder. Usually very fine in texture and pale yellow in color, chickpea flour is used in many Indian snacks and desserts. You can find chickpea flour—both coarse and fine varieties—in supermarkets and Indian markets.

SERVES: 4 • SERVING SIZE: 3 ROLLS • PREP TIME: ABOUT 5 MINUTES • COOKING TIME: 10 MINUTES

1 cup / 92 g **chickpea flour (also called gram or besan flour)**

3 cups / 700 mL **low-fat buttermilk**

5 **cloves garlic, finely chopped**

½ tsp / 2.5 g **ground turmeric**

¼ tsp / 1.3 g **garam masala**

1/16 tsp / 0.4 g **salt**

2 tsp / 10 mL **sunflower oil, divided**

1 tsp / 3.5 g **black or brown mustard seeds**

GARNISH

1 Tbsp / 1 g **chopped cilantro leaves**

KITCHEN TOOLS

Food processor

CHOICES/EXCHANGES
1 Starch
1 Fat-Free Milk
½ Fat

Calories	190
Calories from Fat	50
Total Fat	6.0 g
Saturated Fat	1.4 g
Trans Fat	0.0 g
Cholesterol	5 mg
Sodium	240 mg
Potassium	510 mg
Total Carbohydrate	24 g
Dietary Fiber	3 g
Sugars	11 g
Protein	12 g
Phosphorus	250 mg

1 Using a food processor or hand mixer, combine chickpea flour, buttermilk, garlic, turmeric, garam masala, and salt to form a batter.

2 Pour batter into a wide, heavy-bottomed pan and cook over low heat, stirring or whisking constantly, about 7 minutes, until batter becomes thick and begins to pull away from the sides of the pan.

3 Grease a 9 × 13-inch baking pan with ½ tsp / 2.5 mL oil and add batter, using a spatula to spread evenly.

4 Let batter cool down for 2 minutes, then cut dough into 12 (9-inch-long / 22.8-cm-long) strips. Carefully roll up each strip using your hands and transfer these rolls onto a serving platter.

5 Heat remaining 1½ tsp / 7.5 mL oil in a small, deep heavy-bottomed pan over medium-high heat. Add mustard seeds and sauté, covered, about 1–2 minutes. When they start to splutter, remove from heat.

6 Sprinkle mustard seed mixture on the rolls. Garnish with cilantro leaves and serve.

COOK'S NOTES

You can cover the pan when cooking the mustard seeds to keep the oil from spluttering. Make sure the dough is not overmixed.

Chana (Chickpea) Pilaf GF

This is a great special occasion recipe for vegetarians who eat dairy! It's very festive.

SERVES: 9 • SERVING SIZE: 2 OZ / ¼ CUP / 56 G
PREP TIME: 8–10 HOURS OR OVERNIGHT • COOKING TIME: ABOUT 55 MINUTES

1 cup / 200 g **dried chickpeas**

⅛ tsp / 0.6 g **baking soda**

¾ tsp / 5 g **salt, divided**

2¼ cups / 535 mL **water**

½ tsp / 2.5 mL **sunflower oil**

¾ cup / 140 g **brown basmati rice**

1½ Tbsp / 23 g **plain low-fat Greek yogurt**

¼ tsp / 1.3 g **garam masala**

½ tsp / 2.5 g **smoked paprika**

1 (½-inch / 13-mm) **cinnamon stick**

1 small **blade mace**

1 **bay leaf**

3 **cloves**

2 **green cardamom pods**

½ cup / 80 g **packed chopped onions**

2 **garlic cloves, finely chopped**

½ cup / 75 g **finely chopped fresh tomatoes**

½ tsp / 2.5 g **cayenne pepper**

¼ tsp / 1.3 g **ground turmeric**

1 medium **potato, quartered**

1 tsp / 1.7 g **grated fresh ginger**

1 tsp / 1.8 g **crushed dried fenugreek leaves**

1 small **red bell pepper, finely diced**

2 Tbsp / 18 g **golden raisins**

1 Tbsp / 10 g **toasted silvered almonds**

KITCHEN TOOLS

Pressure cooker

CHOICES/EXCHANGES

2 Starch
½ Fat

Calories	170
Calories from Fat	20
Total Fat	2.5 g
Saturated Fat	0.3 g
Trans Fat	0.0 g
Cholesterol	0 mg
Sodium	220 mg
Potassium	320 mg
Total Carbohydrate	32 g
Dietary Fiber	5 g
Sugars	5 g
Protein	7 g
Phosphorus	155 mg

COOK'S NOTES

If you do not have a pressure cooker, use a heavy-bottomed pot to cook the chickpeas with the baking soda, ½ tsp / 3.3 g salt, water, and oil (see ingredient list). The chickpeas will need to cook for roughly 45–50 minutes or until fork tender. Once the chickpeas are cooked, drain and reserve the liquid. Set both the chickpeas and liquid aside.

While I suggest using dried chickpeas, you can use the canned variety instead. You will not have to soak canned chickpeas, but make sure you rinse them before adding to the Dutch oven. In place of the chickpea cooking water added in step 7, you can use chicken/vegetable stock or plain water.

1. In a large bowl, add chickpeas and cover with water. Soak 8–10 hours or overnight.

2. Drain chickpeas, discarding soaking water. Add chickpeas, baking soda, ½ tsp / 3.3 g salt, water, and oil to a pressure cooker. Cook over medium heat for 2–3 whistles, or until chickpeas are fork tender (about 20 minutes). Set aside when finished cooking. Reserve the water from cooking the chickpeas.

3. Rinse basmati rice 2–3 times under running water until water runs clear. Add rice to a large bowl and soak in 1½ cups / 350 mL water for 15 minutes.

4. Meanwhile, mix yogurt, garam masala, and paprika in a small bowl. Set aside.

5. In a wide heavy-bottomed Dutch oven over medium heat, add cinnamon stick, mace, bay leaf, cloves, and cardamom pods. Cook until the spices crackle and release their aroma, about 10 seconds. Add onions and garlic and cook for 6 minutes, until they start to brown. Add tomatoes, cayenne pepper, and turmeric, and cook for 2–3 minutes, just until tomatoes begin to soften. Reduce heat to low and add yogurt mixture. Slowly stir until all ingredients are incorporated. Cook for another 2 minutes until the masala turns a brownish color. Add

potatoes and ginger and cook for 1–2 minutes. Remove whole spices.

6. Drain rice. Add rice and chickpeas to the Dutch oven. Do not stir.

7. Measure out an appropriate quantity of the water reserved from cooking the chickpeas and add to the Dutch oven. The quantity of water you add depends on the directions on the rice package. (Usually the ratio of rice to water is 2:1, and I add 2 Tbsp extra water.) Once you have added the water, add fenugreek leaves and stir gently.

8. Cover the pot with a lid and bring to a boil over high heat. Once boiling, reduce heat to low and let cook, covered, for another 8 minutes.

9. Add bell peppers to the pot and very gently incorporate them using a fork. Cover again and cook on low for another 2 minutes.

10. Turn off the heat and let sit, covered with a tight-fitting lid, for at least 15 minutes to steam. (You can wrap a clean kitchen towel around the lid to help it steam without the heat escaping.) Open the lid and add raisins, almonds, and remaining ¼ tsp / 1.7 g salt. Gently fluff pilaf with a fork and serve warm.

Lemon Brown Rice with Curry Leaves

SERVES: 3 • SERVING SIZE: ⅓ CUP / 70 G • PREP TIME: NONE • COOKING TIME: 5 MINUTES

1 Tbsp / 15 mL **sunflower oil**

½ tsp / 1.8 g **black mustard seeds**

1 tsp / 4 g **split chana dal (split chickpeas)**

1 tsp / 4 g **split urad dal (black lentils)**

2 **dried red chilies**

1 tsp / 5 g **finely minced fresh ginger**

¼ tsp / 1.3 g **ground turmeric**

4 Tbsp / 36.3 g **roasted almonds**

10 **curry leaves, torn in half**

3 Tbsp / 45 mL **lemon juice**

⅓ tsp / 2.2 g **salt**

1 cup / 205 g **cooked brown basmati rice (slightly undercooked)**

1. Heat oil in a large heavy-bottomed pan or Dutch oven over medium-high heat and add mustard seeds, chana dal, urad dal, and chilies. Stir-fry until seeds begin to splutter and ingredients are lightly browned, about 1 minute.

2. Reduce heat to medium. Add ginger, turmeric, almonds, and curry leaves, and stir well. Combine lemon juice and salt in a small bowl, then add to the pan and cook for 1 minute.

3. Add cooked rice and stir gently to incorporate. Cook until rice is heated through, about 2 minutes. Remove chilies and serve hot.

CHOICES/EXCHANGES

1½ Starch
1½ Fat

Calories	190
Calories from Fat	90
Total Fat	10.0 g
Saturated Fat	1.0 g
Trans Fat	0.0 g
Cholesterol	0 mg
Sodium	260 mg
Potassium	140 mg
Total Carbohydrate	22 g
Dietary Fiber	3 g
Sugars	1 g
Protein	5 g
Phosphorus	120 mg

COOK'S NOTES

Make sure you remove the whole chilies before serving. If you have leftover brown rice in your refrigerator from another meal, this is a great recipe to make use of it.

Jeera Brown Rice Pilaf Ⓥ

SERVES: 6 • SERVING SIZE: 3 OZ / 84 G • PREP TIME: 1 HOUR • COOKING TIME: 45 MINUTES

1 cup / 190 g **brown basmati rice**

1 Tbsp / 15 mL **sunflower oil**

1 **cinnamon stick**

1 **bay leaf**

2 **cloves**

2 tsp / 4 g **cumin seeds**

2 cups / 475 mL **water or vegetable stock**

½ tsp / 3.3 g **salt**

½ cup / 55 g **store-bought crispy onions**

1. Rinse basmati rice under running water until water runs clear. Add rice to a large bowl, cover with water and soak for 1 hour. Drain rice and set aside.

2. Preheat a Dutch oven over medium-high heat and add the oil. Add cinnamon stick, bay leaf, and cloves and stir.

3. Immediately add cumin seeds. When seeds start to splutter, add rice and sauté over medium heat until rice is well coated with oil. Then add 2 cups / 475 mL water and the salt and bring mixture to a boil.

4. When water starts boiling, reduce heat to low and simmer, covered, for 30 minutes. Remove cinnamon stick, bay leaf, and cloves.

5. Remove from heat and set aside, covered, for about 10 minutes to steam the rice. (You can wrap a clean kitchen towel around the lid to help it steam without the heat escaping.) Garnish with crispy onions and serve.

COOK'S NOTES

Traditionally, this dish is topped with fried onions, but store-bought crispy onions work well for this recipe. If you want to make your own crispy onions, slice 1 red onion into very thin slices, coat in 1 Tbsp / 15 mL oil and sprinkle with salt. Cook in a 400°F / 200°C oven for 10 minutes, then reduce the heat to 350°F / 180°C and continue cooking for 20 more minutes.

CHOICES/EXCHANGES
1½ Starch
1 Fat

Calories	160
Calories from Fat	50
Total Fat	6.0 g
Saturated Fat	1.1 g
Trans Fat	0.0 g
Cholesterol	0 mg
Sodium	240 mg
Potassium	90 mg
Total Carbohydrate	25 g
Dietary Fiber	1 g
Sugars	1 g
Protein	3 g
Phosphorus	110 mg

Quinoa Mushroom Pilaf Ⓥ ⒼⒻ

SERVES: 6 • SERVING SIZE: 3 OZ / 84 G • PREP TIME: 10 MINUTES • COOKING TIME: 25 MINUTES

1 Tbsp / 15 mL **sunflower oil**

1 small **shallot, peeled and chopped**

1 tsp / 5 g **ginger-garlic paste (p. 34)**

½ cup / 43.5 g **cremini mushrooms, wiped clean and thinly sliced**

1½ cups / 255 g **quinoa, rinsed well and drained**

1 Tbsp / 1.5 g **finely chopped mint**

1 **bay leaf**

½ tsp / 3.3 g **sea salt**

½ tsp / 2.5 g **ground turmeric**

½ tsp / 2.5 g **ground black pepper**

3 cups / 700 mL **low-sodium vegetable stock or water**

2 Tbsp / 18 g **golden raisins**

1 Tbsp / 10 g **toasted slivered almonds**

CHOICES/EXCHANGES

2 Starch
1 Fat

Calories	190
Calories from Fat	45
Total Fat	5.0 g
Saturated Fat	0.6 g
Trans Fat	0.0 g
Cholesterol	0 mg
Sodium	230 mg
Potassium	360 mg
Total Carbohydrate	32 g
Dietary Fiber	4 g
Sugars	4 g
Protein	6 g
Phosphorus	245 mg

COOK'S NOTES

This dish is great for special occasions. You can serve it with Thakkali Chutney (Tomato Chutney; p. 242) or any chutney of your choice. You can use chicken stock in this recipe instead of the vegetable stock if you'd prefer.

1 Heat a Dutch oven over medium-high heat. Add oil and swirl it around to make sure the entire cooking surface is covered with oil.

2 Add shallot and cook until translucent but not brown, about 1 minute. Add ginger-garlic paste and sauté for 1 minute, stirring well. Add cremini mushrooms and cook until brown, 2–3 minutes.

3 Add quinoa, mint, bay leaf, salt, turmeric, and black pepper and stir. Saute for 1–2 minutes to coat everything in the oil and bring out the fullest flavors from the ingredients.

4 Slowly and carefully add stock and bring to a boil. When mixture comes to a full boil, reduce heat to low and simmer, covered, for about 15 minutes.

5 After 15 minutes, turn off the heat, uncover, and remove bay leaf. Fluff quinoa, cover again, and allow to rest for about 10 minutes.

6 Garnish with golden raisins and slivered almonds and serve.

CHAPTER 12
Slaws and Salads

Cabbage and Onion Slaw (V) (GF)

SERVES: 6 • SERVING SIZE: 2 OZ / 56 G • PREP TIME: 30 MINUTES • COOKING TIME: NONE

1 medium (2½-lb / 1130-g) **cabbage**

2 medium (6-oz / 170-g) **red onions**

2 Tbsp / 30 mL **apple cider vinegar**

1 **green chili, seeds removed and finely julienned**

⅛ tsp / 0.5 g **sugar**

½ tsp / 3.3 g **salt**

KITCHEN TOOLS

Food processor

1. Using a food processor, process cabbage and onions to get 2-inch-long / 5-cm-long shreds, or you can shred or thinly slice the cabbage and onion manually into long thin shreds.

2. Add cabbage, onions, vinegar, chili, sugar, and salt to a large bowl and mix well.

3. Set aside for 30 minutes at room temperature to allow flavors to marry and for slaw to reach the right texture. Serve.

COOK'S NOTES

This slaw is great served alongside grilled seafood or meat. Leftover slaw can be enjoyed the next day as well; the flavors taste even better the next day. Remove the seeds from the chili if you want to reduce the heat level.

CHOICES/EXCHANGES
3 Nonstarchy Vegetable

Calories	60
Calories from Fat	0
Total Fat	0.0 g
Saturated Fat	0.1 g
Trans Fat	0.0 g
Cholesterol	0 mg
Sodium	220 mg
Potassium	360 mg
Total Carbohydrate	15 g
Dietary Fiber	5 g
Sugars	7 g
Protein	3 g
Phosphorus	55 mg

Indian Cuisine Diabetes Cookbook

Carrot and Beet Slaw

SERVES: 4 • SERVING SIZE: 2 OZ / 56 G • PREP TIME: ABOUT 5 MINUTES • COOKING TIME: NONE

2 medium **carrots**
1 small **red beet**
1 medium **red onion**
1 medium **green chili**
Juice of 1 medium **lime**
⅛ tsp / 0.5 g **sugar**
1 Tbsp / 1 g **chopped cilantro**
¼ tsp / 1.7 g **salt**

KITCHEN TOOLS
Food processor

1   Using a food processor, shred carrots, beet, onion, and chili into 2-inch-long / 5-cm-long shreds, or you can shred or thinly slice the carrots, beet and onion manually into long thin shreds.

2   Add shredded vegetables, lime juice, and sugar to a wide bowl and mix well.

3   Mix in chopped cilantro and salt and serve.

COOK'S NOTES

This slaw pairs well with grilled meats and seafood. When you buy green chilies, look for medium-sized chilies, the smaller green chilies can be very spicy.

CHOICES/EXCHANGES
2 Nonstarchy Vegetable

Calories	45
Calories from Fat	0
Total Fat	0.0 g
Saturated Fat	0.0 g
Trans Fat	0.0 g
Cholesterol	0 mg
Sodium	180 mg
Potassium	270 mg
Total Carbohydrate	10 g
Dietary Fiber	2 g
Sugars	5 g
Protein	1 g
Phosphorus	35 mg

Raw Papaya and Mango Salad

The mango originated in the foothills of Himalayas. Literature traces the use of mangoes in Indian cuisine back to ancient times. This bright side dish highlights the versatility of sweet fruits such as papaya and mango.

SERVES: 4 • SERVING SIZE: 2 OZ / 56 G • PREP TIME: ABOUT 5 MINUTES • COOKING TIME: NONE

½ medium (21-oz / 590-g) **unripe papaya**

2 medium (7-oz / 200-g) **green mangoes, peeled**

1 **green chili, thinly sliced**

1 Tbsp / 10 g **crushed roasted peanuts**

1 (1-inch / 2.5-cm) **piece fresh ginger, grated**

1 tsp / 2 g **cumin seeds, toasted and crushed**

1 Tbsp / 15 mL **lime juice**

¼ tsp / 1.7 g **salt**

⅛ tsp / 0.5 g **sugar**

KITCHEN TOOLS

Julienne slicer

1 Remove skin and seeds from unripe papaya. Julienne the papaya and unripe mango using a julienne slicer or medium serrated grater.

2 Mix all the ingredients together in a large bowl and serve.

COOK'S NOTES

This salad can be served with any grilled meat or seafood dish. Remove the seeds from the chili if you want to reduce the heat level. You can use roasted pumpkin or sunflower seeds instead of peanuts, if desired. For even more color and fresh flavor, try garnishing this salad with 1 Tbsp / 1 g chopped cilantro.

CHOICES/EXCHANGES

1 Fruit

Calories	60
Calories from Fat	15
Total Fat	1.5 g
Saturated Fat	0.2 g
Trans Fat	0.0 g
Cholesterol	0 mg
Sodium	150 mg
Potassium	260 mg
Total Carbohydrate	12 g
Dietary Fiber	1 g
Sugars	7 g
Protein	2 g
Phosphorus	30 mg

Indian Cuisine Diabetes Cookbook

Kachumber Salad (Onion and Tomato Salad) Ⓥ ⒼⒻ

SERVES: 4 • SERVING SIZE: 2 OZ / 56 G • PREP TIME: ABOUT 5 MINUTES • COOKING TIME: NONE

3 medium **tomatoes, diced**

½ **English cucumber, diced**

1 medium **red onion, diced**

1 **fresh green chili, finely chopped**

½ tsp / 1 g **cumin seeds, toasted and crushed**

¼ tsp / 1.3 g **smoked paprika**

½ tsp / 2.5 g **ground black pepper**

1 Tbsp / 15 mL **lime juice**

¼ tsp / 1.7 g **salt**

1 Tbsp / 1 g **chopped cilantro**

1 Gently toss all ingredients except cilantro together in a large bowl. Refrigerate until ready to serve.

2 Garnish with cilantro and serve.

COOK'S NOTES

This salad pairs especially well with curries or kebabs. Remove the seeds from the chili to reduce the heat level.

CHOICES/EXCHANGES
2 Nonstarchy Vegetable

Calories	50
Calories from Fat	0
Total Fat	0.0 g
Saturated Fat	0.1 g
Trans Fat	0.0 g
Cholesterol	0 mg
Sodium	160 mg
Potassium	440 mg
Total Carbohydrate	11 g
Dietary Fiber	2 g
Sugars	6 g
Protein	2 g
Phosphorus	55 mg

Curried Aloo Anardana Salad Ⓥ

The anardana tree, or pomegranate tree, has been cultivated since ancient times throughout the Mediterranean region of Asia, Africa, and Europe. This dish is usually made during the wintertime in India. Traditionally, this dish is made with white potatoes, but I've used sweet potatoes here for a healthier twist.

SERVES: 9 • SERVING SIZE: ⅓ CUP / 75 G • PREP TIME: ABOUT 5 MINUTES • COOKING TIME: 55 MINUTES

1 Tbsp / 15 mL **olive oil**

2 lb / 900 g **sweet potatoes (about 2), peeled and cut into ½-inch / 13-mm cubes**

1 medium **yellow onion, diced into ¼-inch / 6-mm pieces**

1 tsp / 1.7 g **grated ginger**

1 medium **clove garlic, minced**

¾ tsp / 5 g **sea salt, divided**

1 tsp / 5 g **mild curry powder**

1 cup / 190 g **farro, rinsed and drained**

2 cups / 475 mL **low-sodium vegetable stock**

2 cups / 475 mL **warm water**

½ tsp / 2.5 g **ground black pepper**

1 Tbsp / 15 mL **lemon juice**

¼ tsp / 1.3 g **garam masala**

7 **mint leaves, finely chopped**

1 Tbsp / 1 g **finely chopped cilantro leaves**

¼ cup / 40 g **pomegranate seeds**

CHOICES/EXCHANGES
2 Starch
½ Fat

Calories	180
Calories from Fat	20
Total Fat	2.5 g
Saturated Fat	0.3 g
Trans Fat	0.0 g
Cholesterol	0 mg
Sodium	250 mg
Potassium	470 mg
Total Carbohydrate	33 g
Dietary Fiber	6 g
Sugars	6 g
Protein	5 g
Phosphorus	155 mg

1 Preheat oven to 375°F / 190°C and position an oven rack in the center.

2 In a large bowl, combine oil, sweet potatoes, onions, ginger, garlic, ½ tsp / 3.3 g salt, and curry powder and toss until well combined. Transfer mixture onto a rimmed baking sheet, spreading evenly. Roast until fork tender, about 30 minutes, stirring every 15 minutes.

3 Meanwhile, in a medium heavy-bottomed saucepan, combine farro, stock, and water and bring to a boil over medium-high heat. When liquid is boiling, reduce heat to medium-low, cover, and simmer until farro is tender, about 25 minutes.

4 Using a colander, drain farro mixture and transfer to a large bowl. Add remaining ¼ tsp / 1.7 g salt and pepper and mix well.

5 Add sweet potato mixture to the cooked farro. Add lemon juice and garam masala and mix well.

6 Garnish with mint, cilantro, and pomegranate seeds before serving.

COOK'S NOTES

Farro has a complex nutty flavor. You can replace the farro with medium-grain barley, if desired. Keep in mind that barley, like farro, contains gluten, and it should be avoided for those who gluten intolerant. Barley can be soaked for 2–3 hours prior to cooking to reduce cooking time. This salad tastes even better the next day after the flavors have had time to marry in the refrigerator overnight.

Sprouted Mung Dal Salad Ⓥ ㉒

SERVES: 6 • SERVING SIZE: 2 OZ / 56 G MIXTURE + 1 POTATO • PREP TIME: ABOUT 5 MINUTES • COOKING TIME: NONE

SALAD

2 cups / 385 g **sprouted or cooked mung dal**

1 small **bunch watercress, cleaned and stalks removed**

1 small **bunch baby arugula leaves**

1 medium **tomato, finely diced**

1 **red onion, finely diced**

1 **English cucumber, finely diced** (about 1 cup / 150 g)

½ tsp / 0.8 g **finely grated fresh ginger**

DRESSING

½ tsp / 3.3 g **salt**

⅛ tsp / 0.5 g **sugar**

1 tsp / 2 g **cumin seeds, toasted and ground**

2 tsp / 10 mL **lime juice**

1 Tbsp / 15 mL **extra-virgin olive oil**

GARNISH

1 Tbsp / 1 g **chopped cilantro leaves**

CHOICES/EXCHANGES
1 Nonstarchy Vegetable
½ Fat

Calories	50
Calories from Fat	20
Total Fat	2.5 g
Saturated Fat	0.4 g
Trans Fat	0.0 g
Cholesterol	0 mg
Sodium	200 mg
Potassium	220 mg
Total Carbohydrate	7 g
Dietary Fiber	2 g
Sugars	4 g
Protein	2 g
Phosphorus	45 mg

Indian Cuisine Diabetes Cookbook

1 Mix all salad ingredients together in a large bowl and set aside.

2 In a small bowl, whisk the dressing ingredients together until well combined and pour dressing directly over salad.

3 Garnish with cilantro leaves and serve.

COOK'S NOTES

This salad can be served with any grilled meat or seafood dish. See page 29 to learn the technique for sprouting the mung dal.

You can add 1 chopped green chili (remove seeds from the chili if you want to reduce the heat level) to the salad dressing for even more flavor.

CHAPTER 13
Desserts

Chia Seed Falooda

Falooda is a sweet milk-based dessert common in the northern part of India. It is thought to have originated from a Persian dessert known as *faloodeh*. Traditional Indian falooda contains vermicelli made from wheat, but in this recipe I use buckwheat noodles.

SERVES: 8 • SERVING SIZE: ⅓ CUP / 84 G PUDDING + 3–4 RASPBERRIES + ½ TBSP / 5.5 G NOODLES
PREP TIME: 8 HOURS OR OVERNIGHT • COOKING TIME: NONE

½ cup / 72 g **chia seeds**
2½ cups / 595 mL **low-fat milk**
1 tsp / 5 mL **vanilla extract**
½ cup / 70 g **raspberries**
1 Tbsp / 20.8 g **maple syrup**
2 tsp / 10 mL **rose water**
1½ tsp/ 7.5 mL **lemon juice**
¼ cup / 44 g **cooked soba noodles, rinsed in cold water**
½ cup / 75 g **pomegranate seeds**

1 In a large bowl, combine chia seeds and milk. Soak chia seeds for 8 hours or overnight in the refrigerator.

2 After chia seeds have soaked, add vanilla extract. Mix well and set aside.

3 In a medium bowl, combine the raspberries, maple syrup, rose water, and lemon. Stir gently to combine and set aside.

4 In a short glass, add a layer of chia seed mixture, a thin layer of raspberry mixture, and a thin layer of soba noodles. Repeat for each serving and garnish each serving with pomegranate seeds.

CHOICES/EXCHANGES
1 Carbohydrate
1 Fat

Calories	120
Calories from Fat	45
Total Fat	5.0 g
Saturated Fat	0.9 g
Trans Fat	0.0 g
Cholesterol	5 mg
Sodium	40 mg
Potassium	210 mg
Total Carbohydrate	15 g
Dietary Fiber	5 g
Sugars	7 g
Protein	5 g
Phosphorus	190 mg

COOK'S NOTES

Some varieties of soba noodles contain wheat flour. If you follow a gluten-free diet, look for 100% buckwheat soba noodles. You can use cellophane noodles made of bean threads instead of soba noodles in this recipe.

Mango Peach Sorbet (V) (GF)

This refreshing dessert recipe was inspired by an fragrant fruity Indian drink called *sharbat*, which is flavored with rose water.

SERVES: 8 • SERVING SIZE: ½ CUP / 96 G • PREP TIME: 6 HOURS • COOKING TIME: NONE

2 **mangoes, peeled and pitted** (reserve 8 thin slices for garnish)

5 small or 3 medium **peaches, peeled and pitted** (about 1 cup / 150 g finely chopped, reserve 8 thin slices for garnish)

1 Tbsp / 12.5 g **stevia white sugar blend**

2 Tbsp / 30 mL **lime juice**

2 tsp / 10 mL **rose water**

1 Tbsp plus 1 tsp / 19 g **fresh lime zest, divided**

2 **sprigs fresh mint leaves, stems removed**

KITCHEN TOOLS

Food processor
Ice cream maker

CHOICES/EXCHANGES
1 Fruit

Calories	50
Calories from Fat	5
Total Fat	0.5 g
Saturated Fat	0.1 g
Trans Fat	0.0 g
Cholesterol	0 mg
Sodium	0 mg
Potassium	180 mg
Total Carbohydrate	13 g
Dietary Fiber	2 g
Sugars	11 g
Protein	1 g
Phosphorus	15 mg

1 In a food processor or blender, purée mangoes and peaches. This should yield about 3 cups / 700 mL fruit purée.

2 Add stevia blend, lime juice, rose water, and 1 tsp / 5 g lime zest and process to combine into a smooth purée.

3 Pour mixture into an ice cream maker and freeze (according to manufacturer's instructions) until firm, about 30 minutes. Transfer to an airtight container and freeze until ready to serve. If you don't have an ice cream maker, you can pour the purée into an ice tray and freeze for 5–6 hours before serving.

4 Garnish with remaining lime zest, mango and peach slices, and mint.

COOK'S NOTES

You could replace the mangoes and peaches with any fresh seasonal fruits. Pineapple is another great choice!

Shrikhand (Sweetened Hung Curd) with Poached Peaches (GF)

Shrikhand an Indian dessert made of strained homemade yogurt called hung curd. It is one of the main desserts in the cuisine of western India. Shrikhand is thought to have originated in ancient India.

SERVES: 8 • SERVING SIZE: ABOUT ⅓ CUP / 85 G YOGURT + ¼ PEACH
PREP TIME: 5 HOURS OR OVERNIGHT • COOKING TIME: 22 MINUTES

4 cups / 980 g **plain low-fat yogurt**

¼ tsp / 0.2 g **saffron thread**

2 Tbsp / 30 mL **low-fat milk, warmed**

2 Tbsp / 13 g **superfine raw stevia**

3 **green cardamom pods, husked and seeds extracted**

2 **ripe peaches, skinned and sliced into wedges**

1 tsp / 7.1 g **honey**

Juice of ½ **lemon**

⅓ cup / 80 mL **water**

¼ cup / 40 g **pomegranate seeds**

KITCHEN TOOLS

Cheesecloth

CHOICES/EXCHANGES
½ Fruit
½ Fat-Free Milk
½ Fat

Calories	100
Calories from Fat	20
Total Fat	2.0 g
Saturated Fat	1.2 g
Trans Fat	0.0 g
Cholesterol	5 mg
Sodium	60 mg
Potassium	310 mg
Total Carbohydrate	15 g
Dietary Fiber	1 g
Sugars	11 g
Protein	6 g
Phosphorus	155 mg

COOK'S NOTES

Raw stevia can be powdered in a food processor to reach the superfine consistency called for in this recipe. For an even sweeter twist on this dessert, try drizzling 1 Tbsp / 21 g pomegranate molasses over the finished dishes.

1. Place a strainer lined with cheesecloth over a pan and add yogurt to strain. Cover and set the strainer and pan in the refrigerator for 5 hours or overnight to continue to strain.

2. Add saffron thread to a heavy-bottomed pan and toast over medium heat for 2 minutes.

3. Add toasted saffron thread to a small bowl with the warm milk and set aside for 10 minutes.

4. Combine strained yogurt, stevia, and saffron milk in a large bowl and mix well.

5. Crush cardamom seeds and sprinkle over the yogurt mixture. Set aside in the refrigerator until ready to serve.

6. Heat a heavy-bottomed pan over medium-low heat and add peaches, honey, lemon juice, and water. Cook for about 10 minutes, then cover and continue cooking until peaches are tender, about 10 minutes.

7. Open the lid and make sure most of the cooking liquid is absorbed. Serve roasted peaches on top of shrikhand and decorate with pomegranate seeds.

Spiced Maple Custard (GF)

This easy-to-make custard is popular all over India. This dessert is similar to flan, a baked custard that is popular in Latino cultures. Traditionally, this custard is steamed, but in modern Indian kitchens (and in this recipe) the custard is baked in the oven. In India this custard is usully made with caramel, but I use maple syrup in this recipe instead to reduce the sugar content. My mother used to make this recipe for us as a sweet treat when I was a child.

SERVES: 12 • SERVING SIZE: 1 RAMEKIN + ½ TSP / 3.5 G MAPLE SYRUP
PREP TIME: 3 HOURS OR OVERNIGHT • COOKING TIME: 40 MINUTES

5 **whole eggs**
2 **egg yolks**
2 Tbsp / 25 g **stevia bakeable blend (Pyure)**
1 tsp / 5 mL **vanilla extract**
¼ tsp / 1.3 g **ground nutmeg**
1 ¼ cups / 300 mL **fat-free half and half**
1 cup / 240 mL **whole milk**
¹⁄₁₆ tsp / 0.4 g **sea salt**
2 Tbsp / 41.5 g **pure maple syrup**

CHOICES/EXCHANGES
½ Carbohydrate
1 Fat

Calories	80
Calories from Fat	30
Total Fat	3.5 g
Saturated Fat	1.5 g
Trans Fat	0.0 g
Cholesterol	110 mg
Sodium	75 mg
Potassium	115 mg
Total Carbohydrate	6 g
Dietary Fiber	0 g
Sugars	5 g
Protein	4 g
Phosphorus	105 mg

COOK'S NOTES

If you want your maple syrup to have a slightly thicker consistency, try chilling it in the refrigerator for at least 30 minutes before drizzling over the custard.

1 In a large bowl, whisk together eggs and egg yolks. While whisking, add stevia blend slowly until fully incorporated and dissolved.

2 Add vanilla, nutmeg, half and half, milk, and salt and continue to whisk. To get rid of the air bubbles in the mixture, transfer it to another large bowl through a fine strainer.

3 Slowly fill 12 (3-oz / 84-g) ramekins (small ceramic custard cups) about ⅔ full with the mixture. (Pour slowly to avoid creating air bubbles.)

4 Preheat oven to 350°F / 180°C.

5 Place ramekins in a shallow baking pan. Place the pan in the oven, then carefully fill the pan with enough boiling water to reach halfway up the ramekins. The hot water bath will allow custard to cook evenly in the oven. Bake for 40 minutes.

6 Remove from oven and allow the ramekins to cool in their water bath until they are cool enough to handle. Then transfer the ramekins to the refrigerator to chill for at least 3 hours or overnight.

7 Once cool, place each ramekin on a serving plate and drizzle each serving with ½ tsp / 3.5 g maple syrup before serving.

Garam Masala Grilled Fruit

SERVES: 8 • SERVING SIZE: ABOUT ⅓ CUP / 50 G FRUIT + ½ TBSP / 7.7 G YOGURT MIXTURE
PREP TIME: ABOUT 5 MINUTES • COOKING TIME: 5 MINUTES

1 tsp / 5 g **ghee (p. 30)**

½ medium **ripe pineapple, cored and cut into 1-inch / 2.5-cm cubes**

1 medium **ripe mango, skin removed and cut into 1-inch / 2.5-cm cubes**

3 medium **peaches, skin removed and cut into 1-inch / 2.5-cm cubes**

1 Tbsp / 11.5 g **truvia brown sugar blend**

1 tsp / 5 g **garam masala**

1 cup / 245 g **plain fat-free Greek yogurt**

1 tsp / 5 mL **pure vanilla extract**

1 pinch **saffron, soaked in ¼ tsp / 1.3 g warm water**

1 Tbsp / 20.8 g **maple syrup**

1 **sprig mint leaves, stems removed**

1. Preheat a cast iron griddle or grill pan over medium-high heat.

2. Melt ghee, and brush on pineapple, mango, and peach cubes. Grill fruits, being careful not to overcrowd the griddle, until you get grill marks, about 3 minutes.

3. Meanwhile, combine brown sugar blend and garam masala in a small bowl. Sprinkle sugar mixture on fruits and grill for another minute.

4. Remove grilled fruit to a large bowl and set aside, uncovered.

5. In another small bowl, mix yogurt, vanilla, saffron water, and maple syrup together. Beat well with a spoon or whisk until you get a smooth consistency.

6. Drizzle yogurt mixture over each serving of fruit just before serving. Garnish with mint.

CHOICES/EXCHANGES
1½ Starch
1 Lean Protein

Calories	130
Calories from Fat	20
Total Fat	2.5 g
Saturated Fat	0.3 g
Trans Fat	0.0 g
Cholesterol	0 mg
Sodium	120 mg
Potassium	190 mg
Total Carbohydrate	20 g
Dietary Fiber	3 g
Sugars	1 g
Protein	8 g
Phosphorus	150 mg

COOK'S NOTES

Ripe fruits are recommended for this recipe, but make sure they are not overripe, otherwise they will fall apart during cooking.

Chukandar Ka Halwa (Beetroot Halwa)

The word *halwa*, similar to the Yiddish *halva*, means a sweet confection. Beetroot halwa is a traditional sweet Indian dish that is commonly made for Indian festivals like Navratri and Diwali. Beetroot is not just a savory ingredient. It actually pairs well with milk, sugar, and cardamom. You'll love the unique flavor of this sweet treat. It's great for special occasions!

SERVES: 8 • SERVING SIZE: 2 OZ / 56 G • PREP TIME: NONE • COOKING TIME: 40 MINUTES

1 Tbsp / 15 mL **sunflower oil**

1 tsp / 5 g **ghee (p. 30)**

8 **raw unsalted cashews, broken into bits**

¼ cup / 36.3 g **golden or regular raisins**

2 medium **beetroots, grated** (about 2 cups / 180 g)

1 cup / 240 mL **low-fat milk**

¼ cup / 50 g **stevia bakeable blend (Pyure)**

½ tsp / 2.5 g **ground cardamom**

CHOICES/EXCHANGES
½ Carbohydrate
½ Fat

Calories	70
Calories from Fat	30
Total Fat	3.5 g
Saturated Fat	0.9 g
Trans Fat	0.0 g
Cholesterol	5 mg
Sodium	30 mg
Potassium	160 mg
Total Carbohydrate	8 g
Dietary Fiber	1 g
Sugars	7 g
Protein	2 g
Phosphorus	50 mg

1 Combine sunflower oil and ghee in a small bowl, then add mixture to a heavy-bottomed Dutch oven over medium-high heat. Once ghee and oil are hot, add cashews and raisins and stir until cashews turn golden brown. (Make sure they don't burn.) Remove the cashews and raisins from the pan and set aside.

2 Add grated beetroots to the same pan and sauté over medium-low heat for 10 minutes.

3 Add milk, reduce heat to low, and cook, stirring occasionally (so that mixture does not stick to the bottom of the pan), for 5 minutes. Milk should be absorbed.

4 Add stevia blend and cardamom and mix well. Continue to simmer over medium-low heat, stirring, as sugar melts and beetroot mixture begins to thicken and glisten. When the mixture begins to pull away from the sides of the pan (this could take approximately 20 minutes), add roasted cashews and raisins. Mix well and serve.

COOK'S NOTES

Don't like beets? Traditionally, halwa is made with carrots instead of beets, so feel free to replace the beets in this recipe with carrots.

Anjeer Khajoor Barfi (Fig and Date Bars)

Barfi (also called barfee, or burfi) is a dense, sweet India dessert usually made with milk and various other ingredients depending on the type of barfi. Plain barfi is made with condensed milk or milk reduced with sugar; the ingredients are cooked down in a heavy-bottomed pan until the mixture solidifies. There are several different varieties of barfi including: besan barfi (made with gram flour), kaaju barfi (made with cashews), pista barfi (made with pistachios), and sing barfi (made with peanuts). This healthier version of the dessert is made without the condensed milk, but you'll still love every bite!

SERVES: 10 • SERVING SIZE: 2 OZ / 56 G • PREP TIME: 15–20 MINUTES • COOKING TIME: 25 MINUTES

1 cup / 150 g (about 15) **dried figs, chopped**

1 cup / 150 g (about 18) **dates, pitted and chopped**

1 Tbsp / 15 mL **water**

1 Tbsp / 15 mL **sunflower oil**

1 tsp / 5 g **ghee (p. 30)**

3 Tbsp / 30 g **finely chopped unsalted almonds**

2 Tbsp / 20 g **finely chopped raw and unsalted cashews**

2 Tbsp / 20 g **finely chopped unsalted pistachios**

3 **green cardamom pods, seeds extracted and finely crushed**

CHOICES/EXCHANGES
1 Fruit
1 Fat

Calories	110
Calories from Fat	40
Total Fat	4.5 g
Saturated Fat	0.7 g
Trans Fat	0.0 g
Cholesterol	0 mg
Sodium	0 mg
Potassium	210 mg
Total Carbohydrate	19 g
Dietary Fiber	3 g
Sugars	14 g
Protein	2 g
Phosphorus	40 mg

1. Soak figs and dates, separately, in bowls of hot water (use just enough water to cover the fruit) for 15–20 minutes. Drain water and grind figs and dates together using a food processor to form a smooth paste. Add 1 Tbsp / 15 mL water to reach the right consistency.

2. Combine sunflower oil and ghee in a small bowl, then add mixture to a heavy-bottomed pan over medium heat. Add the fig and date purée. Cook, stirring frequently, until mixture dries out, about 15 minutes.

3. Stir in almonds, cashews, pistachios, and cardamom seeds and mix well to combine. Continue cooking over medium-low heat, stirring frequently, for another 10 minutes, or until mixture starts to pull away from the sides of the pan.

4. Transfer mixture to a greased plate or pan and press down to form the barfi. Set aside to cool completely. Once cool, cut into squares or diamonds and serve.

COOK'S NOTES

You can keep these delicious bars in the refrigerator for up to a week. If you don't like figs or dates, try other dried fruits such as apricots or prunes.

CHAPTER 14
Sweet and Savory Drinks

Pomegranate Limeade

SERVES: 12 • SERVING SIZE: ABOUT 4.5 OZ / 135 ML • PREP TIME: ABOUT 5 MINUTES • COOKING TIME: 5 MINUTES

½ cup / 100 g **stevia sugar blend (Pyure)**

1 cup / 240 mL **water**

2 **bunches fresh mint leaves, divided**

2 cups / 280.6 g **crushed ice**

1 **lime, cut into ½-inch / 13-mm rings**

1 quart / 950 mL **unsweetened pure pomegranate juice**

Juice of 4 **limes**

1 quart / 950 mL **sparkling mineral water**

1   To make simple syrup, combine stevia blend and water in a saucepan over medium heat. Stir until the stevia dissolves, about 5 minutes. Set aside to let mixture cool.

2   In a large pitcher, combine 1 bunch mint leaves, crushed ice, and lime slices. Add simple syrup and stir.

3   Add pomegranate juice and lime juice and mix well. Top with sparkling mineral water. Garnish with remaining mint leaves.

CHOICES/EXCHANGES
1 Fruit

Calories	50
Calories from Fat	5
Total Fat	0.5 g
Saturated Fat	0.1 g
Trans Fat	0.0 g
Cholesterol	0 mg
Sodium	10 mg
Potassium	200 mg
Total Carbohydrate	13 g
Dietary Fiber	0 g
Sugars	12 g
Protein	0 g
Phosphorus	10 mg

Jal Jeera (V) (GF)

In Hindi, *jal* means water and *jeera* means cumin. This spice-infused water is often served as an aperitif on hot summer days.

SERVES: 6 • SERVING SIZE: 5 OZ / 150 ML • PREP TIME: ABOUT 5 MINUTES • COOKING TIME: NONE

½ tsp / 2.5 g **ground black pepper**
¼ tsp / 1.7 g **black salt**
½ tsp / 2.5 g **ground cumin**
22 **mint leaves, divided**
1 **green chili, seeds removed**
1 small **bunch cilantro, stems removed**
1 tsp / 5 g **crushed jaggery**
30 oz / 900 mL **warm water**

KITCHEN TOOLS
Mortar and pestle

1 Grind all the ingredients except water and 12 of the mint leaves to a fine paste using a mortar and pestle (or food processor).

2 In a large bowl, combine warm water and paste. Let mixture steep for 3 minutes.

3 Strain the liquid and serve garnished with mint leaves.

COOK'S NOTES

Jaggery is type of unprocessed sugar that is available in Asian and Indian markets. You can replace the jaggery in this recipe with dark brown sugar. Black salt is a special variety of salt with a strong flavor. You can replace the black salt in this recipe with sea salt or Himalayan salt.

CHOICES/EXCHANGES
Free food

Calories	5
Calories from Fat	0
Total Fat	0.0 g
Saturated Fat	0.0 g
Trans Fat	0.0 g
Cholesterol	0 mg
Sodium	95 mg
Potassium	5 mg
Total Carbohydrate	1 g
Dietary Fiber	0 g
Sugars	1 g
Protein	0 g
Phosphorus	0 mg

Nimbu Pani (Ginger Limeade) Ⓥ ㉖

In Hindi, *nimbu* means lemon and *pani* means water. This drink is a refreshing aperitif that is popular in all regions of India. In northern India they add a bit of crushed cardamom and/or black pepper to this recipe.

SERVES: 6 • SERVING SIZE: ABOUT 8 OZ / 240 ML • PREP TIME: 8 HOURS OR OVERNIGHT • COOKING TIME: NONE

Juice of 3 **limes**

1 (2-inch / 5-cm) **piece ginger (skin on), crushed**

5 cups / 1.2 L **water**

¼ tsp / 1.7 g **salt**

1 cup / 140.3 g **crushed ice**

1 (12-oz / 350-mL) **can club soda**

12 **mint leaves**

1 In a glass jar, combine lime juice and crushed ginger. Cover and refrigerate overnight.

2 Strain the ginger-infused juice into a large pitcher and add water. Stir well.

3 Add salt and crushed ice and pour into 6 tall glasses. Top each serving with club soda and garnish with mint leaves.

COOK'S NOTES

You can store the lime juice and ginger mixture in the refrigerator for up to 1 week before serving this drink.

CHOICES/EXCHANGES
Free food

Calories	5
Calories from Fat	0
Total Fat	0.0 g
Saturated Fat	0.0 g
Trans Fat	0.0 g
Cholesterol	0 mg
Sodium	110 mg
Potassium	20 mg
Total Carbohydrate	1 g
Dietary Fiber	0 g
Sugars	0 g
Protein	0 g
Phosphorus	0 mg

Fenugreek Tea GF

2 tsp / 7.4 g **fenugreek seeds**
½ tsp / 2.5 g **grated nutmeg**
2 cups / 475 mL **cold water**
Juice of ½ **lemon**
1 tsp / 7.1 g **honey**

KITCHEN TOOLS
Mortar and pestle

1 Crush fenugreek seeds together with grated nutmeg using a mortar and pestle or the bottom of a clean heavy pan.

2 Add fenugreek and nutmeg mixture and cold water to a small saucepan and let it steep for 1 hour.

3 Place the saucepan over medium heat and simmer for about 3 minutes. Turn off the heat, add lemon juice, and let steep for 15 minutes.

4 Strain the mixture, add honey, and serve hot.

CHOICES/EXCHANGES
Free food

Calories	10
Calories from Fat	0
Total Fat	0.0 g
Saturated Fat	0.0 g
Trans Fat	0.0 g
Cholesterol	0 mg
Sodium	0 mg
Potassium	15 mg
Total Carbohydrate	2 g
Dietary Fiber	0 g
Sugars	1 g
Protein	0 g
Phosphorus	5 mg

Chaas (Savory Yogurt) ⓖⓕ

Chaas is a savory buttermilk drink popular all across India. It is traditionally made by churning buttermilk and cold water together in an earthenware pot, using a hand-held whipping utensil called a madhani. Chaas can be eaten plain or seasoned with a variety of spices and herbs such as the cumin and mint in this recipe.

SERVES: 8 • SERVING SIZE: 4.5 OZ / 135 ML • PREP TIME: ABOUT 5 MINUTES • COOKING TIME: NONE

CHAAS

1½ cups / 368 g **chilled plain fat-free Greek yogurt**

2 cups / 475 mL **cold water**

1 cup / 140.3 g **crushed ice**

¼ tsp / 1.7 g **black salt**

½ tsp / 1 g **cumin seeds, toasted and ground**

1 small **bunch mint leaves, stems removed** (about 1 oz / 28 g)

GARNISH

1 small **bunch mint leaves, stems removed** (about 1 oz / 28 g)

1 Combine all chaas ingredients in a blender and purée to get a smooth consistency.

2 Using a fine strainer, strain out any bits of mint.

3 Pour equal quantities of the chaas into 4 individual glasses, garnish with mint leaves, and serve immediately.

COOK'S NOTES

To toast the cumin seeds, heat a heavy-bottomed pan over medium heat and add cumin seeds. Toast until the seeds turn light brown, about 1 minute. Then grind the seeds to a fine powder using a mortar and pestle. You can use powdered cumin instead, if desired. For more information of this technique, see p. 25.

You can use low-fat buttermilk instead of yogurt in this recipe, but you will need to reduce the water to 1 cup / 240 mL. Check the nutrition information on the buttermilk to make sure it works with your meal plan. You can replace the black salt in this recipe with sea salt or Himalayan salt, if desired.

CHOICES/EXCHANGES
Free food

Calories	25
Calories from Fat	0
Total Fat	0.0 g
Saturated Fat	0.0 g
Trans Fat	0.0 g
Cholesterol	5 mg
Sodium	85 mg
Potassium	65 mg
Total Carbohydrate	2 g
Dietary Fiber	0 g
Sugars	2 g
Protein	4 g
Phosphorus	60 mg

Masala Kappi (Spiced Coffee) (GF)

The use of coffee in India can be traced as far back as the 17th century. This is a traditional Keralan brewed coffee recipe. Some recipes call for adding ginger powder as well as the garam masala. The southern part of India, especially the Mysore, or Mysuru, region, is home to many coffee plantations. In the month of January, the coffee plants in this region blossom and the coffee plantations begin to look like jasmine flower gardens. It's so beautiful and fragrant.

SERVES: 6 • SERVING SIZE: 8 OZ / 240 ML • PREP TIME: ABOUT 5 MINUTES • COOKING TIME: ABOUT 10 MINUTES

1 tsp / 5 g **garam masala**
5 tsp / 25 g **ground coffee**
5 cups / 1.2 L **water**
1 cup / 240 mL **low-fat milk**
2 tsp / 8.4 g **stevia**

1   Mix garam masala with ground coffee. Then, following brewing directions for your coffee maker, brew the coffee with 5 cups / 1.2 L water.

2   In a small saucepan, bring milk to a boil and mix in stevia. Add milk mixture to the brewed coffee and serve hot.

CHOICES/EXCHANGES
Free food

Calories	20
Calories from Fat	5
Total Fat	0.5 g
Saturated Fat	0.3 g
Trans Fat	0.0 g
Cholesterol	0 mg
Sodium	20 mg
Potassium	160 mg
Total Carbohydrate	2 g
Dietary Fiber	0 g
Sugars	2 g
Protein	2 g
Phosphorus	45 mg

COOK'S NOTES

Use 1 tsp / 5 g garam masala for every 5 cups of coffee you brew.

Lassi Namkeen (Savory Lassi) 🟢GF

SERVES: 6 • SERVING SIZE: ABOUT 4 OZ / 120 ML • PREP TIME: ABOUT 5 MINUTES • COOKING TIME: 1 MINUTE

2 cups / 490 g **plain fat-free Greek yogurt**

½ tsp / 1.2 g **black peppercorns**

½ tsp / 1 g **cumin seeds**

1 tsp / 2.2 g **superfine sugar**

1¼ cups / 300 mL **water**

¼ cup / 35 g **ice cubes**

6 **sprigs thyme leaves**

KITCHEN TOOLS

Mortar and pestle

1 Dry-roast black peppercorns and cumin seeds in a heavy-bottomed pan over medium heat for about 1 minute, or until spices release their aroma.

2 Crush peppercorns and cumin seeds into a coarse powder, using a mortar and pestle or the bottom of a clean heavy pan, and set aside.

3 Using a food processor or blender, blend all ingredients except thyme leaves until smooth.

4 Garnish each serving with 1 sprig thyme leaves and serve.

COOK'S NOTES

This refreshing lassi is very popular on hot summer days in India. You can use a food processor to grind the peppercorns and cumin seeds if you'd like. Traditionally, lassi namkeen uses curry or mint leaves, but I like the flavor of thyme leaves in this recipe.

CHOICES/EXCHANGES

½ Fat-Free Milk

Calories	50
Calories from Fat	5
Total Fat	0.5 g
Saturated Fat	0.1 g
Trans Fat	0.0 g
Cholesterol	5 mg
Sodium	30 mg
Potassium	115 mg
Total Carbohydrate	4 g
Dietary Fiber	0 g
Sugars	3 g
Protein	8 g
Phosphorus	105 mg

Papaya Lassi (GF)

LASSI

1 small (8-oz / 230-g) **ripe papaya, seeds removed and cut into ½-inch / 13-mm cubes**

1 cup / 245 g **plain fat-free Greek yogurt**

1 tsp / 7.1 g **honey**

1 cup / 240 mL **water**

Juice of ½ **lime**

¼ cup / 35 g **ice cubes**

¼ tsp / 1.3 g **ground cardamom**

GARNISH

1 **bunch mint leaves, stems removed**

¼ tsp / 1.3 g **ground cardamom**

1 Combine all lassi ingredients in a food processor and blend until smooth.

2 Serve in 6 tall thin glasses and garnish with mint leaves and ground cardamom before serving.

COOK'S NOTES

You can substitute mango or any seasonal fruit for the papaya in this recipe. You can use whole cardamom pods for this recipe instead of ground cardamom, but make sure you remove the husks and crush the seeds before combining them with the other ingredients.

CHOICES/EXCHANGES
½ Carbohydrate

Calories	40
Calories from Fat	0
Total Fat	0.0 g
Saturated Fat	0.1 g
Trans Fat	0.0 g
Cholesterol	0 mg
Sodium	15 mg
Potassium	110 mg
Total Carbohydrate	6 g
Dietary Fiber	1 g
Sugars	4 g
Protein	4 g
Phosphorus	55 mg

Mixed Berry Lassi 🅖🅕

This delicious lassi makes a great quick breakfast. Just blend the ingredients and go!

SERVES: 6 • SERVING SIZE: ABOUT 8 OZ / 240 ML • PREP TIME: ABOUT 5 MINUTES • COOKING TIME: NONE

2 cups / 280 g **mixed berries**
½ cup / 122.5 g **plain fat-free Greek yogurt**
2½ cups / 590 mL **low-fat milk**
1 cup / 140.3 g **crushed ice**
1 Tbsp / 20.8 g **maple syrup**
Juice of ½ **lime**
½ tsp / 2.5 g **ground cardamom**
1 **sprig mint leaves, stems removed**

1 Combine all ingredients except mint leaves in a blender and blend to a smooth consistency.

2 Pour into 6 tall thin glasses and garnish with mint leaves before serving.

COOK'S NOTES

You can substitute any seasonal berries in this recipe. You can use whole cardamom pods for this recipe instead of ground cardamom, but make sure you remove the husks and crush the seeds before combining them with the other ingredients.

CHOICES/EXCHANGES
½ Fruit
½ Fat-Free Milk

Calories	90
Calories from Fat	15
Total Fat	1.5 g
Saturated Fat	0.7 g
Trans Fat	0.0 g
Cholesterol	5 mg
Sodium	55 mg
Potassium	260 mg
Total Carbohydrate	14 g
Dietary Fiber	2 g
Sugars	11 g
Protein	6 g
Phosphorus	135 mg

CHAPTER 15
Condiments, Chutneys, and Raitas

Coconut Chutney GF

SERVES: 16 • SERVING SIZE: 2 TBSP / 30 G • PREP TIME: ABOUT 5 MINUTES • COOKING TIME: NONE

CHUTNEY

1 cup / 83.3 g **unsweetened freshly grated coconut**

1 cup / 245 g **plain fat-free Greek yogurt**

1 **green chili**

1 (1-inch / 2.5-cm) **piece ginger, peeled**

1 medium **shallot**

½ tsp / 3.3 g **salt**

1 **sprig curry leaves, stems removed**

¼ tsp / 1.3 g **tamarind paste**

GARNISH

1 **sprig curry leaves, stems removed**

KITCHEN TOOLS

Food processor

1 Using a food processor, grind all chutney ingredients into a coarse, grainy paste (not too smooth).

2 Garnish with curry leaves and serve.

COOK'S NOTES

Unsweetened grated coconut can be found in the frozen section of most grocery stores and Indian markets. Remove the seeds from the green chili for a more mild chutney. You can use mint leaves instead of curry leaves and juice from 1/2 lemon instead of the tamarind paste.

CHOICES/EXCHANGES
Free food

Calories	20
Calories from Fat	15
Total Fat	1.5 g
Saturated Fat	1.2 g
Trans Fat	0.0 g
Cholesterol	0 mg
Sodium	65 mg
Potassium	40 mg
Total Carbohydrate	1 g
Dietary Fiber	0 g
Sugars	1 g
Protein	1 g
Phosphorus	20 mg

Lemon Chutney

The Maharashtra region in India is home to cities such as Mumbai (Bombay) and Pune. The cuisine of this mid-western state is very distinctive. Many dishes from this area have a specific flavor profile called *aamti*, which is a little spicy, a little sweet, and a little tangy. This lemon chutney recipe is inspired by the flavors of this region.

SERVES: 32 • SERVING SIZE: 1 TBSP / 15 G • PREP TIME: ABOUT 5 MINUTES • COOKING TIME: NONE

6 **whole organic lemons, washed, cut into quarters, seeds removed**

2 Tbsp / 28 g **smoked paprika**

1 tsp / 5 g **cayenne pepper**

¼ tsp / 1 g **sugar**

1 tsp / 6.7 g **salt**

KITCHEN TOOLS

Food processor

1 Combine all ingredients in a food processor and grind into a coarse paste. Serve.

COOK'S NOTES

The best way to grind the chutney is to pulse all the ingredients, so that you get a coarse consistency. This chutney can be served with breads as well as rice dishes.

Because the lemons are added to the food processor with the skin on, I recommend using organic lemons for this recipe. Make sure you wash them well.

CHOICES/EXCHANGES

Free food

Calories	5
Calories from Fat	0
Total Fat	0.0 g
Saturated Fat	0.0 g
Trans Fat	0.0 g
Cholesterol	0 mg
Sodium	75 mg
Potassium	50 mg
Total Carbohydrate	3 g
Dietary Fiber	1 g
Sugars	1 g
Protein	0 g
Phosphorus	5 mg

Thakkali Chutney (Tomato Chutney)

This chutney comes from southern India and is very popular in the Chettinad region. It is relished alongside breakfast delicacies like idlis (steamed lentil dumplings).

SERVES: 8 • SERVING SIZE: ¼ CUP / 60 G • PREP TIME: 30 MINUTES • COOKING TIME: 8 MINUTES

3 **dried guajillo chilies**

1 cup / 240 mL **hot water**

2 tsp /10 mL **sunflower oil**

1 tsp / 3.5 g **brown or black mustard seeds**

1 **stalk curry leaves, cleaned and leaves separated**

2 **shallots, finely diced**

3 large **tomatoes, finely diced**

¼ tsp / 1.3 g **tamarind paste**

2 Tbsp / 10.4 g **frozen grated unsweetened coconut**

½ tsp / 3.3 g **salt**

KITCHEN TOOLS

Blender (or food processor)

CHOICES/EXCHANGES
1 Nonstarchy Vegetable
½ Fat

Calories	35
Calories from Fat	20
Total Fat	2.0 g
Saturated Fat	0.5 g
Trans Fat	0.0 g
Cholesterol	0 mg
Sodium	150 mg
Potassium	210 mg
Total Carbohydrate	5 g
Dietary Fiber	1 g
Sugars	2 g
Protein	1 g
Phosphorus	30 mg

1 Soak chilies in 1 cup / 240 mL hot water for 30 minutes.

2 Heat oil in a heavy-bottomed pan over medium-high heat and add mustard seeds. When mustard seeds begin to splutter, add curry leaves and sauté until they turn light brown, about 1 minute.

3 Add shallots and tomatoes and sauté for about 7 minutes, or until tomatoes are cooked.

4 Using a blender or food processor, blend the cooked mixture with the remaining ingredients, including the soaked chilies. Grind to a smooth consistency and serve.

COOK'S NOTES

The guajillo chilies in this recipe can be replaced with 1 Tbsp / 14 g smoked paprika.

Green Mint and Coriander Chutney

SERVES: 8 • SERVING SIZE: 1 TBSP / 15 G • PREP TIME: ABOUT 5 MINUTES • COOKING TIME: NONE

2 cups / 16 g **packed cilantro leaves**
½ cup / 12 g **packed mint leaves**
1 small **green chili**
¼ tsp / 1.3 g **ground cumin**
Juice of 1 **lime or lemon**
¼ tsp / 1.7 g **salt**

KITCHEN TOOLS
Food processor

1 Mix all ingredients in a food processor and grind to a smooth paste.

COOK'S NOTES

For a variation on this chutney you can add 2 garlic cloves, a pinch of sugar, and/or 1 small onion. For a milder version, add 2 Tbsp / 30.6 g plain fat-free yogurt or 2 Tbsp / 24 g reduced-fat sour cream. Add another green chili if you like your chutney more spicy. This chutney pairs wonderfully with breads and grilled meat and seafood.

CHOICES/EXCHANGES
Free food

Calories	10
Calories from Fat	0
Total Fat	0.0 g
Saturated Fat	0.0 g
Trans Fat	0.0 g
Cholesterol	0 mg
Sodium	80 mg
Potassium	105 mg
Total Carbohydrate	2 g
Dietary Fiber	1 g
Sugars	1 g
Protein	1 g
Phosphorus	10 mg

Anar Ka Raita (Pomegranate Raita)

The pomegranate, which is native to Persia, the western Himalayas, and modern-day Iran, has also been cultivated in places such as Russia, the Mediterranean region, and India. The arils (seeds) of this fruit are used in many dishes—both savory and sweet—throughout India and are considered highly nutritious.

SERVES: 16 • SERVING SIZE: 2 TBSP / 30 G • PREP TIME: ABOUT 5 MINUTES • COOKING TIME: NONE

1½ cups / 368 g **plain low-fat Greek yogurt**

½ tsp / 3.3 g **kosher salt**

1 large **pomegranate, seeds extracted** (about 1 cup / 150 g seeds)

3 **bunches scallions, finely chopped**

3 **sprigs mint, cut into a chiffonade**

1/16 tsp / 0.3 g **sugar**

1 tsp / 2 g **cumin seeds, toasted and crushed**

1 In a large bowl, combine yogurt and salt and beat well with a fork or whisk.

2 Add all remaining ingredients except cumin and mix well.

3 Stir in cumin and serve.

COOK'S NOTES

For a little heat, try adding 1 minced green chili to this recipe. To learn the technique for roasting and crushing the cumin seeds, see p. 25. You can replace the toasted, crushed cumin seeds with store-bought ground cumin.

CHOICES/EXCHANGES
½ Carbohydrate

Calories	30
Calories from Fat	5
Total Fat	0.5 g
Saturated Fat	0.3 g
Trans Fat	0.0 g
Cholesterol	0 mg
Sodium	70 mg
Potassium	105 mg
Total Carbohydrate	4 g
Dietary Fiber	1 g
Sugars	3 g
Protein	3 g
Phosphorus	40 mg

Cucumber Raita GF

Raita is a yogurt-based condiment enjoyed throughout India. The word *raita* is derived from the Sanskrit words *rājikā*, meaning black mustard, and *tiktaka*, meaning sharp or pungent. Cucumber raita is a popular condiment in many Indian restaurants and in the U.S. as well.

SERVES: 8 • SERVING SIZE: ¼ CUP / 60 G • PREP TIME: 8 HOURS OR OVERNIGHT • COOKING TIME: NONE

1 (14-oz / 394-g) **seedless English cucumber**

1 Tbsp plus ½ tsp / 23.3 g **salt, divided**

2 cups / 490 g **plain low-fat Greek yogurt**

½ tsp / 1 g **cumin seeds, toasted and crushed**

¼ tsp / 1.3 g **cayenne pepper**

½ tsp / 1.7 g **chopped green chilies**

1 Tbsp / 12 g **fat-free sour cream**

⅛ tsp / 0.5 g **sugar**

1 Tbsp / 1 g **chopped cilantro**

1 Using a coffee filter, drain yogurt for at least 1 hour (up to 8 hours or overnight) in the refrigerator to reduce excess moisture.

2 Peel and grate the cucumber. (If you're not using a seedless cucumber, remove seeds before grating.) Mix cucumber with 1 Tbsp / 20 g salt, then let cucumbers drain in a colander for at least 1 hour.

3 Rinse cucumbers in cold water. Drain them and squeeze out as much moisture as you can. Transfer to a bowl.

4 Add all remaining ingredients, including yogurt, and mix well. Taste to check the seasoning. Keep in the refrigerator until ready to serve.

COOK'S NOTES

For a quicker version of this recipe, you can grate the cucumber, mix with 1 tsp / 6.7 g salt, and skip the draining of the water from the cucumber. The consistency of the raita will be a little thinner if you use this method.

To learn the technique for roasting and crushing the cumin seeds, see p. 25. You can replace the toasted, crushed cumin seeds with store-bought ground cumin. Traditional recipes for raita include mustard seeds; you can add about ½ tsp / 1.8 g toasted and crushed mustard seeds to the recipe if you'd like.

CHOICES/EXCHANGES
½ Fat-Free Milk

Calories	45
Calories from Fat	10
Total Fat	1.0 g
Saturated Fat	0.7 g
Trans Fat	0.0 g
Cholesterol	5 mg
Sodium	130 mg
Potassium	105 mg
Total Carbohydrate	3 g
Dietary Fiber	0 g
Sugars	2 g
Protein	6 g
Phosphorus	80 mg

Gajar Ka Raita (Carrot Raita) **GF**

Gajar means carrot in Hindi, and carrot is the main ingredient in this refreshing raita. If you don't like carrots, you can replace the carrot in this recipe with cucumber or raw beetroot.

SERVES: 9 • SERVING SIZE: ⅓ CUP / 80 G • PREP TIME: ABOUT 5 MINUTES • COOKING TIME: NONE

1½ cups / 368 g **plain low-fat Greek yogurt**

½ tsp / 3.3 g **kosher salt**

1 tsp / 3.5 g **black or brown mustard seeds, toasted**

1 cup / 83.3 g **finely grated carrots**

1 medium **onion, grated**

3 **sprigs cilantro, leaves separated and minced**

1/16 tsp / 0.3 g **sugar**

KITCHEN TOOLS

Mortar and pestle

1 In a large bowl, mix yogurt with salt and beat well with a fork or whisk.

2 Using a mortar and pestle or the bottom of a clean heavy pan, crush mustard seeds and add to yogurt mixture.

3 Add all remaining ingredients and mix well.

CHOICES/EXCHANGES
½ Carbohydrate

Calories	45
Calories from Fat	10
Total Fat	1.0 g
Saturated Fat	0.5 g
Trans Fat	0.0 g
Cholesterol	1 mg
Sodium	130 mg
Potassium	125 mg
Total Carbohydrate	4 g
Dietary Fiber	1 g
Sugars	3 g
Protein	4 g
Phosphorus	65 mg

COOK'S NOTES

You can replace the whole mustard seeds in this recipe with ground mustard.

Turmeric Chutney GF

SERVES: 16 • SERVING SIZE: 1 TBSP / 15 G • PREP TIME: ABOUT 5 MINUTES • COOKING TIME: 5 MINUTES

1 cup / 245 g **plain low-fat Greek yogurt**
1 tsp / 7.1 g **honey**
1 tsp / 5 g **finely chopped fresh ginger**
1 Tbsp / 0.5 g **finely minced mint leaves**
½ tsp / 3.3 g **salt**
1 tsp / 5 mL **sunflower oil**
1 tsp / 3.5 g **brown or black mustard seeds**
½ tsp / 2.5 g **ground turmeric**
1 tsp / 5 mL **lemon juice**

1 In a large bowl, whisk yogurt, honey, ginger, mint, and the salt together. Set aside.

2 Heat oil in a small pan over medium heat and add mustard seeds. When they begin to splutter, add turmeric and stir. Remove from heat and set aside to cool.

3 Once mustard seed mixture is cool, add to yogurt mixture. Mix in lemon juice just before serving.

CHOICES/EXCHANGES
Free food

Calories	15
Calories from Fat	5
Total Fat	0.5 g
Saturated Fat	0.2 g
Trans Fat	0.0 g
Cholesterol	0 mg
Sodium	80 mg
Potassium	25 mg
Total Carbohydrate	1 g
Dietary Fiber	0 g
Sugars	1 g
Protein	1 g
Phosphorus	20 mg

COOK'S NOTES

Turmeric chutney tastes great served with any grilled seafood or meat. You can use ½ tsp / 2.5 g ground mustard instead of the mustard seeds in this recipe. For a slight variation on this recipe, add ¼ tsp / 0.9 g fenugreek seeds instead of the mustard seeds and follow the same cooking process.

Pomegranate Vinaigrette

SERVES: 6 • SERVING SIZE: 2 TSP / 10 G • PREP TIME: ABOUT 5 MINUTES • COOKING TIME: NONE

2 Tbsp / 42 g **pomegranate molasses**

½ tsp / 1 g **cumin seeds, toasted and ground**

1 tsp / 5 g **ground coriander**

½ tsp / 2.5 g **ground black pepper**

½ tsp / 2.5 g **ground cinnamon**

½ tsp / 2.5 g **ground cloves**

Juice of 1 **lemon**

2 **cloves garlic, mashed into fine paste**

3 Tbsp / 45 mL **extra-virgin olive oil**

¼ tsp / 1.7 g **sea salt**

1 In a large bowl, mix all ingredients together and whisk well to emulsify and make into a thick liquid.

COOK'S NOTES

Instead of buying premade pomegranate molasses, you can make your own by boiling down store-bought pomegranate juice over medium heat for about 15–20 minutes to make a thick syrup. Use ¼ cup / 60 mL juice to yield 2 Tbsp / 42 g pomegranate molasses. To learn the technique for roasting and crushing the cumin seeds, see p. 25.

CHOICES/EXCHANGES
1½ Fat

Calories	80
Calories from Fat	60
Total Fat	7.0 g
Saturated Fat	1.0 g
Trans Fat	0.0 g
Cholesterol	0 mg
Sodium	95 mg
Potassium	110 mg
Total Carbohydrate	4 g
Dietary Fiber	0 g
Sugars	3 g
Protein	0 g
Phosphorus	5 mg

Onion Chutney (V) (GF)

This is a simple and flavorful chutney. In India, it is usually eaten with roasted tuber vegetables such as sweet potatoes.

SERVES: 16 • SERVING SIZE: 1 TBSP / 15 G • PREP TIME: 30 MINUTES • COOKING TIME: NONE

1 cup / 150 g **finely chopped onion**
1 Tbsp / 14 g **smoked paprika**
½ tsp / 2.5 g **cayenne pepper**
1 tsp / 5.2 g **tamarind paste**
½ tsp / 3.3 g **salt**
1 tsp / 4.3 g **coconut oil**

1 Mix all ingredients together in a large bowl. Set aside for about 30 minutes and serve.

CHOICES/EXCHANGES
Free food

Calories	10
Calories from Fat	0
Total Fat	0.0 g
Saturated Fat	0.3 g
Trans Fat	0.0 g
Cholesterol	0 mg
Sodium	75 mg
Potassium	30 mg
Total Carbohydrate	2 g
Dietary Fiber	0 g
Sugars	1 g
Protein	0 g
Phosphorus	5 mg

COOK'S NOTES

You can replace the tamarind paste in this recipe with 1 tsp / 5.2 g tomato paste.

Metric Equivalents

Liquid Measurement	Metric equivalent
1 teaspoon	5 mL
1 tablespoon *or* 1/2 fluid ounce	15 mL
1 fluid ounce *or* 1/8 cup	30 mL
1/4 cup *or* 2 fluid ounces	60 mL
1/3 cup	80 mL
1/2 cup *or* 4 fluid ounces	120 mL
2/3 cup	160 mL
3/4 cup *or* 6 fluid ounces	180 mL
1 cup *or* 8 fluid ounces *or* 1/2 pint	240 mL
1 1/2 cups *or* 12 fluid ounces	350 mL
2 cups *or* 1 pint *or* 16 fluid ounces	475 mL
3 cups *or* 1 1/2 pints	700 mL
4 cups *or* 2 pints *or* 1 quart	950 mL
4 quarts *or* 1 gallon	3.8 L

Length	Metric equivalent
1/8 inch	3 mm
1/4 inch	6 mm
1/2 inch	13 mm
3/4 inch	19 mm
1 inch	2.5 cm
2 inches	5 cm

Weight Measurement	Metric equivalent
1 ounce	28 g
4 ounces *or* 1/4 pound	113 g
1/3 pound	150 g
8 ounces *or* 1/2 pound	230 g
2/3 pound	300 g
12 ounces *or* 3/4 pound	340 g
1 pound *or* 16 ounces	450 g
2 pounds	900 g

Dry Measurement	Metric equivalent
1 teaspoon	5 g
1 tablespoon	14 g
1/4 cup	57 g
1/2 cup	113 g
3/4 cup	168 g
1 cup	224 g

Fahrenheit	Celsius	Fahrenheit	Celsius
275°F	140°C	400°F	200°C
300°F	150°C	425°F	220°C
325°F	165°C	450°F	230°C
350°F	180°C	475°F	240°C
375°F	190°C	500°F	260°C

Weights of common ingredients in grams							
Ingredient	1 cup	3/4 cup	2/3 cup	1/2 cup	1/3 cup	1/4 cup	2 Tbsp
Flour, all-purpose (wheat)	120 g	90 g	80 g	60 g	40 g	30 g	15 g
Flour, well-sifted, all-purpose (wheat)	110 g	80 g	70 g	55 g	35 g	27 g	13 g
Sugar, granulated cane	200 g	150 g	130 g	100 g	65 g	50 g	25 g
Confectioner's sugar (cane)	100 g	75 g	70 g	50 g	35 g	25 g	13 g
Brown sugar, packed firmly	180 g	135 g	120 g	90 g	60 g	45 g	23 g
Cornmeal	160 g	120 g	100 g	80 g	50 g	40 g	20 g
Cornstarch	120 g	90 g	80 g	60 g	40 g	30 g	15 g
Rice, uncooked	190 g	140 g	125 g	95 g	65 g	48 g	24 g
Macaroni, uncooked	140 g	100 g	90 g	70 g	45 g	35 g	17 g
Couscous, uncooked	180 g	135 g	120 g	90 g	60 g	45 g	22 g
Oats, uncooked, quick	90 g	65 g	60 g	45 g	30 g	22 g	11 g
Table salt	300 g	230 g	200 g	150 g	100 g	75 g	40 g
Butter	240 g	180 g	160 g	120 g	80 g	60 g	30 g
Vegetable shortening	190 g	140 g	125 g	95 g	65 g	48 g	24 g
Chopped fruits and vegetables	150 g	110 g	100 g	75 g	50 g	40 g	20 g
Nuts, chopped	150 g	110 g	100 g	75 g	50 g	40 g	20 g
Nuts, ground	120 g	90 g	80 g	60 g	40 g	30 g	15 g
Bread crumbs, fresh, loosely packed	60 g	45 g	40 g	30 g	20 g	15 g	8 g
Bread crumbs, dry	150 g	110 g	100 g	75 g	50 g	40 g	20 g
Parmesan cheese, grated	90 g	65 g	60 g	45 g	30 g	22 g	11 g

Index

C

Cabbage and Onion Slaw, 206
Cabbage and Peas Sabzi, 186
calamari, 138
cardamom pod, 19, 134–135, 218–219
carrot, 207, 246
Carrot and Beet Slaw, 207
cassia, 18
cauliflower, 79–81, 134–135, 170–171
Centers for Disease Control and Prevention, 6
Chaas (Savory Yogurt), 232
chaat masala, 56–57
Chana (Chickpea) Masala, 76–77
Chana (Chickpea) Pilaf, 198–199
chana dal, 24, 152–153, 200
cheese, parmesan, 58
cheesecloth, 32–33
Chia Seed Falooda, 216
chicken
    Chicken Curry in a Hurry, 68–69
    Chicken Piralen (Traditional Keralan Roasted Chicken), 100–101
    Chicken Tikka Masala, 114–115
    Jaldi Kozhi Biryani (Quick Chicken Biryani), 104–105
    Murgh Malai Kebabs (Chicken Kebabs), 154–155
    Navratan Korma (Mixed Vegetable Braise), 72–73
    Nilgiri Murgh Korma (Chicken Korma), 70–71
    Roasted Chicken Tandoori, 146–147
    Stuffed Keema Parathas (Chicken-Stuffed Parathas), 172–173
chickpea, 58, 76–77, 198–199
chickpea flour, 40–41, 196–197
chili, 44–45, 47, 49–50, 52, 122–123, 152–153, 168–171, 190–191
Chinese five-spice, 18
Chukandar Ka Halwa (Beetroot Halwa), 223

chutney. See condiment, chutney, and raita
cilantro, 17, 47, 70–71, 87, 104–105, 110–111, 148–151, 166–167, 170–171, 229
cinnamon, 18
clove, 19–20
coconut, 46, 122–123, 126–127, 130, 188–189, 240, 242
Coconut Chutney, 240
coconut milk, 52, 68–71, 88–89, 102–103, 124–125, 128–129
coffee, 233
condiment, chutney, and raita
    Anar Ka Raita (Pomegranate Raita), 244
    Coconut Chutney, 240
    Cucumber Raita, 245
    Gajar Ka Raita (Carrot Raita), 246
    Green Mint and Coriander Chutney, 243
    Lemon Chutney, 241
    Onion Chutney, 249
    Pomegranate Vinaigrette, 248
    Thakkali Chutney (Tomato Chutney), 242
    Turmeric Chutney, 247
cooking, experimental, 11–12
cooking, senses, 25
cooking technique, 8–9, 12, 25–26
coriander, 17, 87, 100–101, 106–107, 110–111, 128–129, 193, 243
corn, 63, 90–91, 190–191
Corn Bhutta (Roasted Corn on the Cob), 63
Corn Tikki, 190–191
Country-Style Keralan Crab and Mango Curry, 126–127
crab, 126–127
cucumber, 86, 212–213, 245
Cucumber Raita, 245
culinary education, 12
culture, 1–4
cumin, 20, 106–109, 139, 176–177

curcumin, 16
Curried Aloo Anardana Salad, 210–211
Curried Mixed Lentils and Butternut Squash, 192
curry
    Adraki Gobi (Gingery Cauli), 79
    base, 25–26
    Chana (Chickpea) Masala, 76–77
    Chicken Curry in a Hurry, 68–69
    Country-Style Keralan Crab and Mango Curry, 126–127
    Goan-Style Shrimp Curry, 122–123
    leaves, 20, 39, 47, 88–89, 102–103, 128–129, 200
    Masala Okra, 78
    Navratan Korma (Mixed Vegetable Braise), 72–73
    Nilgiri Murgh Korma (Chicken Korma), 70–71
    Palak Tofu (Tofu in Spinach Sauce), 74–75
    powder, 58, 145, 180–181
    Sweet Potato Aloo Gobi, 80–81

D

Dahi (Indian Plain Yogurt), 31
dal, 24
Dal Makhani, 94–95
Dal Panchmel, 93
Dal Tadka, 96–97
date, 224–225
dessert
    Anjeer Khajoor Bar (Fig and Date Bars), 224–225
    Chia Seed Falooda, 216
    Chukandar Ka Halwa (Beetroot Halwa), 223
    Garam Masala Grilled Fruit, 222
    Mango Peach Sorbet, 217
    Shrikhand (Sweetened Hung Curd) with Poached Peaches, 218–219
    Spiced Maple Custard, 220–221
diabetes, global issues, 6

PRAISE FOR INDIAN CUISINE DIABETES COOKBOOK

Many of us, including myself, react tepidly to cookbooks that make health claims because so many of these books produce bland and uninteresting food; hence the need for May Fridel's Indian Cuisine Diabetes Cookbook. Her book brightens up the kitchen with an array of spices, which come together in logically composed and very tasty recipes. Drawing on many of the traditions and flavors of her native India, she innovates with spices in ways foreign to most Western cooks. Not only is this book an asset for people with diabetes, it is a great cookbook in itself, worthwhile for all home cooks—people with and without diabetes alike.

—James Peterson, chef and award-winning cookbook author

While this beautifully written and designed book is intended for people with diabetes, it will be a valuable resource for anyone who wants to enjoy life-enhancing cuisine while exploring new tastes and flavors. The recipes are drawn from many regions of India, including the author's native Kerala, but they incorporate western techniques and ingredients to create dishes that will delight any palate—vegan, vegetarian, or carnivore. Each recipe is accompanied by a table showing exchanges, calories, fat content, and other nutritional information. Many of the recipes can be made using ingredients found in ordinary grocery stores, while the adventurous cook can experiment with a variety of spices and flavor profiles.

—Colleen Taylor Sen, writer and food historian

No authentic cookbook with a focus on Indian foods has ever been available for patients with diabetes. Indian Cuisine Diabetes Cookbook by May Fridel presents over 100 diabetes-friendly Indian recipes. Indian cuisine is truly diverse and includes a wide variety of traditional and regional recipes; far more than almost any other cuisine in the world. May Fridel has truly succeeded in presenting a glimpse of Indian cuisine from many different states of the country, and the book serves as a quick reference guide for any food-savvy health-conscious individual. The calorie counts and nutrition information provided for each recipe will indeed be helpful for people with diabetes who are trying to make healthier choices.

Readers should bear in mind that same amount of food can impact individuals differently, and individualization is vital when it comes to diet. Glycaemic status is affected by many factors, including diet. Therefore the monitoring of blood glucose is highly recommended, and people with diabetes should consult with their diabetes clinicians when making decisions about diet. The recipes in Indian Cuisine Diabetes Cookbook are suitable in general for people with diabetes. This book will certainly be a great resource for those who want to relish different types of healthy Indian dishes.

I highly recommended this book as it takes on both the huge diversity of Indian cuisine and the prevailing challenges for successful management of diabetes through diet. Let me congratulate May Fridel for her pioneering efforts in coming up with a user-friendly Indian cookbook for people with diabetes.

—Dr. Jothydev Kesavadev, MD, of Jothydev's Diabetes and Research Center